Event Management

FOR DUMMIES®
A Wiley Brand

by Laura Capell

FOR DUMMIES®
A Wiley Brand

Event Management For Dummies®

Published by: **John Wiley & Sons, Ltd.**, The Atrium, Southern Gate, Chichester, www.wiley.com

This edition first published 2013

© 2013 John Wiley & Sons, Ltd, Chichester, West Sussex.

Registered office

John Wiley & Sons Ltd, The Atrium, Southern Gate, Chichester, West Sussex, PO19 8SQ, United Kingdom

For details of our global editorial offices, for customer services and for information about how to apply for permission to reuse the copyright material in this book please see our website at www.wiley.com.

The right of the author to be identified as the author of this work has been asserted in accordance with the Copyright, Designs and Patents Act 1988

Wiley publishes in a variety of print and electronic formats and by print-on-demand. Some material included with standard print versions of this book may not be included in e-books or in print-on-demand. If this book refers to media such as a CD or DVD that is not included in the version you purchased, you may download this material at http://booksupport.wiley.com. For more information about Wiley products, visit www.wiley.com.

Designations used by companies to distinguish their products are often claimed as trademarks. All brand names and product names used in this book are trade names, service marks, trademarks or registered trademarks of their respective owners. The publisher is not associated with any product or vendor mentioned in this book.

For general information on our other products and services, please contact our Customer Care Department within the U.S. at 877-762-2974, outside the U.S. at (001) 317-572-3993, or fax 317-572-4002. For technical support, please visit www.wiley.com/techsupport.

For technical support, please visit www.wiley.com/techsupport.

A catalogue record for this book is available from the British Library.

ISBN 978-1-118-59112-3 (pbk); ISBN 978-1-118-59109-3 (ebk); ISBN 978-1-118-59110-9 (ebk); ISBN 978-1-118-59111-6 (ebk)

Printed in Great Britain by TJ International, Padstow, Cornwall.

10 9 8 7 6 5 4

Contents at a Glance

Table of Contents

Part II: Planning Your Event's Look and Feel 101

Introduction

● ●

*E*vent management used to be a career that people fell into. Few people had any kind of qualification or degree that was related to the industry, and most people found that they ended up in it when they thought they were on a different career path.

I started off working at Toyota (GB) plc in their 'New Media' team – as it was called at the time – back in the days when having a website was considered essential, but also the work of wizards; this was back when ad banners at the top of a page were as exciting as the industry appeared to be. I was challenged with monitoring the online forums (of which Yahoo was by far the main one) that discussed Toyota's products. I remember thinking at the time that the people who used these forums felt like they were trend-setters, but I never appreciated how big communities would be one day be on-line – probably just as well I didn't continue my career in that new-fangled technology!

At the time, Toyota were launching the second version of an electric car and from watching the owners of the first version in the forums, I could see how passionate they were about their cars and how sharing information amongst themselves to help each other was really important. I suggested to the press team that when the new car was to be photographed in the UK, we invite some of these first version owners as advocates, knowing that they'd write about their experience across the forums. I then had the task of working out who to invite and organising them to be in the right place at the right time for the photo shoot. Fifteen or so owners turned up, excited about seeing face to face the people they had been talking to for months online, but also with the anticipation of seeing something to which they knew they had exclusive access, and about which they'd each have opinions they could pass on to everyone else.

That day was the reason I have been working in events ever since. No amount of online stats, increase in web traffic numbers or site usage info could compare to the pure joy that I saw on the faces of those guests, and I had helped make that happen. I started a career in events so I could make people smile.

Since then, not all of the events I have managed have been about making people smile. Nowadays, events are used for many different reasons and as a much more common communication tool. However I always try to remember that someone, somewhere should be smiling because of the event that I've organized – or why do it?

About This Book

This book is primarily about the business of working as an event manager within the event management industry. It covers the crucial areas of briefing, budgeting, scheduling and the thousand-and-one pieces of detail required to successfully meet a client's brief. If you're not an event manager as such, but you have been tasked with organising a particular one-off event, or if you're a marketing professional who would like to know more about the events industry and what it entails, this book is for you, too: Organising a successful event involves the same skills and requirements whatever your job title.

Whatever the background you're coming from, use this book as a reference. *For Dummies* books are designed as reference works, with a get-in, get-out philosophy reflected in the self-contained structure of the chapters. You don't need to read this book in order from front cover to back.

Scattered liberally throughout the main text, you'll find a number of sidebars (grey-tinted boxes) which, while not strictly essential reading, will illustrate and help you to understand further the meat of the book. Many of them are marked as Case Studies, and these involve real-life examples drawn from a career spent in event management. Read them or leave them as you see fit.

Within this book, you may note that some web addresses break across two lines of text. If you're reading this book in print and want to visit one of these web pages, simply key in the web address exactly as it's noted in the text, pretending as though the line break doesn't exist. If you're reading this as an e-book, you've got it easy – just click the web address to be taken directly to the web page.

Foolish Assumptions

Although I'd like to believe that the whole world would love to read my wise words on the joys, trials and tribulations of event management just for the heck of it, fact is I've made a few assumptions about you based on the fact that you're reading this. I think you'll be one or other of the following:

- ✔ Someone who, whatever your current role, has been tasked with organising an event or thinks they might be about to be.
- ✔ A marketing or other professional who aspires to enter the event management industry, or develop your career within it.
- ✔ A student looking to start out on an event management career.

I assume that although you may have a corporate background, that's not necessarily the case, and I make no particular assumptions about previous knowledge of this area.

I also take it as read that you want to know not only the broad outline of the industry, but also all the nitty-gritty things you need to do in order to achieve a successful outcome to your organisational efforts.

Oh, and I also assume that you have a real passion to succeed in your particular event or your longer-term career, that you thrive under pressure, that you love to deal with, influence and work collaboratively with other people, and that you're not afraid of a lot of hard work.

Icons Used in This Book

In this book we use a few icons in the margin to mark information to which we'd particularly like to draw your attention. This is what they all mean:

This icon flags up real-life events, examples or anecdotes which can help you understand the closely-worded info in the surrounding text.

When you see this icon, make sure to take the associated information on board. It's important.

Look out for these little gems. They're nuggets of insider knowledge designed to help you do things more easily or more quickly

Whoa! This icon flags up stuff that can ruin your whole day if you get it wrong. From budgetary pitfalls to health and safety commandments, ignore anything marked with this icon at your peril.

Beyond the Book

In addition to the material in the print or e-book you're reading right now, this product also comes with some access-anywhere goodies on the Internet. To start with, there's the Cheat Sheet, which you can find at www.dummies. com/cheatsheet/eventmanagement, which gives you a range of pithy summaries, checklists and essential info in a single, ready-reference document you can refer to time and again.

You'll also find a few handy items at `www.dummies.com/extras/event management`, including printable versions of some of the more useful forms provided in this book.

Where to Go from Here

Where you go from here is pretty much up to you. If you want advice on how to deal with a particular area of event management, go straight to the relevant chapter and dive in: Getting to know your market is what Chapter 2 is about; budgeting wisdom is in Chapter 5; you can find essential info on health and safety in Chapter 12. Whatever you need, go fetch.

If you're absolutely new to the business and intricacies of event management, you'll probably be well advised to check out Part I first, but beyond that this book – and the world of event management – is your oyster. Enjoy!

Part I

getting started with
with
Event
Management

For Dummies can help you get started with a huge range of subjects. Visit www.dummies.com to learn more and do more with *For Dummies*.

In this part . . .

- ✔ Understand why you'd put on an event in the first place, and why sometimes, face-to-face contact with customers or delegates can achieve so much more than any amount of marketing.

- ✔ Meet the customers: Learn how to target your event at the right people, and how to get their input.

- ✔ From conferences to festivals, formal meetings to brand experiences, the range of events is huge. Learn how to choose the right one to meet your client's brief.

- ✔ Pull together the perfect planning team. Get the low-down on all the key roles and responsibilities.

- ✔ Master budgeting and come to terms with costs.

Chapter 1

Why Put on An Event?

*E*veryone has a different idea of what event management is and what an event is. There's no real need to agree; this range of opinions makes the events industry what it is today – diverse.

Whether you're a wedding planner, fundraiser, secretary, brand manager or even an actual event manager, you can discover a huge amount in this book and from people doing the same things you are. Look around you, see what other people do and try to do it better.

To be successful in the event industry, you need far more than just organisation skills; passion and teamwork are vital, too. This chapter talks you through the skills you need and explores one of the first steps in managing events.

Introducing Events

According to my dictionary, an event is something that takes place – a significant occurrence or happening. I like to think of an event as any particular time when a group of people are brought together.

Many people in the industry don't consider events to be marketing; they focus on production and creating theatre. I believe, however, that trying to communicate a message to a group of people is a form of marketing. If you think of an event as a marketing tool, what people experience and feel becomes a driving force in your decision making.

The benefits of an event are:

✔ It can be much more personal than other forms of communication.

✔ A real occasion stands out in a cluttered world of digital and above the line marketing (for example, advertising).

✔ People enjoy human interaction and face-to-face conversations.

✔ They generate a high level of word-of-mouth response, which is one of the best forms of endorsement?

Many people consider themselves to be event managers, and many types of event exist. (I cover types of events in more detail in Chapter 3.) As events become more popular, the disparity between what one event manager does and what another does can be huge.

This book focuses on corporate events, while leaving weddings and community events to the more experienced. However, the skills and knowledge are transferrable, and once you've mastered how to manage an event, you'll have the confidence and understanding to manage most events that people can throw at you.

Event Management As an Industry

The UK event industry is now worth more than £36.1 billion, according to the 2010 *Britain For Events* report – online at www.aceinternational.org/phocadownload/reports/Britain%20for%20Events%20Report%20final.pdf, if you want to take a look. The main event industry sectors are:

✔ Conferences and meetings (£18.8 billion)

✔ Exhibitions and trade shows (£9.3 billion)

✔ Sporting events (£2.3 billion)

✔ Music events (£1.4 billion)

✔ Incentive travel (£1.2 billion)

✔ Festivals and cultural events (£1.1 billion)

✔ Outdoor events (£1 billion)

✔ Corporate hospitality (£1 billion).

That's a lot of money.

Event industry body Eventia published the 2012 *UK Events Market Trends Survey (UKEMTS)* in June 2012. This major research project, undertaken annually since 1993, provides volume and key trends data for the UK conference and business events market from a supply-side or venue perspective.

An estimated 103 million delegates attended events in 2011. (An average of 80 people attended each of an estimated 1.3 million events in 2011, slightly more than the average 76 delegates in 2010.)

Eventia reports that a resurgence in corporate sector events accounted for 57 per cent of all events staged (51 per cent in 2010, and just 47 per cent in 2009). The number of association events was stable (21 per cent, the same as in 2010), and public sector events showed a substantial fall, down from 37 per cent in 2009 and 28 per cent in 2010 to 23 per cent in 2011. This industry is growing and growing.

Fifteen years ago, some of the biggest names in the academic marketing industry published *Principles of Marketing* (by Kotler, Armstrong, Wong and Saunders; Financial Times/Prentice Hall). That book had over 1,000 pages, and one page mentioned events. Now, an Internet search for 'event management' generates over 30 million results. This shows how much the marketing industry has changed.

The event management industry has grown hugely in the last five years, in part because of the recession, but also because face-to-face marketing and communications are seen as much more impactful and successful methods than previously. The changes are that:

- ✔ Production companies that provide kit such as lighting and sound have started to take the extra step of helping to organise other elements of the event too.

- ✔ PR agencies that were hosting basic press launches and press-worthy stunts have started to try their hand at larger events.

- ✔ In-house teams have been growing as businesses try to save on costs by not paying other companies to run their events for them.

The London 2012 Olympics was a huge boost for the events industry in the UK and Europe. Many companies jumped on the bandwagon and gave events a go to capture the spirit of the nation. Events ranged from speaking to consumers in the street to hosting hospitality-focused events around the Olympics rather than sending out purely written communication. I now see businesses that tried their hand at using events in their marketing plans in the summer of 2012 including events in their budgets for 2013 and beyond.

The events industry is growing. As the amount of communication received daily from companies, increasingly through digital channels, becomes a little overwhelming, there's comfort in speaking to real people at events.

The types of events in the industry have changed dramatically, with more focus on large, interactive experiences rather than smaller meetings. The biggest change, however, is that digital is now an essential part of an event rather than just an add-on, as in times gone by.

Essential Skills for Would-be Event Managers

The event industry is intense and is hard work. Even for those who have been in the industry for many years, something else that you have never seen before always comes along in the next event.

You need common sense in the events industry, although it isn't a skill as such. I have yet to find a way to develop common sense; from what I can see, you either have it or you don't – but it's very useful.

To be the best event manager possible, you need to have or to develop these qualities:

- **Passion:** Being an event manager is incredibly rewarding, but can be tiring as you get closer to show day and your to-do list is never ending. With the constant demands on your time, you often think 'Why am I doing this?' Only those that are passionate about events and about event management as a job feel the true satisfaction and reward that producing a successful event offers. If you are keen to get into the events industry as your career, see Chapter 19 for some ideas.

- **People skills:** Event management is a people business, more so than any other form of communication or channel of marketing. Every part of the process of planning an event involves speaking to and thinking about people, see Chapter 4 to see who some of those key people involved in planning an event. Enjoying spending time with people and understanding what makes people tick helps you think like your target market.

- **Communication skills:** Events are a communication tool. Not only is one of your main objectives likely to be to communicate to your attendees (See Chapter 8 to find out how to make sure people know about your event), but you need to communicate with many people before the event. Whilst contacting people by email is often easier, I'm a big believer in picking up the phone (events is a people not computer business, after all). Knowing how to get the information you need out of people and then being able to cascade that information down to other people such as your client or suppliers makes your life much easier. See Chapter 11 for information on how to communicate with your team on-site at your event.

✔ **Problem solving skills:** The event industry has a saying that there are no problems, only solutions. One of the most rewarding parts of event management is coming up with solutions to what often feel like impossible requests. Sitting with your team and brainstorming ideas on how you want the event to run or how you can get around the fact that your deliveries are all delayed by a road traffic accident on the main motorway into your event site takes skill. Being the kind of person who gets a thrill out of finding solutions helps make you a good event manager. It also helps when trying to think of all the potential problems before they occur, a role we called contingency planning. This is covered in chapter 13.

✔ **Attention to detail:** When I started my career in event management, I had a sticky note on my computer screen saying ATD. It stood for Attention To Detail. This note reminded me constantly to triple-check everything and to think about all the small things. Maybe you have no choice over the big things such as what venue to use, and you have to make the best of a bad option. Small things and attention to detail can transform a mediocre venue into the perfect venue for your event. It's easy to skim over small things when you're busy in the run-up to an event, but take your time to pay attention to the detail, and everyone notices the difference. Designing an experience that will be truly memorable is an art and I cover this in Chapter 7.

✔ **Time management:** Any potential event manager who turns up to an interview late is probably not in the right industry. Time management is a crucial element of events, not simply on your show day when you have to make sure it all runs to time. When planning your event, you need to work around the fixed deadline of the show day; you can't change the day to fit your planning. Not being ready on show day is not an option. See Chapter 9 for some ideas on how to manage your time.

✔ **Resourcefulness:** For those who remember *Challenge Anneka*, imagine that being an event manager is like being on one of these shows all the time. You need to be able to think on your feet and source yellow and green stripy table cloths with only two days to go. Resourcefulness is closely linked to problem solving but, in events, even when you've worked out the solution, you still need to put it into action. Resourcefulness, if you can hone this skill, is a lifesaver for you, your clients and your suppliers.

✔ **Organisation:** Often in interviews, I ask candidates why they want to get involved in events, and I regularly hear the answer 'Because I'm organised.' Don't join the industry just because you're organised, but organisational ability is definitely a good skill to have (although not the most important). Knowing what tasks you need to complete and how is a very good stepping stone to a successful event. Documents such as status reports and timing plans help with this immensely; see Chapter 4 for more information.

✔ **Negotiation skills:** Budgets can always be bigger. Things always cost more than you'd like, so being able to get the most for your client's money is an important skill. Many people are natural negotiators. Negotiation is an art, but one that you can develop. See Chapter 5 for the steps to creating a good negotiation plan.

✔ **Responsibility:** Taking a client's budget and spending it is a big responsibility in any industry. Events tend to have so many costs involved that it can be easy to lose track of what you've spent. A responsible approach to budget management helps you keep stress levels to a minimum, Chapter 5 will show you what costs you may need to consider but also how to potentially make money.

As an event manager, you're also responsible for lots of people. You may not have a big team to manage, but you're responsible for the guests at your event. See Chapter 12 for more information on health and safety.

I also believe that you have a responsibility to the environment around you when planning events. Thinking about what impact your event will have on local tourism, on the local residents and also on local facilities makes you a more considerate event manager.

✔ **Respectfulness:** One of the great things about events is that there's rarely a right or wrong way of doing things. If you have lots of people in a team, you often have many different ideas. Respecting other people's ideas and the support you receive from team members helps create good long-term relationships, see Chapter 4 for ideas on who to include in this key team of people during the planning stage.

You also need to respect your client. You may not agree with what clients want for their events, but remember that they are paying. Making sure that clients are happy is just as important as the event being planned to perfection. That isn't to say that you can't make suggestions for improvements, but remember who's boss.

✔ **Delegation:** There are no supermen or women in the event industry, as far as I know, so it's important to acknowledge that you can't always do everything. Think about who in your team can help you, and don't be afraid to ask for that help. See Chapters 4 and 11 for more information on team management, before and during the event.

✔ **Flexibility:** Event managers are often control freaks; to want to organise everything and be in control of all the different influences on the success of the event is in their nature. Being a control freak is no bad thing, but you need to be flexible and not let your controlling nature stop you from seeing and taking good opportunities. For example, you may have planned for all your table cloths to be white, but a supplier may offer the right number of black table cloths for free. Is the money saving worth the change in colour? Quite often it is, with just a slight tweaking of perception.

✔ **Efficiency:** This is a skill that I think you must be born with. It is the art of understanding in what order it is best to do things and doing them as quickly as possible. You could be organised and know what needs to be done, but still not get all the jobs done as quickly as someone who is efficient. Some people are efficient, and others aren't. Efficiency helps in event management, because you're often very busy and have only limited time in the day to complete all your tasks. It's not a case of multi-tasking but of doing what's required in the quickest way in the long term, not just the short term.

For example, you may have a huge list of things to do in the office, but you need to visit your supplier, who is two hours away. There are a couple of things you can do here. The first is to travel by train whenever possible, to give you the maximum time in which to work on your laptop and make phone calls. Second, see what other meetings you can fit into your day. If you're out for part of the day, you may as well be out for all of it and save another half day in the future.

✔ **Endurance:** The event industry can be tough, because the more passionate you are, the more you strive for perfection in all areas of your event. This often means very late nights and long days, with little sleep. I always make sure that I have bags of sweets on hand for the team if it's going to be a late night – I know that the combination of determination and sugar will get us to a successful event. See Chapter 18 for a list of 10 key things to have in your event kit.

Getting Started: Figuring Out Your Event's Objectives

Having reasons for doing something is always a good first step. The event industry refers to these reasons as *objectives*.

You're most likely going to be organising an event for someone else, whether that's your boss or someone from another company. The person who asks you to put on the event is *the client*.

Organising an event can be quite daunting, but the task is a lot easier if you have a clear brief to identify what you're doing and why. Make sure your brief is SMART: The acronym SMART is often used in the business world to help people write clear objectives and goals. It stands for:

- ✔ **Specific:** Often your client will have a very clear idea of what they want you to achieve, try to coax this out of your client through the briefing process because you may find however perfect your solution or answer is, if it doesn't match up to what they want, your client won't be happy. The clearer the initial brief, the better response you will be able to provide.

- ✔ **Measurable**: Ensure that your objectives in what you are trying to achieve are clear. Ask your client to tell you exactly what they want to achieve and discuss how you can measure this: For example, it is simply a certain number of people attending that is going to be classed as a success?

- ✔ **Attainable**: You have two areas to consider here: One, that the client's brief is achievable within the budget parameters they have set (see Chapter 5 for advice on budget management), and two, that it is the type of event that your audience will want to attend, and in which you are able to spark their interest through a basic marketing campaign. See Chapter 8 for information on how to get people to attend your event.

- ✔ **Relevant:** See Chapter 2 for information on knowing your target audience. You and your client may think a particular style event would be great fun but are you a good representation of your target audience? Will what you think is appealing, be appealing and relevant to those that you want to attend?

- ✔ **Timely**: (When working with your client on the initial brief, make sure it will work in terms of time in a couple of different areas. First, is it physically possible to do in the lead time they have provided you? Second, is the time that your client proposes for the event appropriate for the customer or delegate that you're trying to attract? See Chapter 9 for advice on how to decide when your event should be.

By ensuring that your client's objectives are written against these criteria, you have a clear checklist against which to make all your future decisions. If your Client provides you with a brief that doesn't match this, go back and ask as many questions as you can to extract the information you require. 'We ask a lot of questions' is one of the things I tell our clients up front, but I explain to them that I'm doing it so that I can provide the best possible solution, and not to annoy them!

The quality of briefs varies dramatically. Often, one of the first steps to guide your client through is writing the brief. It sounds back to front – and it kind of is – but a clear brief helps you going forward.

When you've received the brief from your client, first decide whether an event can actually meet all the client's objectives and requirements. It's not a question of trying to do yourself out of a job; it's important to decide whether you can do right by your client and the client's brief.

Figure 1-1 and 1-2 show two very different briefs, one that's incredibly thorough and explains clearly what the client is trying to achieve, and one that's much more open and doesn't provide you with all the information you would need. In the case of Figure 1-1, I would push the client to provide me with much more information to make it a SMART brief. Everyone prefers a particular type of brief: some people prefer more direction, whilst others like the space to decide on their own route.

Dear Laura,

Thanks so much for your time just now. As promised, I'm just sending over a bit more information about the idea we are looking at.

We want to set up a two-day 'pop-up' branded workspace, outdoors at Canary Wharf, at some point during this summer. Ideally we would provide areas to work, sunshades and lunch to office workers from the local area. We would also need an area to run iPad-driven demos.

Just wondered if you were able to give a rough figure of how much an event like this would cost to execute,

Many thanks,

Figure 1-1:
A simple
event brief.

		Experiential Brief
Key Business objective:		To increase penetration of Product A by 500,000 people by focusing on recruitment of our new target market (details to be provided separately).
Brief Objective		• To develop an experiential sampling campaign that creates cut through to continue to drive reappraisal by the new target market of Product A and specifically drives trial of Product A. • The communication should reinforce the over-arching brand message and also highlight Product A as a sub-brand that is desirable and relevant for our target market's needs. The campaign should feel consistent with the above the line communication. • The activity must communicate the key campaign message of XXX. • The campaign should recognise that although primarily an adult consumed product, it does also appeal to the whole family • The campaign should build brand engagement- it must link the deliciousness of our products to our sustainability credentials and the values at the heart of the brand. • Drive data capture through sign up to our e-newsletter/promotion of the new website. Prompted awareness of our brand is high, but saliency and conversion to purchase are low. To drive penetration, this campaign must reposition the brand in our target market's mind as a more desirable and relevant brand for them. In order to do this most effectively, the communications idea should be campaignable and provide a consistent and rich creative territory that is rooted in the brand consumer insight & brand position.

Total budget		£200,000 including product and coupon costs. Production cost of Product A variant B: Production costs of Product A variant C: We would like to include a 20p MONP coupon with each sample. Redemption costs @ 20p + handling charges will need to be accounted for in the budget.
Timings		Campaign to run from late March through April 2014.
Actions		Client to send brief: w/c Jan 6th 2014 Event Manager to present proposal w/c Jan 20th 2014 Client to confirm next steps w/c Jan 27th 2014

Figure 1-2:
A more
complex
event brief.

Chapter 2

Knowing Your Audience

*H*aving a clear idea of who your event is targeting helps make decision making and planning an easy process. It allows you to develop a checklist that is appropriate for your target market. This chapter shows you how to identify and categorise your target market, plus it gives some useful tips on how you can refer to them.

Zeroing In On Your Target Market

The term *target market* is often used in marketing, and is a good one to be familiar with when planning an event. It's impossible to appeal to everyone when putting on an event, and why would you want to? Your client's brand, company and product or service doesn't appeal to everyone, so why expect your event to?

Hopefully, clients provide a lot of background information about who they want to target; however, often they don't, especially if the event isn't part of their day-to-day remit.

Alphabet soup: B2B, B2C and B2E

What do all these letters mean? Well, long story short, B means business, C means consumer or customer, and E means employee. Therefore:

> ✓ **B2B:** Business to business marketing, in which an organisation seeks to interest other organisations in its goods or services.
>
> ✓ **B2C:** Business to consumer marketing, in which an organisation promotes its products and/or services to the end consumer.
>
> ✓ **B2E:** Business to employee marketing is also known as internal communication marketing and is when an organisation talks to its team of employees.

In event management, you may have to lay on events for any of the target markets – businesses, consumers or employees. The client's target group affects what type of event you plan and all the detail within it.

You may be required to talk to more than one of these groups of people. For example, you may be asked to organise an exhibition about innovation that's open to the public but also encourages small businesses to network with each other and start new projects. This is perfectly normal. It is possible to talk to more than one group of people at once. You need to tailor both your marketing plan and the content of the event, so that both groups benefit from attending your event.

Delving into demographics

In marketing and events, *demographics* help us categorise people and decide how to treat and interact with them. Information in five key areas helps you build up a good idea of how you can interact with groups of people. The characteristics to use are:

> ✓ Age
>
> ✓ Gender
>
> ✓ Income level
>
> ✓ Race
>
> ✓ Ethnicity

By dividing up your audiences in this way you are able to adapt your marketing approach as necessary.

Some clients may refer to groups of people such as the *baby boomers* (people born in the 20 years after the Second World War) and *Generation X* (those born after the baby boomers, up to the 1980s). These generational *cohorts* (groups) refer to people of a particular age, and for whom research has proven that they have certain beliefs based on their upbringing.

Exceptions always exist to the rules of demographics. Use groupings as a general indication only of the potential trends in interest and personality type that may be similar across your target audience.

Social classifications

Your client may often refer to people by letters and numbers. Often clients and marketers refer to people's social grade using the guidelines in Table 2-1. Again, this is useful to help establish the appeal of certain brands to particular groups, and the likely disposable income of different groups.

The classifications are referred to as NRS social gradings (because the National Readership Survey originally developed them). The gradings are based on the occupation of the person who earns the most in the household.

Table 2-1	NRS social gradings	
Grade	**_Social Class_**	**_Chief Income Earner's Occupation_**
A	Upper middle class	Higher managerial, administrative or professional
B	Middle class	Intermediate managerial, administrative or professional
C1	Lower middle class	Supervisory or clerical and junior managerial, administrative or professional
C2	Skilled working class	Skilled manual workers
D	Working class	Semi-skilled and unskilled manual workers
E	Those at the lowest levels of subsistence	Casual or lowest-grade workers, pensioners and others who depend on the welfare state for their income

The grades are often grouped into ABC1 for the middle class, and C2DE for the working class.

Creating identities for your target market

Once you've identified some target market groups, it's often helpful to be even more specific and pick out exactly the type of person you want to target. By building up a picture of a representative person in your target market, you can use it as a checklist for all your future planning and decision making. Think about what the person's family is like, and what hobbies and interests he or she has. Give your target a name as well, so he or she becomes a real person.

For example, Figures 2-1 and 2-2 give examples of two different targets for a breakfast cereal company: A traditional customer (Patricia) and a current target customer (Libby). The company was able to check whether its marketing plans targeted Patricia or Libby, as appropriate.

Patricia

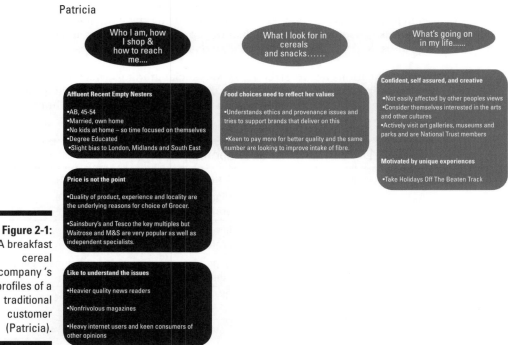

Figure 2-1:
A breakfast cereal company 's profiles of a traditional customer (Patricia).

The example in Figure 2-1 shows how important it is to review the target market profile if your client changes its product or service. If one of the objectives is to attract new customers with your event, you need to be clear exactly what type of customers your client wants to attract.

This process of identifying a target profile also works for internal communication events such as sales and marketing conferences. Think of the typical person within the organisation and then consider how long he or she has been with the company, the size of his or her family, what he or she does at the weekends, and so on.

Libby

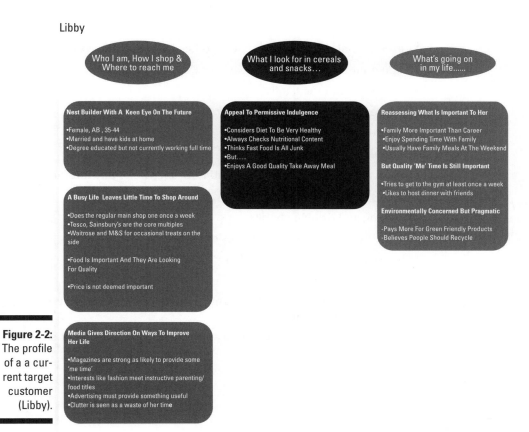

Who I am, How I shop & Where to reach me

What I look for in cereals and snacks...

What's going on in my life......

Nest Builder With A Keen Eye On The Future

•Female, AB , 35-44
•Married and have kids at home
•Degree educated but not currently working full time

Appeal To Permissive Indulgence

•Considers Diet To Be Very Healthy
•Always Checks Nutritional Content
•Thinks Fast Food Is All Junk
•But.....
•Enjoys A Good Quality Take Away Meal

Reassessing What Is Important To Her

•Family More Important Than Career
•Enjoy Spending Time With Family
•Usually Have Family Meals At The Weekend

But Quality 'Me' Time Is Still Important

•Tries to get to the gym at least once a week
•Likes to host dinner with friends

Environmentally Concerned But Pragmatic

-Pays More For Green Friendly Products
-Believes People Should Recycle

A Busy Life Leaves Little Time To Shop Around

•Does the regular main shop once a week
•Tesco, Sainsbury's are the core multiples
•Waitrose and M&S for occasional treats on the side

•Food Is Important And They Are Looking For Quality

•Price is not deemed important

Media Gives Direction On Ways To Improve Her Life

•Magazines are strong as likely to provide some 'me time'
•Interests like fashion meet instructive parenting/food titles
•Advertising must provide something useful
•Clutter is seen as a waste of her time

Figure 2-2:
The profile of a a current target customer (Libby).

Use the following checklist to get you started. Try to come up with answers (imagine you're making their Facebook profile page) but don't worry if there are some you can't complete yet. Imagine that you are describing a friend or a family member; by the end of your event planning, you should be referring to them by name. For example, 'Sarah from Manchester wouldn't like that, so how about we do it like this?' Try to list or describe the person's:

❑ Name

❑ Age

❑ Gender

❑ Place of residence

❑ Type of accommodation

❑ Co-residents: Who does he or she live with?

❑ Level of education

❑ Career: What does he or she do, and has he or she always done this?

❑ Annual/monthly income

❑ Position within the family

❑ Number of hours a week spent at work

❑ Leisure activities

❑ Hobbies

❑ Friendship group: How big is it and how does he or she interact with it?

❑ Diet

❑ Smoking and drinking habits

❑ Online behaviour: What websites does he or she visit?

❑ Shopping habits: Online or offline? How often?

❑ Club memberships (if any)

❑ Holidays: How often does he or she go on holiday? What kind of holiday does he or she go on?

❑ Religion: Is he or she religious? If so, what religion does he or she follow?

❑ Life ambitions

❑ Fears

Conducting Research

When you start event planning, you see how much research and planning is involved in each element. Every time you make a decision, consider whether you have made the right decision and check that you've not made an assumption.

We have a saying in the industry: When you assume, you make an ass of u and me.

This advice may sound straightforward and sensible, but it's amazing how easy it is to make assumptions or to forget to check information.

Guard against mistakes by making clear to your clients that you ask a lot of questions and double-check every single point. This verification isn't just needed at the detail-planning stage, such as when checking the entry time to the venue, or whether you've printed the final version of the event safety plan; you need to have this mind-set from the start, when your client tells you who the target market is and what the members of it believe.

Working with focus groups

Whenever you can you should try to get a group of your target market together as a *focus group* – people who you can test ideas against to see their reactions before you get too far down the planning process. If you are planning an internal communications event, see whether you can get a steering group together made up of people from various departments and of various ages, to get a good variety of opinions. It's not always possible, but the information you get is valuable. Chapter 14 investigates focus groups in more detail.

Bribe people with tea and biscuits, and you almost always get 15 minutes of someone's time and some honest opinions.

Looking at competing events

In marketing and communication, there's no problem with looking at what your competitors are doing and using it for inspiration. I'm not saying copy it, but the likelihood is that your client's competitors have done some research too, so at the least it's a good place to start for generating ideas.

First establish who the competition is. Your client is likely to have a pretty good idea, and a good brief includes this information. You can always double-check the information you've been provided to ensure that you understand. Before you start your event planning, make sure you know the following:

- ✔ Who your client's top five competitors are, and whether each is an employer or an alternative supplier for the same product
- ✔ Where your client's company/brand fits in the market place
- ✔ Market trends and size of the market place

Sign up to any newsletters available online for the main competition, so you receive regular updates and see first hand how your client's competitors treat people. It's useful to know what your competitors are offering their customers or employees, so you can accurately assess what will get cut through and what will appeal to your target market.

Where possible, attend events that are in competition with yours, so you know exactly what you are competing with.

Use the information you have

Having gathered information through focus groups and competitor/industry research, you need to use this knowledge to improve your event plan.

For a new family festival, focus groups, interviews and online research were conducted:

- ✔ The event logo that the organisers had designed was presented to parents in a focus group and the organisers sought their opinions. The feedback was that it looked vibrant but the colours were 'quite young', that is they would be more suitable for an audience of 2–7 year olds. This research allowed the organisers to update the logo with new colours to reflect the slightly older age group that they were targeting.

- ✔ Parents were asked in focus groups what ticket price they would pay for the event. To the organiser's amazement, they proactively suggested a price that was more than double the original ticket price. This research encouraged the organiser to review the ticketing model and opened up a greater opportunity for ticket revenue.

Starting With Who You Know

Not all the events you plan are trying to attract members of the public who have never heard of your event. You may be in the lucky position of already having a captive audience or an audience of people who have attended previous versions of the event. Speak to your client to see who is on the list of previous attendees.

Mandatory attendance

Not all events are open to everyone. If you are organising an event for a team of internal employees, their attendance may not be optional. However, don't completely disregard marketing to them. You still need to communicate with this group to tell everyone when the event is, what to expect and where to go. In this case, think of your marketing strategy as more of a communications strategy.

People at work are always being asked to attend meetings or events that they don't want to attend: Often, though, when they're there they see the benefit. You need to consider how to communicate the benefits before the event to stop people considering ways to get out of attending – you want people to look forward to it. Even when attendance is mandatory, you should still send out a 'save the date' message but focus more on encouraging employees by communicating how their long-term issues or concerns may be solved by them attending.

Customer relationship marketing

For repeat events, the previous guest base is a good place to start your marketing efforts. Previous guests already have a relationship with you, and if they had a good experience at the last event, they will have told other people about it.

Trying to convince this group of people to attend your event is a longer-term but easier process than attracting new guests. Previous attendees look for information to confirm their decision to attend the event again. For example, they may look for reasons to convince their boss that they should attend again. Past attendees want to know that other people in the industry of the right calibre will be attending. People who have attended in the past also expect the experience to be better than before. They may want to see testimonials from others who attended, to show it wasn't just them who had a good time, and photos to remind them of the event.

Loyal fans of brands

Among previous attendees, there may be a group of loyal and influential fans. These are the best type of brand ambassadors. Harness their enthusiasm and interest by asking them to share their experiences and help to shape the next event. Ask your client whether any previous attendees are interested in taking more of an active role. A quick search across online channels, such as chat groups, Facebook and LinkedIn groups, normally identifies any of these individuals, because of the high level of interaction they have.

Loyal fans are important to you, so treat them as VIPs: Give them a discount code for their tickets or give them a behind-the-scenes opportunity. Such special treatment is a small cost to you but makes a big difference in terms of added value to your loyal fans.

Chapter 3

Deciding on the Type of Event To Put On

*T*he scope for face-to-face interaction makes an event unique as a marketing and communications tool. In no other form of marketing communications do you have the ability to have such a close and personal relationship with your target market. On the down-side, however, there's no other way to create such a quick negative impact if the event's not pitched or executed correctly. Make sure you consider your objectives and the appropriate tone of the event to ensure that you select the right approach. If you are planning on communicating with a large number of your internal employees, for example, you're not likely to take the same approach as if you are speaking to members of the press/media.

In this chapter, you find out a little more about the types of event that you can put on and some of the lingo that's useful when talking about each approach. Many more types of event exist than we can cover here, but the selection should give you options for the most common objectives. I also provide some detailed information on giveaways, which can be a big part of any programme, including exhibitions and conferences.

Challenging the Brief

You may have already been given a specific enough brief by your boss to know exactly what type of event she has been expecting, but often you will be told to 'put on an event' with little guidance. My advice would be to challenge your brief: Find out from your boss or the rest of the organising committee what they have been imagining when they think of the event. This simple questioning process will quickly highlight any differences in their expectations are and what the objectives of the event are leading you to believe would be the perfect solution. It's much better to know about this at the start of your planning rather than when you have spent days or weeks researching and planning a different type of event. You will then need to decide how to handle the situation if there is a difference in approaches. This is likely to come down to your confidence and position within the business. If you strongly believe that their expectations do not match the objectives and/or budget, then you do have a responsibility to advise them of your recommendations. Often a way of convincing them is to discuss the Return on Investment (ROI) with them and use facts and figures to lead them down the right approach. This is covered in more detail in Chapter 5.

Objectives and budget should be at the heart of any decision you make.

Figure 3-1 gives you an outline of the type of event you should consider, but this is by no means exact.

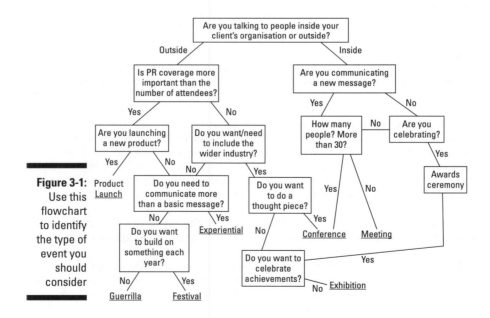

Figure 3-1: Use this flowchart to identify the type of event you should consider

Managing Meetings

If you work within a business environment, it is likely that you spend some of your time at work going from meeting to meeting, so you may wonder why I've classed meetings as events. Well, any time a group of people get together in a planned way, I class it as an event. Meetings don't organise themselves, and this task may well fall upon you! Often meetings and conferences get grouped in together and get confused, so I have approached them separately. You can correct your colleagues when they refer to them incorrectly! In general, meetings:

- Can be informal or formal – formal meetings are those that normally involve external stakeholders and informal meetings tend to include internal colleagues of similar levels
- Involve relatively few people (up to approximately 30)
- Are often held in-house (that is, within the building where the participants normally work)
- Last no longer than a day, normally just a few hours
- Involve minimal if any branding
- Need only very basic technical production

At **larger** events you would normally have signage showing the company name and the name of the event or product, for example, that is being discussed. Providing basic, clear information is the key to organising a successful meeting. Go about it like this:

1. **Discuss with the person who is going to chair the meeting, who the attendees should be.**

2. **Decide where the meeting is to be held and book the meeting room.**

3. **Send invites out to attendees (an Outlook calendar invite works well) but a personal call may be required if it's a more senior or unexpected team member.**

4. **Set a clear agenda and distribute to the team prior to the meeting.**

5. **Order any catering requirements such as tea and coffee, and food such as pastries if it is a breakfast meeting.**

6. **Provide IT support for any person needing to present on a screen (if you have an in-house IT assistant, make sure they are on standby; if it's going to be you, get there early and do a quick test).**

7. **Print out copies of the agenda and leave them on the tables in the meeting room for easy reference.**

8. **Check with the chair of the meeting whether you need to order additional catering at any point throughout the meeting.**

9. **Ensure that any follow-up information has been distributed after the meeting.**

Crafting a Conference

You've probably been to conferences at which you felt like you were back at school, sitting at the back of the class, not really wanting to be there and planning what you were going to do that evening when you escaped. Well, that's a badly planned conference. Let me introduce you to an interesting conference where your guests (or delegates as we call them in conference circles) are learning, inspired and networking all day.

An internal conference is for your client's colleagues, that is internal employees in an organisation. An external conference is open to a wider audience and often open to the public generally. Whether it's an internal conference for your sales and marketing department or an event open to the public, conferencing can and should be creative and inspiring. A conference is normally made up of some basic elements:

- ✔ A plenary session
- ✔ Breakout sessions or seminars
- ✔ Networking opportunities
- ✔ A team-building session

It's your job to make each session as effective as possible.

If the conference is for an internal audience, a lot of your colleagues are likely to have taken a whole day or more out of the office to attend, so it is important for them (and your career) that they feel that it has been worthwhile.

Common reasons/objectives to host this type of event would be:

- ✔ Bring a diverse group of people together in one geographic location.
- ✔ Network and meet like-minded people.
- ✔ Communicate with a large group of people at one time.
- ✔ Motivate a team/extended team of employees.
- ✔ Be able to take top-line information and create working groups to discuss sub-sections in more detail.

Energisers

These can be really useful during a conference when you need to wake your audience up a little! They tend to only last a few minutes and should be planned into your schedule after a lengthy plenary session, and before delegates listen to another speaker. You should get your host to introduce them.

It could be as simple as:

✔ Making the whole audience get on their feet and clap their hands 10 times.

✔ Getting every person to turn to their right and shake the hand of the person next to them.

✔ Asking your audience to hold up a piece of coloured card in response to a question about the previous plenary topic (you need to provide tables with coloured card if you are going to do this!)

Energisers also give you an opportunity to do a quick stage-set change in the background if you need to.

Planning the Plenary

Plenary is the term we use to describe the part of the day when all the delegates are sitting in the main conference room listening to a speaker. The plenary tends to be at the start of the conference and can be used to update the whole team on sales figures, targets and strategy plans for the following year. It is a good way of communicating with everyone at once and should be inspiring.

Consider carefully who will host these plenary sessions to make sure they don't become several hours of being preached at.

✔ For internal conferences, you will often find the Board of Directors will speak, such as the Sales and Marketing Director, the Finance Director, and the Digital Director.

✔ When your conference is directed to delegates from outside your organisation, particularly when they are expected to pay for attending, it is important to consider who the audience want to hear from.

Check what each speaker is intending on speaking about to ensure they are not repeating each other.

Organising breakout sessions

Breakout sessions are when you split your delegates up into smaller groups and normally move them to different rooms within your venue. They're often referred to as *workshops*. A breakout session is a term that tends to be used when discussing conferences for your internal team. These working groups enable activities to be run and are a good way to mix different departments so that a session on New Product X may involve delegates from sales, marketing, market research and customer service. When these departments mix, participants can hear and consider different points of view.

Breakout sessions are a good way to tackle difficult subjects that may need more detailed information and question and answer sessions.

The number of breakout sessions to plan into your day will depend on how many delegates you have attending and how much content you've got to talk about.

Seminars

Seminars are like breakout sessions for external conferences. For example, you may be putting on a conference where the main topic of conversation will be 'How Manufacturing in Great Britain is supporting the Economy'. You may look to host individual sessions after the plenary sessions about the more detailed facets of this, such as, 'The impact Manufacturing has previously had on the Economy', 'How Manufacturing varies around the country' and 'What are the current trends in Manufacturing?'

Seminars tend to be less interactive than breakout sessions and are like miniplenaries. As with breakout sessions, the number of seminars you should plan into the day will depend on the amount of space for delegates in each room and how many topics of conversation you would like to offer.

If you want to run multiple at the same time, you could offer your delegates the choice of which seminars to attend. This allows your delegates to plan their day around what most interests them. By asking your delegates to prebook their attendance at these, you will be able to gauge which ones are the most popular and you may potentially be able to swap rooms around to maximise the space for the most popular seminars.

Team-building

When planning this part of your day for an internal conference, remember it's about team-building. Don't be tempted to pick an activity just because it sounds fun or easy; remember it needs to actually bring your team members together – to motivate them, ideally in a skill/knowledge sharing and personable way so that your team feel closer after. As we know, teams that get on better, do better work.

There are many great team-building companies out there that specialise in running this part of your conference and are normally very self-sufficient. However, if your budget doesn't allow you to bring a company in to help, make sure you have some little helpers and you can run something yourself.

Not all activities need to be expensive or difficult to organise, but as always in event planning, ensure you refer back to your objectives and information on your audience to make sure your choices are appropriate.

Three main reasons exist for using a team-building activity:

- ✔ **Improving group communication skills:** An example of a team-building activity for improving group communication would be to describe a situation where you are recruiting for a job – it doesn't need to be their current industry and the interviewer can only ask one question. It will make the team realise how important questions are and how a cleverly considered question can provide a large amount of information. Give each of your teams 5 jobs to interview for and encourage everyone to share their answers and how they got there after approximately 30 minutes.

- ✔ **Problem solving as a team:** A popular and low-cost exercise would be to ask your delegates to identify who they think might be the target market for a new product the company is launching.

  - **Step one:** Split your audience up into smaller groups of 5–10 delegates

  - **Step two:** Provide them with a stack of newspapers or magazines, cardboard, scissors, glue and pens

  - **Step three:** Give the team a time limit of 1 hour to put relevant words and photo clippings onto an A3 board that represents the new target market

  - **Step four:** Display all the A3 boards on easels during the next tea-break for other delegates/team members to look at

  - **Step five:** Hold up the best example on stage and offer a prize to the winning team

- ✔ **Building trust between team members:** Making eye contact is a big part of good communication but also for developing trust and respect. Some people find it very difficult and so a great exercise for helping build trust is focusing on this. Pair your team up and make them look into each other's eyes for 60 seconds and make them start again if they break eye contact. Then do it again but making them hold eye contact for 90 seconds.

You need to establish which one of these fits your objectives and design your team building around performing various tasks that are fun but also challenging. By running these activities as a group, you should see the benefits of different personality types helping add different approaches and opinions into a situation.

 The team-building activity is a good way to integrate your company's Corporate Social Responsibility (CSR) policy into your event. The company CSR policy may relate to giving back to the community or reducing waste by a certain amount.

Networking Knowledgably

Whether your event is for delegates inside your business or outside your business, networking is just as important. Often with large businesses, an annual conference may be the only opportunity for delegates to meet their peers from other countries and colleagues in other departments. New opportunities and relationships can be developed and can often lead to sales and thus profit, so this element of an event should never be a second thought.

If you are running a networking event that is independent of any other event – that is, not part of a larger conference, you may wish to consider charging people to attend. Delegates will pay to attend if they are confident that they will meet people that will prove profitable in the future.

To allow delegates to plan their approach to the networking event, think about how much information you communicate with them prior to the day. You may wish to send an email, which lists those companies that have representatives attending. This will enable those pro-active attendees to plan who they want to target and do basic research before they attend.

A networking session can either be an event in its own right or part of a larger conference or exhibition. Both types will require a similar approach in terms of your role. You need to consider:

✔ Are there sets of people that you feel it is essential for them to meet? You may want to consider a more structured approach to the networking session where people are pre-matched to those that they should meet.

✔ Will certain people be in higher demand than others? Make sure your attendee list is balanced so one person doesn't feel under too much pressure whilst everyone else is left disappointed.

✔ What will you do if no-one talks to each other? If you decide to take a fluid approach to the session and let everyone do it for themselves, you and your team may still end up needing to assist with some people starting off conversations. Always try to introduce people with an interesting fact so immediately both parties know why they are being encouraged to speak to each other.

In Chapter 6 I run through digital techniques to facilitate networking but at this stage, you need to decide if you think it will be of benefit to your delegates.

Network to extend your network – it's about conversations, not the presentation of ideas from other people.

Putting Together Great Exhibitions

An exhibition is a collection of similar items. Some are temporary and some are permanent like at a museum. Events are non-permanent so we have focused on temporary exhibitions and trade shows. You could organise an exhibition to be part of a conference or it may be a stand-alone event. It could be anything from a school art exhibition to a chemical engineering industry exhibition; the subject matter does not matter and the scale of it just impacts the time it takes to organise!

The companies or people that exhibit are called exhibitors, which we will also touch on briefly here.

Common reasons/objectives to host an exhibition would be:

✔ Bring together a group of industries or departments that have a common interest

✔ Provide an environment for conversation to happen with like-minded people

✔ Create an event that can happen regularly

✔ Create an event which can encompass many other event facets

It is for you to decide where your exhibitors come from; there is no set way. Detailed below are three common ways of filling your exhibition space with some interesting exhibits.

Self selecting

It may be that you have such a clear idea of how your exhibition should look and what should be involved that you know exactly what companies you want to take part, or it may be that your exhibition is actually an internal business event where different departments are presenting their plans. Either way, the decision on who should be involved has already been made and the next stage is to convince them to take part! Think carefully about what you're asking them to do; being part of an exhibition can take up a lot of time and if it's a small department or company where there may only be a couple of people, asking them to man an exhibition stand for a day or more could have a significant impact on their normal workload.

Using an application process

A democratic approach to take would be to offer all companies in a sector such as engineering to apply for the opportunity to be involved. This would allow all sizes of companies to potentially be involved and wouldn't restrict attendance to those who can afford to pay the highest site fees. It is extremely important to set very clear timings and very clear criteria for success. In essence, it is a pitching process where the companies have to demonstrate why their exhibit would be the most relevant/interesting/suitable to include. This process is generally used when it is for the public sector and favouritism can't be a contributing factor, but you could follow the same principles if you want to include a broad range of companies at your event.

The steps that you need to carry out for this process are:

- ✔ Publicise the exhibition and the opportunity for companies to get involved.

- ✔ Ask all interested companies to submit an *Expression of Interest* form, which details basic information about the company.

- ✔ Identify any companies which do not achieve the basic requirements.

- ✔ Send all qualifying companies a *Submission Pack* for them to complete, which should detail their intended stand design and messaging.

- ✔ Process the packs through a Judging Process with as many stages as necessary to get to the required number of companies.

- ✔ Send letters to all unsuccessful companies thanking them for their interest and efforts.

- ✔ Phone and then write to all successful companies with details of next steps.

Paid-for exhibitions

This is an opportunity to make some money! If your event isn't internal and is aimed at the trade or the general public, many companies will be able to justify spending money to have a presence there as part of their marketing budget. This could be for two reasons: The opportunity to increase brand awareness and to sell product at the event and generate sales during the day.

The way to cost up the spaces at the exhibition can be difficult and research should be done into what exhibitors are paying at other similar events, but contributing factors to setting the cost would be:

✔ Expected number of visitors

✔ Size of space

✔ Positioning of space

Exhibiting at an exhibition

Organising an entire exhibition may be a little bit big for what you need and it may be that there is a suitable exhibition or trade fair in your industry that you want to attend. In which case, you will be one of the exhibitors. Taking a space at an exhibition can be a cost-effective way to get your company in front of a large number of relevant people.

The most common approach for you will be to:

1. **Find a relevant show to attend.**

2. **Apply to attend (either application process or paid for).**

3. **Agree with the organisers the position you want.**

4. **Design your stand.**

5. **Organise your attendance.**

6. **Attend the exhibition.**

7. **Evaluate your gains.**

Before agreeing what space you want at an exhibition, think about the traffic flow around the space and try to think about where people are going to spend most time. Look at spaces around the café areas and near the entrance.

Perfecting Product Launches

The way a product is launched will have a big impact on how the press, industry and public will perceive it. Therefore – hey, no pressure – perfect execution is essential!

Launches tend to come in two forms: Either a stand-alone press launch or as a reveal as part of a larger event such as at a conference or exhibition. Either way, ensuring secrecy and good press coverage are normally the main objectives.

The automotive industry has always focused heavily on how their new products are launched. They range from having a large piece of cloth covering the vehicle and the reveal being pulling off the cover to lowering the new model down from the ceiling into the venue and creating a theatrical effect with the build up. However, recently there has been a trend for using more technology in launches – video mapping and 3D projection are becoming common and impressive.

The Lexus CT 200h launch event in Dubai in 2011 and the Hyundai Accent Launch, also in 2011, were fantastic examples of creating a captivating and memorable launch whilst simply using powerful visual effects.

Powerful product launches aren't just restricted to companies with massive budgets in glamorous locations. You can organise a successful event by also creating something memorable for your audience.

- ✔ **PR is key:** You will need to work closely with whoever manages your PR as it is likely that this will be the key driver for holding a launch event. There is no point creating a fantastic product launch in your company headquarters if you establish that the relevant media won't leave the local city.

- ✔ **Be different to the competition:** Media are likely to be invited to similar events for your competitors all the time so think about how your event will stand out.

- ✔ **Delivery is everything:** It is essential that whilst you are telling the world that your new product is market leading and is the best thing since sliced bread, make sure it works when you are launching it.

However, with the nature of social media, your customers don't always need to wait for the media to release stories about your new product; you may decide to go direct to your customers. If you are promoting a product or service that is very lifestyle focused, but maybe not very unique in offering, it is unlikely that you will get vast press coverage unless the launch is spectacular.

Common reasons/objectives to host this type of event would be:

- ✔ Launching a new product or service to the public or media
- ✔ An alternative to Above the Line (ATL) advertising, or to kick-start an ATL campaign
- ✔ Achieving high levels of brand awareness and coverage for the product/ service (press and social media)

TNT: Launching with a bang

A great example of a product launch comes from Belgium. A big red button, on a plinth, was positioned in the middle of a town square. A large arrow hung above the button with the word 'Push', to add drama. Curious members of the public would come up to the button and push it, and a series of events unfolded on a screen in front of them. People got knocked over, ambulances appeared, a fight broke out, a woman in underwear on a motorbike drove past, amongst other strange things. As the minute-long scene finished, a banner dropped down from the side of a nearby building which read 'Your daily dose of drama from 10/04 on TNT'.

The TV channel TNT's launch went viral and had far more impact in launching the new brand than a traditional, media-focused press release would have had, with over 10 million YouTube hits to date. This is a great example of how a product launch can also be seen as a PR stunt and as a piece of experiential activity to spark attention and interest from the public. (See later on in this chapter for more information on experiential marketing events.) In essence, whatever you call it, it has created content that is engaging and memorable.

Appreciating Award Ceremonies

We've all seen the Academy Awards (Oscars) and the buzz that surrounds it; the glamour, the celebrities, the red carpet, the gold envelopes, the emotional speeches and the fake smiles of those that didn't win!

Whilst it's unlikely your first award ceremony is going to be quite on that scale, it's good to have the potential in mind because if your awards ceremony become so renowned, you never know how big it's going to grow! However there is no need to feel intimidated because in essence, as long as you have some awards, some guests, some winners and losers – you have yourself an awards ceremony! For interest – the first Academy Awards were presented on May 6, 1929 with an audience of only 270 people and the winners had been announced 2 months before, so every event starts somewhere.

As with press launches, an awards dinner can be an event on its own or part of a larger conference and/or exhibition. It may be for the industry or for your own company.

Common reasons/objectives to host an awards ceremony would be:

- ✔ To recognise achievements of individuals or groups of people
- ✔ To bring together a company or industry in unified support

Some of the questions to ask are:

✔ **What are the awards going to be for?** A very basic question but very important. If you're only giving one award away, do you really need to do an entire ceremony? Would people come and would it get enough interest?

✔ **How formal is the event going to be?** This comes down to what is appropriate for your audience and the awards that are being presented.

  • Is it going to be black tie and a sit-down meal? This is the most common approach as your finalists want to feel that there was some grandeur in winning their award. They need to feel that it really is a prestigious moment.

  • Or is it going to be more relaxed and a standing event? This is a good option if your ceremony isn't expected to last more than an hour and you want to save money. Food, furniture and even the venue can cost less as it doesn't need to be a big ceremony.

✔ **How are people going to be nominated/shortlisted?** Options are:

  • An online entry process

  • Face-to-face presentations

  • Make a shortlist of nominees and give the final choice to someone else.

You could also consider charging people to enter the awards; this is common practice in industry awards, but not with internal communication events.

✔ **Who is going to decide on the finalists for each category?** There are three main options:

  • You employ a judging panel (if it's an internal event, it could be the Board of Directors or it could be leading figures in the industry)

  • You put it to a public vote

  • You decide the winners

Ensure your process is rigorous because all it takes is a bad loser to question the integrity of the finalist selection process and you may have much more press than you had ever thought possible for your awards – in awards, not all press is good! You need to feel confident that if challenged, you are confident that your process was fair to all involved.

✔ **How many finalists are you going to have for each category?** Three to five finalists per awards are normally sufficient. It's important to remember that the more you have, the longer the ceremony is going to take and the more prep/attendees that will be needed!

✔ **How are you going to introduce the finalists?** You could:

   • Have a host – external or internal

   • Have a *Voice of God* (a voice over the PA system who doesn't stand on stage)

   • Use video content with photos or short videos of the entrants (remember someone will need to produce and run these films)

✔ **Who is going to present the award?** Someone who is respected in the industry should present the award, whether or not this is an internal team member or from another organisation. This choice will often come down to costs and relationships. Make sure you get a photographer to take a photo of the special moment!

Sizing Up Sporting Events

As the name would suggest, a sporting event is only appropriate when the prime purpose of your event is to have people competing and potentially spectating one or multiple sports. This can range from a School Sports Day, to a Premiership Football match to the most high-profile sporting event – The Olympics.

Sporting events are a very bespoke type of event and it is unlikely that you will have to organise one unless you work specifically in a sport-related industry. They do, however, offer some interesting elements for you to consider when planning other events.

Sports events rely on two things – competition and community. Whilst it is the case for all events, in sports events, the atmosphere is something that can change dramatically minute-by-minute, more so than in any other execution.

Basic elements such as visitor flow and catering are of particular importance at sports events because very tight windows of opportunity exist during which everyone is trying to achieve exactly the same thing. Ensuring you can cope with capacity expectations and potential security risks will make for a smooth-running event.

Common reasons to host this type of event would be:

✔ To bring together competing teams

✔ To create a sense of community

Festival Fun

When most people think of festivals they have visions of tents, rain, mud and music stages. There are many festivals like this, but they aren't the only ingredients that make up a festival.

A festival simply refers to a celebratory event, normally relating to a particular theme.

So it's not surprising that there are festivals out there for comedy, literary, art etc. Contrary to popular belief, a festival doesn't always need to be on one site either; multi-venue festivals are very common in literary and comedy circles but again, they can be any theme. In fact multi-venues are normally internal sites, which are a great protection against the English weather!

There is also a pretty even split between paid for and free festivals. Your decision on which route you take should be based on budgeting restrictions and your main objectives. We cover more about ticketing in Chapter 8.

All of these different types of festivals can be joined up as content areas or zones within a more eclectic festival.

Common reasons/objectives to host this type of event would be:

- ✔ To create a community event
- ✔ To make money
- ✔ To highlight the needs or skills of an industry or group of people

You will not make money in your first year. It takes on average three years to make a profitable festival.

Music festivals

Content and atmosphere are the two things that will contribute to a successful music festival. If you are intending on starting from scratch, ask yourself if you know enough of the right people. More than in any other type of event planning, who you know is vital. If you don't know the right people, come up with a plan as to how you could meet the right people.

CASE STUDY

Just making it happen: the Edinburgh Fringe

The Edinburgh Festival Fringe is part of the largest arts festival in the world and takes place every August for three weeks in Scotland's capital city.

Every year thousands of performers take to a multitude of stages all over Edinburgh to present shows for every taste. From big names in the world of entertainment to unknown artists looking to build their careers, the festival caters for everyone and includes theatre, comedy, dance, physical theatre, musicals, operas, music, exhibitions and events.

In 1947, eight theatre groups turned up uninvited to perform at the (then newly formed) Edinburgh International Festival, an initiative created to celebrate and enrich European cultural life in the wake of the Second World War. Not being part of the official programme

of the International Festival didn't stop these performers – they just went ahead and staged their shows anyway. Year on year more and more performers followed their example and in 1959 the Festival Fringe Society was created in response to the success of this growing trend.

The Society formalised the existence of this collective of performances, provided information to artists, published the Fringe programme and created a central box office. Its constitution was written in line with the ethos that brought these theatre companies to Edinburgh back in 1947: That the Society was to take no part in vetting the festival's programme. To this day that policy remains at the core of the Fringe festival and anyone with a story to tell and a venue willing to host them will be included in the programme. (www.edfringe.com, 2012)

A music festival is made up of multiple performers, scheduled to play in either one or multiple venues across the course of the event. There should be a genre of music that glues all the acts together in one venue. That is not to say that you can't have an eclectic mix of music at your event, but try to make sure that you're not sending your audience off all around your event to listen to their favourite type of music.

Artists and their management teams need to believe that performing at your event will further their career. The ideal line-up will include some big names that draw in the crowds and some smaller acts that complement the headliners and could potentially get their big break by playing at your event.

REMEMBER

It takes time to build up enough of a reputation to command the most respected and popular artists.

Two common approaches to music festivals are a remote venue and multi-city-venues. Take Glastonbury Festival of Contemporary Performing Arts and The Great Escape in Brighton as examples; two very different music festivals, but both successful in their own right. Table 3-1 compares the two festivals.

Table 3-1	Comparing festivals
Glastonbury	*The Great Escape*
One large outdoor site, miles away from city life	Over 30 indoor venues across the town
Only weekend tickets sold	Tickets sold per day or as a weekend deal
Food and drink can be taken on the site but is available to also purchase	Food and drink has to be purchased in the venues
Music, comedy, arts and literature	Music only
Family friendly	Adults only

Both are successful but both have very different approaches. You can take elements of either of these approaches to develop your ideal music festival; just check that each decision is linked back to your objectives and target market.

Comedy festivals

Comedy is a tricky business: What one person finds funny, another person may find offensive. Doing thorough research into the types of acts that your target market are interested in is essential. A comedy festival where no one laughs is not a successful event, regardless of how fantastic your stage set looks.

Literature festivals

This type of festival generally has a niche audience and so is best approached by starting small and building up. It is most commonly spread across multiple venues that have a connection to literature, allowing people to pick and choose the authors who really interest them.

You should always try to consider how you can get local businesses involved in your event.

Making Hay

Hay Festival is one of the most famous literature festivals in the UK. It has a programme of debates and conversations with poets and scientists, novelists and historians, artists and gardeners, comedians and musicians, filmmakers and politicians. In 10 days it hosts over 900 individual events and everything is hand picked. The main festival site is free to everyone and the individual events have a cost attached, which allows the visitors to spend as much, or as little, as they want. It also caters for families and children of all ages.

Many local venues get involved and host events, so as well as being an event that brings visitors to the area, it encourages involvement and pride from the locals.

Food festivals

Food festivals are becoming common in local council calendars. They are a great opportunity to bring communities together around a subject matter that everyone can become engaged in. Everyone has to eat and by ensuring a wide variety of foods is available, they can be a very inclusive event.

Small events can be created where local traders are contacted and asked to bring a mobile unit to a public space such as a town centre. This can be then scaled up to the size of an event such as Taste of London where restaurants and other lifestyle brands, come together to create immersive experiences.

Experiential Field Marketing

There are two phrases that often get discussed – field marketing and experiential marketing. Both have very similar values – that sending a team of people out in to the field is the best way to communicate a message, but that is where their similarity ends.

These two types of events are very often confused and you may find companies claiming they do one, when actually it is the other they can offer. This is particularly the case when companies claim they are running a brand experience programme, but there is such a limited customer experience that it is basic field marketing. As with many things, companies are often trend followers without real knowledge as to what the trends entail.

Field Marketing

Field marketing involves sending out a team of people, often called *brand ambassadors* (BAs), into the market place to ensure that messages are being communicated correctly. Field marketing is a traditional discipline in marketing, involving people distributing, auditing, selling or sampling promotions in the 'field'.

Imagine that a product for washing up is being sold with a free laundry bag. The field marketing team will be the team of people that visits all the supermarkets around the country to ensure that the laundry bags are being displayed correctly next to the washing-up tablets.

A Field Marketing programme is normally something organised by the distribution or sales team rather than the marketing team. It also lends itself more to FMCG (fast-moving consumer goods, such as toiletries) products where samples can be easily and cheaply distributed. For more information on this, please see 'Sampling' further on in this chapter.

Experiential Marketing

Experiential Marketing is the process of engaging with your target audience in a memorable and interactive way. The target audience should come away from it feeling like they have had an experience that they would never have had without your company.

There is a fine line between having a poster and a BA handing out samples in the town centre and a BA asking you to take part in a game in front of the poster, where a sample is your prize. The first is a form of advertising and the second is a basic form of experiential marketing.

However it can go so much further than that: experiential marketing needs to have creating interesting experiences at the heart of the planning but location is actually of equal importance. We will cover creating content and how to decide where to host your event in more detail in Chapters 6 and 10.

innocent, the smoothies and drinks company, is one of the most loved brands in England. It's been voted the brand people most want to work for and is a company that many other companies want to be like. innocent have created a cult following by their fans even though their product is at a premium price point. One of the reasons for this is that they treat their customers like part of the family.

When innocent decided to create a brand experience, they made sure that their brand was at the heart of it and helped to determine every decision that was made. They created the *innocent Village Fete*, which was a brand experience, a festival and a sampling event all in one.

By not investing money into headline acts but investing money into areas creating activities for people to take part in, whatever age they were, innocent managed to maximise the reach they could achieve. Rather than having a VIP area, they invited guests into their VNP area – for Very Nice People, keeping their friendly and non-pretentious tone intact in the live environment. Small additions like creating a tagged puggy park and by allowing visitors to reminisce about the village fetes of their youth with ferret racing and welly-wanging, it had the ultimate easy, feel-good factor.

Through clever marketing and impeccable attention to detail in the delivery, innocent created a sell-out event that has since gone on to win many awards. Nearly 50,000 bought tickets for the event with over £1m worth of press generated from over 80 journalists from top dailies. Over 1,500 photos were uploaded to Flickr website by those that attended with even more content on Facebook and YouTube.

So you can see how, because of the many crossovers, field marketing and sampling are often confused with experiential marketing. Typically, both involve deploying BAs into the market places and both will involve a lot of logistical planning.

Interactivity is key.

Therefore the phrase that is most useful to describe the likely type of event that you would be asked to organise is Experiential Field Marketing – a live activity where face-to-face human interaction is a main focus and a brand message is communicated in an engaging and memorable way, potentially with some sampling too.

The location option for this type of activity is vast but proximity to purchase points of the product is often a contributing factor. If customers decide they like your product, where can they buy it nearby? Imagine shopping centres, town centres, theme parks, public spaces such as parks, the list is endless if you are truly offering your customers an experience that is more immersive than if they were in a shop that sold your products.

You should consider carefully the reasons why your customers may want to engage with your experience. Unlike other events, your audience is unlikely to be actively choosing to engage in the experience so it needs to be drawn in. Content and appearance will be major factors in this (see Chapter 6), so try to put yourself in your customer's shoes – if you were invited to take part, would you, would it change your opinion of the company/brand and would you remember it?

Common reasons/objectives to host this type of event would be:

✔ To raise awareness of a product/service or company

✔ To create positive memories connected to the product/service or company

The Pop-Up Phenomenon

Pop-up shops and restaurants have become a trend in the last 10 years across the globe. The trend involves 'popping-up' one day, then disappearing anywhere from one day to several weeks later. They started off as shops where companies were able to create a truly bespoke and interesting experience for a short period of time. Particularly useful when a product is launched and you want to make it stand out more than the current range, pop-ups tend to be very creative and very interactive.

Recently, as the trend has taken off, this concept has become more common in big cities. If you live outside of a major town, you still may have never seen one. They rely heavily on marketing to support them and very often there are refer a friend and word of mouth type schemes to encourage knowledge.

innocent smoothies used this concept to great success, to promote their move from drinks into food. They set up a pop-up café for 10 days, which had a limited amount of tickets available. They were sold out every day with people waiting at the door to see if they could get a cancellation booking. It created a vast amount of press and positive brand awareness. A brand which has historically been connected to fast food, made a successful move into the world of fine dining all through an event in a temporary venue. The space is now a permanent restaurant for another chef, so in essence, innocent tested the concept and space for another brand.

Giveaways

Everyone likes free things; whatever it is, people's natural instinct is to take it if it's free. It is likely that you will have relatively large numbers of giveaways and the basics of where these are going to be stored and then how they are going to be given out need to be considered in your planning. Can they be prepared weeks in advance or is it a perishable, refrigerated sample that can only be distributed in a certain way. Giveaways can be summed up as two different approaches: Goody bags at events and sampling, but the two can be combined.

Goody bags

If you are organising an exhibition and you have lots of sponsors who want a way to communicate with all visitors about their service/product/offer, providing the guest with a bag of literature is an easy way to do this. It is commonly done at events such as the Ideal Home Show® and can be a cheap method of communication.

Goody bags are another example of where attention to detail is important. Overstuffing a bag and it breaking as your visitor walks home, doesn't give off a good impression. It may seem like a good cost-saving method to go for the cheap plastic bag but actually if you have some weighty literature, it may be worth investing in a stronger, paper bag with rope handle or even a tote bag. If it is attractive and a practical size, your visitor may re-use this bag the next day for carrying their lunch into the office and what was a simple goody bag, is now a piece of branding being carried around and endorsed by someone.

Think about when you want to distribute your goody bags: On the way in to your event so they can read some of the literature whilst there or on the way home so your guests don't have to carry the bag around all day?

Samples can be included in goody bags. If you are working with a brand that needs to get access to lots of people but doesn't want to have a physical presence at an event (such as a running race), there are companies that specialise in pulling these goody bags together and will sometimes include your sample for free if they are looking to bulk up the bag.

Goody bags don't have to be just for mass-market communication; remember when you were a child and you went to a birthday party, you got given a party bag? It's the same concept. If you want to say thank you to your guests, it can be a way to extend your generosity after the event. Luxury brands will often be seen doing this with celebrities at parties. They are hoping that the celebrity or influencer, will publicly talk about their product. If you are organising an event where you know your guests are likely to be of great interest to a brand, don't be shy about asking them if they'd like to get involved. (For more information on brand partnerships, look at Chapter 5.)

Sampling

Traditionally linked with field marketing and experiential marketing, sampling is a great way to get large numbers of people to trial your product. It tends to work best for FMCG (fast moving consumer goods) products due to cost. Many companies are confident that when someone tests/tastes their product, they will think it is good and, as such, it is worth giving them a free trial. There is an element of risk for a consumer to purchase a product or variant of which they have no knowledge; sampling reduces risk and has a direct influence on purchase consideration.

As with all types of marketing, your target market and their mind-set need to be considered. Train stations during rush hour are great venues for sampling cereal bars to busy commuters, but not so good for sampling nappies. The way your sample is presented needs to be considered: Are you trying to communicate something new? Do you need to educate the consumer? Dump bins of samples such as drink cans work really well when it's very clear what you need to do with the product. When the sampling campaign is to educate the consumer on a new method of consumption or use, having someone there to demonstrate this will be more beneficial. This approach is often found in supermarkets, where demonstrators will have a small stand at the end of an aisle and, for example, will show you how a new flavour of soup goes really well with a particular brand of bread.

Sampling is often connected to coupons and redemption offers. This gives the consumer that extra encouragement/push to purchase that is sometimes needed. Using coupons can be controversial – many companies feel that offering money off can lessen a brand's image, but even Harrods has The Sale. If a company such as this can offer money off when it is appropriate, there's no reason why other brands can't follow suit.

Due to the nature of a money-off coupon, there are ways of tracking the success of the campaign, down to finite detail. It is not uncommon to see an increase in sales of a particular product in a region where sampling has taken place in the previous week. This shows the success of the campaign in a way no one can argue with.

Guerrilla Marketing

Guerrilla marketing is about creating experiences out of the unexpected to attract attention and deliver word of mouth. Not often used on a large scale, it is a great technique to consider when communicating something like a brand name or a simple message. It may be used when speaking to customers outside your organisation, but isn't often used for communicating with internal employees.

Not often considered to be an event on its own, when used creatively guerrilla marketing can be part of a larger event/campaign in either the lead up or during the actual live day.

Zero to hero

Coke Zero promoted their partnership with Skyfall – a James Bond franchise film – by encouraging customers to *Unlock the 007 in You*. A branded vending machine was placed in a train station. Customers had to fill in their contact details electronically on the screen and were then sent on a 70-second, Bond-style mission around the station to win tickets to the film's premiere. There were obstacles all around and the final part of the challenge was to hum the Bond theme-tune.

Just because you want to create something that is non-permanent and likely to only exist for a few minutes, it is still important to consider the implications of your actions and any permissions/permits that you will need to apply for – it should still be legal!

There has been a trend recently of brands using vending machines to communicate with their customers in an interactive way. By taking something that is normally so self-sufficient and easy to understand, customers are being surprised by the new use and therefore it sticks out in their day as being even more memorable.

The video on YouTube accompanying the event gathered over 3 million hits – a perfect example of how a simple piece of live marketing can be amplified much further than the one person involved in the experience.

Flash Mobs

Flash mobs are a relatively new concept and can be traced back to the early 2000s. Whilst starting out as a social experiment, they have quickly become an area of consideration for adventurous marketers. They refer to when a large group of people meet in a pre-arranged space and disrupt the norm by undertaking an unusual activity for a few minutes then disperse as if nothing happened.

Time to organise them can be high but the costs are minimal and they are a great opportunity for content development. Content could be used in other parts of a marketing campaign. They may also be referred to as PR stunts and with the rise in smartphones, the activity is likely to be shared online without your control.

Flash dance

T Mobile developed one of the first famous UK flash mob marketing campaigns. A flash mob of 350 people met in Liverpool Street Station, London, on a Thursday morning and danced amongst the normal commuters. By the Friday evening, footage of the flash mob from ten hidden cameras was played in an extended ad slot. Those present on the Thursday morning saw first hand the brand trying something new. By using dance the event was brought to life and had reached millions of TV viewers the following day, through integrating it into part of a much larger marketing activity.

T Mobile then continued this campaign by hosting activity in Trafalgar Square, London and Heathrow Terminal 5.

You need to question whether or not your target audience will engage with this type of activity. Not used for internal communications, this technique is more likely to be suitable if you have a young demographic target who can engage through social media and help you to extend the experience.

Sustainable events

The impact that humans have on the world has long been noted and is something that you should be aware of too when planning your event. You can help make an event more sustainable by considering the alternative options for each supplier. It may be as simple as ensuring there is a recycling option present on the site or even having a solar powered music stage. Be aware that it is very likely to cost more to put on a more sustainable event. You will need to speak to your client to find out how much of a priority image and impact has. Corporate Social Responsibility (CSR) is on the agenda for many businesses but they do not often have an additional budget to support this.

Here are a few ways to make your event more sustainable:

- Consider carefully your venue choice based on your target market to reduce transport costs.

- Help the local community in a team-building event such as painting a local village hall.

- Use water fountains rather than bottled water.

- Encourage car sharing amongst your guests.

- Don't date any of your event branding or printed information so it could be re-used.

- Print all information double-sided.

- Provide bike racks to promote green transport.

- Using fairtrade tea and coffee.

Chapter 4

Managing Your Team to Manage Your Event

*Y*ou know the saying 'There's no 'I' in team'? That's what they say. They're right, but you may be a one-man team and therefore have no choice! Planning an event is the most rewarding job I have ever done but it can be very intense unless you have the right team around you. The important thing to remember is that you are never alone; you can always ask people for help; they might not be part of your official team, but other people can help make your life a little easier when planning your event.

The team is important in events, so make sure that the team you work with contains the most suitable people you can find. Over time, as you work on more and more events, you'll start to understand your strengths and weaknesses; this makes it easier when you're planning the day and deciding what roles everyone should have.

This chapter looks at the roles to fill when planning any event. The name next to them all in an organisational chart may be yours, but the tasks need doing to some degree in all type of events.

Clear communication should be a mantra. The art of being able to communicate effectively and managing to maintain that level of excellence while planning an event is crucial.

In this chapter, I run through the simple steps you can follow to make sure everyone knows what's going on and the right decisions are made on time.

Key Roles and Responsibilities

The events industry is made up of many different specialisms. Depending on the type of event you're planning, different sets of skills are required. The larger the event, the larger the team. In a large team people can maintain a specialism, rather than having people handling multiple roles. For example, for a very small event you may be the event manager, the creative director *and* the producer. If you're lucky enough to have the budget and team resource available, however, you can have three different people performing these roles.

The following sections introduce a few of the main characters in larger events. For large events, you may have more than one person in each role, and with different skill levels: For example, you might have a junior producer and an executive producer, or a production manager and a more junior production co-ordinator.

The client

The client is your boss. Although he, she or it may not be your actual boss at work, when you're organising the event, the boss is the person in ultimate control – the person who has briefed you on the event, and the person paying for it. (See later in the chapter for more detail on this.) Your client may be an internal team of directors that has asked you to organise the Christmas awards event, or you may work at an agency where a client has asked you to manage a product launch for a new vacuum cleaner.

The client has the prerogative to change his or her mind at the most annoying time. For the event manager, that can be very frustrating! A good event manager guides the client through the planning process, working with the client to decide the best possible event for the budget. Managing your client is just as important as managing the event, and you can't manage one without the other. We refer to client management as *client servicing* or *account management*.

Depending on the event you're organising and also the size of your business, your client can fit lots of types of role. Your client may work in marketing, human resources, internal communications or even sales. It's rare that your client works in events, but it does happen.

If your client is a colleague with whom you have an existing relationship, you may already have done some of the groundwork in getting to know what the client likes and dislikes.

The following are some simple steps to help you work better with your client:

- ✔ **Listen to what your client says:** This is crucial in getting to know him or her. For example:

    - Find out whether your client prefers formal emails and meetings or is more relaxed. Can you use Christian names or should you say Mr and Mrs?

    - Does the client use any buzzwords? If you use these words in conversation, the client feels comforted by the similar language.

    - Try to identify any internal politics that may have an impact on the approval process, depending on the sign-off level your client has on budgets and branding.

    - Understand the company culture. Who does your client dislike going to for sign-off or help? Is there a way to sidestep that person?

    - Empathise with your client. Find out general personal details, as you would with a friend. Listen to their plans for the weekend, for example, and on Monday remember to ask how they went.

- ✔ **Set guidelines and processes:** Each client has a preferred way of working. Be adaptable with your processes but agree at the start of the planning phase what is expected and when. If your client always has a meeting with her boss on Tuesday, make sure you update your client on the Monday so she is prepared.

- ✔ **Be proactive:** Your client is paying you to help guide her through the process of putting on an event, and expects good service! Try to always be one step ahead.

- ✔ **Go above and beyond:** Clients like to feel special and that they are your priority. Whilst routine is important, try to surprise your client every so often with a recommendation or email a link to something you think she may be interested in.

If your client believes you care about and listen to him or her on a personal level, he or she will assume you do so on a professional level too.

The procurement pros

Procurement managers are often the most feared people in a business. I don't agree that you should fear them; however, I recommend you try extra hard to have a good relationship with them, because they are powerful people.

Procurement is buying on a professional level and in events there are two places you may come across Procurement Managers:

- ✔ **When you are trying to be 'bought' by a company for your services:** That is, hired by a potential client. At this point, the procurement team will be looking to see if you and your employer are a good investment and have stable financial backing. They don't want you to start planning an event for one of their colleagues and for your company to then go bust. They are also there to make sure that they get the best deal i.e. they will haggle and negotiate until they have got what they want. They therefore have the ability to drive down your margin or to say no to you, full-stop.

- ✔ **When you are buying items for your event:** At this stage you are a procurement manager in essence, as you will be trying to get the best deal from the best suppliers.

Not every company has a procurement team or procurement person, but there's likely to be someone who has control over the choice of event manager or other suppliers – potentially a hands-on finance manager. Make it your mission to make friends with this person.

If your client isn't an internal colleague and is from a different company, you're likely to have to get approval from your client and from the person who manages the purchasing process on any budgets you submit. The person who manages procurement may also give you a purchase order number to confirm that you're contracted to work on the event. Your client may decide who to do business with, but the procurement team decides how much budget you are allocated and what contracts you require to commence work.

Even before this stage, the procurement team is likely to decide whether your company can pitch for a piece of work.

Take a proactive approach with procurement, suggest budget updates and provide details of any cost changes before the team ask you, always copying them into emails regarding budget changes.

Many procurement managers are incentivised on the amount of money they save from their suppliers. So be aware: They are in the business of saving money wherever they can and will challenge you on all aspects of your costings.

The event (or account/project) manager

This is you! This may not be your day-to-day job title, but you are the event manager.

So what does your role entail? That's difficult to answer without knowing how big your team is and what event you're organising. But in essence, your role is to ensure that the planning and execution of the event is on time, on brief and on budget.

Your organisation or team may include junior and senior event managers. Your position in the team needs to be established early in the planning process. It's likely that some roles will be split across different members of the team, or you may be supervised on a particular area and thus share responsibility.

In the following sections, I outline a framework of categories of work that an event manager may undertake. I also identify in brackets which roles you can delegate to other team members, if you have the opportunity.

Research

The research function is concerned with finding out as much as possible about the aim and requirements of the event, and how it needs to capture the attention of its audience. The decisions you make involve:

- Considering the competitive landscape for your event – not just against the industry, but also think about what else your audience may spend its time doing
- Sourcing suppliers, venues and entertainment options (or production manager and producer)
- Identifying and securing speakers or special guests (or producer)

Co-ordination

Co-ordination involves ensuring that everything that needs to happen for a successful event does happen, at the time and place that it needs to. Successful co-ordination involves:

- Accepting and interrogating the brief from the client
- Managing suppliers (or production manager)
- Sourcing, briefing and managing staff
- Managing the venue (or production manager)
- Managing site facilities for car parking, traffic control, security, first aid, hospitality, and so on (or production manager)
- Stand/set/branding designer management and production management (or production manager)
- Producing detailed timing plans (producer or production manager)
- Creating the marketing plan and materials for the event

✔ Planning room layouts and the entertainment programme; scheduling workshops and demonstrations

✔ Selling sponsorship and stand and/or exhibition space to potential exhibitors and/or partners

✔ Preparing delegate packs and papers

✔ Overseeing the dismantling and removal of equipment at the event, and clearing the venue efficiently (or production manager)

✔ Carrying out post-event evaluation, including data entry and analysis and producing reports for event stakeholders

Financial and legal management

Whatever the type of event you're running, it needs to come in on budget. You also need to get paid for the work you do, and make sure that everything you do is legally correct and properly insured. Financial and legal management covers:

✔ Developing the budget and agreeing it with the client

✔ Managing the securing and payment of suppliers

✔ Agreeing the payment schedule and invoicing the client, but only if your client is not in the same business as you

✔ Managing the budget on a weekly basis

✔ Ensuring insurance is in place

✔ Adhering to health and safety requirements (or production manager)

The perfect production team

In events, the term *production* means the design, creation and build of an event. This includes elements such as managing the lighting designers and picking and managing the company who might supply your stage.

Depending on the scale and technical complexity of the event, you're likely to need a production team to support you when briefing, sourcing and managing specialist technical suppliers. No one expects you to have an in-depth understanding of generators or video production, for example. Try to surround yourself with experts who can help guide the event planning from the production side.

Many more people are involved in the technical delivery of the event, who you may consult in the planning of the event when required.

Production manager

Your production manager (PM) is involved in all technical decision making and makes the wishes of you and your client a reality at your event.

- ✔ Take the PM on a visit to your venue, so he or she can check that it's fit for purpose. If necessary, the PM can advise you of what's required when you source a new venue.

- ✔ Brief your PM on your client's intentions for the event, and talk through your plans and any thoughts on how you want the event to look and run. The PM can then alert you to any problems and make any recommendations.

- ✔ The PM starts the quoting process with the necessary technical suppliers and recommends which suppliers to use.

- ✔ The PM handles all supplier queries and any venue queries during the planning of the event.

- ✔ Your PM may be able to create computer aided design (CAD) plans of your venue, which show where all the equipment, sets, tables and so on will be positioned – or this may be done by a different CAD designer. Either way, your PM has input into these plans, because further technical decisions, such as the capacity of the room, and positioning of tables are based on information.

- ✔ If your PM is a qualified health and safety officer, he or she can write the required health and safety documentation. You are likely, however, to need an independent health and safety advisor, who the PM briefs and manages.

- ✔ The PM writes a production schedule which details when all deliveries, activities, and so on need to happen over the build of the event. This schedule ensures that loading bays can cope with the number of vehicles at any one time and that things happen in the right order on site.

- ✔ Your PM is on site during the whole build (which can last from a couple of hours up to weeks, depending on the event) and is the main point of contact for all suppliers.

- ✔ The PM is responsible for the quality of the technical delivery during the event.

Producer

The producer takes the client's key messages and tries to help communicate them during the event in an engaging and memorable way.

- ✔ The producer, ideally, works with the creative team to help create an identity or theme for your event. By being involved in this stage, the producer can consider how the content can be developed based on the theme.

✔ The producer runs brainstorming sessions and planning sessions for the content development.

✔ If guest speakers and/or entertainment are required, the producer suggests speakers, DJs and other talent that fit with the event's objectives.

✔ The producer creates and collates any content required. The producer does not need to be a specialist in the client's business or industry (basic information and understanding never hurts, though). A large part of the producer's role is doing the groundwork with the client and online research to become a quick specialist, but most importantly trying to understand what the audience wants to hear and see.

✔ If your event is part of an integrated campaign, the producer is responsible for liaising with the other marketing partners so that all elements of the campaign are in line.

✔ The producer provides any speaker support required on-site during rehearsals to make sure that your speakers don't just have good content to deliver, but deliver it in a way on stage that ensures everyone wants to pay attention.

✔ The producer manages the running order on the day, working closely with the production manager.

✔ For small shows, the producer can also show-call the show, which means ensuring that all presenters, acts, video clips, and so on, appear on time by giving countdowns and telling people the exact moment to go on stage.

The dream design team

One of the fun parts of managing events is coming up with the creative ideas. Thinking up a concept that is incorporated in your event can make you proud. Design is a skill, however, and you may not be the most appropriate person to design and develop the creative theme. Even if you aren't the person tasked with devising the creative theme, there's no harm in getting involved in the brainstorming!

Strategy director

A strategy director is a great addition to the team, if you can afford one. The strategy director is responsible for helping to delve deeply into the client's company and messages, and considers what's happening in the market place at the moment. The strategy director works with the creative director to help define the reasoning (the strategy) to explain how you've decided a creative direction. Essentially, the strategy director comes up with a gap in the industry/unique selling point of the event/campaign and an idea, and the creative director translates that into how it may look in a live environment.

Creative director

This person brings your event objectives to life with an identity, theme and/or branding.

The creative director aims to understand your client's brand and the key messages that need to be communicated. You work closely with the creative director, and your detailed knowledge of your client is invaluable.

The creative director leads an internal brainstorming session and develops the overall creative strategy. The creative strategy identifies the most appropriate techniques; the creative director briefs the designer and art-workers in the team. The creative director also reviews the final designs and artwork to ensure they're of the highest quality, before signing them off.

Spatial designer

Also often called a *3D designer*, this person helps your client see what you all imagine happening at the event. The spatial designer can create 3D models of the space and show what the environment could look like.

Such 3D models may not be needed if you're using an existing conference venue with a built-in stage and you don't intend to bring any branding, additional props, staging, and so on. However, a spatial designer can look at a room or space and design and visualise how the space may best work for your event. Maybe it's ideal for the tables to be in a different direction to normal, or for the stage to be in the centre of the room.

Print designer

Some pieces of artwork always need to be created for an event. You may have a go on the computer yourself; the more professional approach is to have a designer work on the designs.

A print designer can help create a logo for your event if you need one, and is able to ensure that your logo and brand are represented properly through all printed material. You can create some items yourself – small things such as toilet and cloakroom signs – but the print designer can design the more complex elements such as any brochures or tickets.

Deciding the Scale of the Planning Team

The size of the planning team is directly related to the size of the project you're organising and, most importantly, the resources you have available – such as the budget. Throughout this chapter I've detailed the team members that you'll ideally have, but you can do all roles to a basic level on your own.

1. **First establish the client brief: This firms up what your client is expecting the event to look like and how much budget they have to spend.**

   Read the later section in this chapter for more information on how to create a brief.

2. **Break down the role into easy-to-understand sections.**

   I suggest using a status report as a template, as a good starting point (see further on in this chapter for example status reports and some hints about how to use them to your advantage). A status report sets out all the actions that need to be completed, by whom and by when.

3. **Write a timing plan showing what actions need to happen and when for you to hit your deadline.**

   This plan doesn't need to be exact at this stage; you just need enough detail to check whether sufficient time is available. Chapter 9 gives you examples of what a timing plan consists of and the level of detail you would need when actually producing the event.

4. **Identify how long you think each task will take, and compare the time against how much time is available.**

   A good tool for this is a *time scope* document. This can be difficult on your first couple of events as it's always the small things that take the longest. For your first few events, imagine how much time you think it will take then double it until you have tried. The time scope shows how much time is needed for each task rather than when the jobs need to be completed; this helps you work backwards from your deadline dates. See an example of this over the page.

5. **There may be more than you can manage on your own; if so, you need to start looking at how many other people you may need and with what skill sets.**

   Refer back to earlier in this chapter where we talk through the various roles that may help you when planning your event. Many of these people might not be available in your company so you would need to look at contracting them as freelancers. Therefore their availability will impact on your timings and your budget. Speak to your client and discuss whether other assistance or budget is available.

Don't be afraid to ask for help if you need it to do a good job; your client will thank you for flagging it earlier rather than when it's too late. If assistance isn't available at the level required, look again at the event brief and try to identify areas that may be changed or removed to reduce the time needed to manage the event. Using a time scope framework such as the one in Figure 4-1 will help you identify the time needed to plan the event but also how time will add up

Project Time Scope – Event Management
Client:
Job name and number:

Project Dates:

Role	Days:	Notes:
Event Manager		
Meetings (client)	3	
Internal team liaison	2	
Co-ordination of event	10	
Logistics planning	3	
Subtotal:	18	
Producer		
Creative support	3.5	
Content develpment – meetings	4	
Content develpment – research	5	
Content develpment – writing	7	
Subtotal:	19.5	
Production Manger:		
Health and Safety	1	
Scheduling	1.5	
Venue management	2	
Documentation	1.5	
Stand Production	4.5	
Subtotal:	10.5	
GRAND TOTAL:	48	

Figure 4-1: A typical time scope framework.

The Power of an Organisation Chart

Clarity and efficiency in communications reduces stress levels and helps the speed of decision making. Have you ever been on the phone to a customer service helpline and been passed from person to person and still not received an answer to your question? It's frustrating, and the experience makes you more sensitive and distressed than before you made the call. If when you have a question you can speak to the person who can answer it straight away, it saves everyone a lot of time and frustration.

When planning your event, you can help reduce the time taken to resolve issues by clearly identifying who to direct questions to. If you create an organisation chart or a communication flowchart, all members of the team can see who to direct their questions to. The scale of the event and the size of the team are intrinsically linked so will vary from event to event. Figure 4-2 shows such a chart.

Figure 4-2:
This chart will help communicate to all team members who everyone is and also who are the decision makers

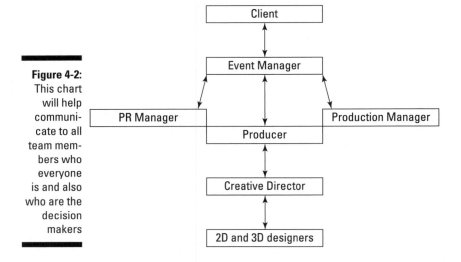

You should be the main contact point for your client, to ensure consistency and ease of communication. You may have a team of a production manager and two production co-ordinators or some more junior creative designers. You are unlikely to want these junior team members asking you all their questions, so they can feed their questions directly to the production manager or creative director, who then feeds into you.

In terms of team culture, you need to create a friendly working environment for everyone. Don't forget the junior team members, and include them in the process.

Circulate the organisation chart when you provide information on roles and responsibilities to your client. If you're the only team member, it's sufficient to send an email to your client to confirm the best method of contacting you.

Deciding the Decision-making Chain

Making decisions quickly, efficiently and according to plan takes time. Each client is different, and clients expect to be involved in the decision-making process to different extents. Some clients are happy that when they've signed off a budget, you make all the decisions. Others want to approve every single decision or suggestion you make. The latter type is much more time consuming and can easily slow the process down, thus increasing the risk of stress on a job.

If your client likes to know the detail, you can still run a smooth planning process, but it takes a little more careful management. Think about building contingency time into the timing plan. Also be aware when your client has holidays and meetings – anything that may affect how quickly you receive feedback.

You may also find that, for example, your client's boss may be the person who's interested in the detail and doesn't empower your client to approve the planning procedure. This can have a huge knock-on effect on approval times and the opportunity for missing deadlines.

Any of these situations can be dealt with as long as you know about them at the start of the planning process.

Ask this question at the start of the project: 'What is the decision-making process?' Also find out how many levels of sign-off you need to go through and how long the client expects the process to take. This is totally dependent on your client, so I can't tell you how long it will take, but I can advise that it always takes longer than you think.

By getting to know your client, you'll also discover any areas that are particularly important to him or her. You can then decide whether to assign more time to sign-off on these elements. For example, if you know that your client is much more interested in, or has more opinions on, branding than catering, you know which element to build more contingency time into.

Good practice is to have a sign-off sheet for each major decision. This can be impractical, however, especially if a lot of the communication with your client is by email. You could consider having a set template email that you ask your client to send every time something is being approved. This should make the flippant 'that's fine' comment a little more structured.

Always insist on a written record of approvals. If your client gives approval by phone or in a meeting, make sure you confirm this in an email or contact report.

It doesn't happen often, but you may get into a situation where your client has approved a decision but then changes his or her mind after you've ordered or booked something. You may be able to change the plan with no cost incurred. However, if a cancellation cost is incurred, by having written proof of approval you are justified in adding this cost to the budget.

Communicating During the Planning Process

Often people say they're interested in a career in events management because they like organising things; well, hopefully you like communicating too, because it's probably more important than good organisational skills.

Being a good communicator is a skill. If you're not naturally good at communicating, try to find a person in your organisation who you can learn from. Identify someone who always seems to get what he or she wants, and then ask what techniques to use.

Nowadays, with so many communication methods available, it's often difficult to know which to use and when. Depending on the size of the project, you might consider using meetings on a weekly or fortnightly basis, conference calls for the times when a meeting isn't possible, and text-based tools throughout. Also bear in mind other team members' preferred styles, the size of the team and the nature of the event.

Human contact

In a world of technology, it's possible to organise an entire event without any human contact, using only technology. Putting on an event is about engagement, inspiration and collaboration, however. As tempting as it may be to only use technology, I recommend that you have some face-to-face contact with your client, however busy you both are.

Be flexible about where you meet your client; make it difficult for your client not to meet you. You often get a lot more out of a face-to-face meeting than a telephone call. Offer to take tea and cake if it helps create some time in your client's diary.

Meetings

The old-fashioned ways are often the best. Even in the age of digital and technology-enhanced communications, a meeting with your client can be productive.

If you ask for opinions in a face-to-face meeting, you'll receive a quicker and more honest response than if people hide behind emails.

Also, by having multiple personalities in a room, a meeting may generate more ideas than an email exchange would.

Conference calls

With so many demands on their time, your client and/or stakeholders may be reluctant to commit to a face-to-face meeting. Conference calls are an effective and easy way to enable a group of people who cannot physically be in the same place to talk.

Before the meeting, circulate your agenda in case people don't have time to look back through old emails.

The pros of conference calls are that they:

- ✔ Are often free to set up (apart from the cost of a local call). Search online for different options; companies such as powwownow (www.powwownow.co.uk) and conferencegenie (www.conferencegenie.co.uk) are reliable.
- ✔ Reduce the costs of travel compared with people attending a meeting.
- ✔ Encourage efficiency of all the points on the agenda covered on the call.
- ✔ Allow more people (if they're available) to participate.

The cons of conference calls include that:

- ✔ It's difficult to convey emotion over the phone.
- ✔ Some people may jump ahead in presentations if they've received documents by email ahead of the call. So if you are trying to build up to a momentous visual or moment in your presentation, some of the impact may be lost.
- ✔ Often the sound quality can be poor, depending on where the participants are dialling in from.
- ✔ You can't monitor how engaged people are – they may be multi-tasking and not paying full attention to the discussion.

Paperwork, paperwork, paperwork

Being an events person, I'm a fan of face-to-face communication and speaking to people on the phone. I think it helps to build stronger relationships with team members and suppliers. However, written communication is important in events and does help with smooth planning. There are many components to planning an event. Even if you can remember everything that needs to be actioned, this doesn't help other people to know what to do.

Everyone has his or her own style and ways of working, but I've included a selection of documents that you can use as a starting point. Even if your client is an internal client, use these same documents; don't be afraid to formalise the planning with people you're normally more informal with.

Client brief

What your client wants is one of the first things you need to understand. Your client may communicate the brief verbally, but you should still complete and agree a written version.

If your client provides a verbal brief, write up a *return brief* (the same as a client brief, but you write it) for your client to agree. You can then be sure that you understand the brief clearly.

The information that your client provides in this brief is the blueprint for many of your future decisions, and as such should be as thorough and accurate as possible. If you don't have enough information, ask your client for further details and interrogate the brief as much as possible. Often, what you think the client means is different from what the client actually does mean. Always replay what you think the client is asking for – there's no space for misunderstandings.

The better the brief, the better the response. Figure 4-3 shows a template for a client brief.

Status report

This document is my 'things to do' list. If designed and used correctly, it's a great tool to organise any size of event.

You can distribute status reports as often as you like. I recommend a weekly status report sent to all stakeholders on a Monday morning, so that everyone can plan their week.

On a large project, the status report may run to many pages. Some stakeholders may ask to only be shown part of this document each week. I suggest, however, that stakeholders see the whole document so that they have a good overview of all actions; everything is connected when organising events, and something that you think has no impact may be significant to a different team.

The benefits of a status report are that:

✔ **It keeps everyone in the loop:** When a large number of stakeholders are involved in a project, the status report helps ensure that everyone knows the major issues for the week, and also what role to play in addressing the issues.

✔ **It helps provide a great paper trail:** This can help if you need to get someone up to speed quickly with the project. They are also excellent documents to help encourage your clients to complete the actions they need to before you can take your next steps. There's always an action that your client needs to take, even if it's as simple as agreeing to what you'v e recommended.

creative brief

Client:	Job Name:
Job No:	Total Job Budget:

Type of execution *e.g. print 3D*	
First Review:	Final Approval:
Acc Dir:	Creative Time Allowed in Budget:

What is our task?

Who are we talking to?

What do they currently believe?

What must the communication say?
(proposition)

What do we want them to believe?

What tone of voice should the communication have?

What practical considerations should be borne in mind?

Mandatory Requirements *e.g. logo, strap-line*

Assets available and where they can be found

Figure 4-3:
A template for a client brief

Figure 4-4 shows a standard status report.

status report

Client: Report issued:
Job name: Version:
Distributed by:
Distribution list:

No.	Element	Action	Lead (Who)	Deadline
1.	Holidays and Key Calendar Dates			
2.	Finance and Legal			
3.	Creative Development			
4.	Content			
5.	Marketing and Communications			
6.	Digital			
7.	Sponsorship			
8.	Venue			
9.	Logistics			
10.	Production - Set and Staging			
11.	Production - AV			
12.	Branding and Print Production			
13.	AOB			

Figure 4-4:
A standard status report

As with all communication, adjust your tools and style to that most useful for you and your client.

Agenda

Before attending a meeting, make sure that you distribute an agenda. People are much more likely to attend your meeting if they know what is being discussed. It is also an opportunity for you to make sure that any subjects that need to be discussed get covered rather than be missed off due to lack of time at the end of the meeting.

I'm a fan of saving on paperwork whenever possible, so you may want to use your status report as an agenda. If you do, it also means that you cover all aspects each week, even if briefly. If you take this approach, make sure you start the meeting with the most important topics for that week, so they get the most time.

Contact report

After every client contact, such as a conference call or meeting, you should write a contact report. This is the simplest way of creating a paper trail. Paper trails can sometimes be needed if your client or supplier changes their mind/requirements later on in the planning process and tries to backtrack on agreements that have been made. The contact report can be a formal report or an email. You are the most likely person to be responsible for writing it.

At times when you're organising an event, someone forgets or misunderstands an agreement. Without any written communication, it's difficult to establish who's at fault and therefore who's responsible.

A simple email after a call to thank your client or supplier for his or her time and to say that you look forward to receiving further information by the end of the week allows you, if you don't receive the information by the end of the week, to chase the client.

As a general rule, a call during which only one subject is discussed can be followed up with an email; for anything longer, use a more formal report.

The email or document should be sent to all team members who were either in the meeting or who need to know the outcomes of what was discussed.

The contact report should be sent out within 24–48 hours to prompt action, and before you forget what was discussed! Figure 4-5 shows an example you can use.

contact report

[Add Company name here]	Report date: [Add report date here]
[Add project name here]	Meeting Date: [Add meeting date]
[Add reason for meeting here]	cc: [Add CCs initials here]

Client attendees	Event Management team attendees
[Attendee 1]	[Attendee 1]
[Attendee 2]	[Attendee 2]
[Attendee 3]	[Attendee 3]

No.	Detail	Action (who/when)
1.	[Insert item agreed during meeting here] • [Use bullets to show lists]	
2.	[Insert item agreed during meeting here] • [Use bullets to show lists]	
3.	[Insert item agreed during meeting here] • [Use bullets to show lists]	
4.	[Insert item agreed during meeting here] • [Use bullets to show lists]	
5.	[Insert item agreed during meeting here] • [Use bullets to show lists]	
6.		
7.		

Figure 4-5: A contact report template

Drawing Up a Clear Scope of Work

The scope of work details all the actions and the plan that you are going to follow to achieve the agreed objectives. There may be many versions of your response to your client's brief, but when you and your client have agreed the final approach, it's important to document the detail.

You should write and own this document, but you and your client should take equal responsibility for it. If written well, the scope of work is useful as a contract.

The scope of work covers areas such as:

- **Project lead:** Record who the client is and who's responsible for the approval process.

- **Objectives:** Objectives are often difficult for a client to agree, because the client is likely to want to do everything for a fixed budget. By writing the objectives down and obtaining your client's signed agreement, you help your client to focus on what is important.

- **Services:** Detail what you or your team will do to deliver the event, such as '1. Hire the Business Design'.

- **Cost:** Include full information about the cost you and your client have agreed, and detail the payment schedule that your client's agreed to, including any bonuses discussed.

- **Milestones:** Detail all the agreed timings and critical dates in the planning process. By making it clear up front that certain delivery dates must be achieved you focus everyone on ensuring that the process is followed smoothly.

- **Exclusions:** Or also what you expect the client to do to help with planning of the event. If you're responsible for sponsorship activation areas at an event but not for finding, negotiating with and contracting sponsors, make it clear that you expect the client to provide information on the sponsors.

- **Key performance indicators (KPIs):** List the KPIs and how they'll be measured. KPIs are like a set of objectives that show if the event has been a success. For example, 2,500 delegates to attend the event over 3 days. It's important to agree KPIs at the start of the project.

Your client should sign this document. You should then refer to the scope of work at regular intervals in the planning process (monthly, for example), to ensure that you're on track. Figure 4-6 shows a typical scope of work document.

Scope of Work (SOW)

Name of SOW:	
Company:	
Brand:	
Client Contact:	
Project Period:	
Territory:	
Management & Delivery of:	
Services description:	
Estimate of costs and disbursements:	
Timetable for completion of each stage of the SOW:	
Payment Schedule:	
Service Levels:	
Key Performance Indicators:	
Key Client Personnel:	
Status Meetings / Reports Requirements:	

ADDITIONAL INFORMATION

For and on behalf of
Client

For and on behalf of
Event Manager

....
Name

....
Name

....
Signature

....
Signature

....
Date

....
Date

Figure 4-6:
A template
for a scope
of work
document

Chapter 5

Budget Planning and Management

. . . .

In This Chapter

▶ Clarifying at the outset what you're trying to achieve

▶ Discovering what should be in your budget

▶ Negotiating for beginners

▶ Working out when you need to get paid

▶ Helping to offset the costs of your event

▶ What ROI means

. . . .

*Y*ou don't need to be a maths genius to be able to write and manage a budget for an event. However, you *do* need some clear tools and you need to research costs and options. It takes time to pull your budget together, but investing the time at the beginning has a positive impact on your event planning and budget management going forward. The closer your original budget is to the final budget, in terms of cost, the better.

Variances will occur as you go through the process of planning your event. Ideas will be developed, and therefore the kit and team that you need changes over time. Remember to flag with your client anything that pushes you over your agreed budget. The client then needs to agree to, and find, the additional budget.

In this chapter I give you some example budget templates, payment schedule templates and revenue model options. I also mention some common areas of over-spend in budgets, so that you can watch them closely as you plan your event.

Being Realistic: Are You After Champagne on a Beer Budget?

An endless supply of money would be great in our personal lives and our work lives. Meanwhile, in the real world, you need to be as sensible about how you spend money when planning an event as you are with your own money. It's very easy to spend money on events. If you spend money well, it can enhance your visitors' experience, but the expenditure isn't what makes an event.

One of the first steps when planning any event is to establish how much money is available – the *budget*. Obviously, everyone always wants events to cost as little as possible; however, before you venture into planning any event, ensure you understand what budget has been put aside for the job.

Until you've done some investigation into how much the elements of the event cost, you may not know whether the figure you've been given is realistic.

Over time and after reading multiple quotes and budgets, you'll begin to get a feel for what seems realistic. For example, a budget of £2,000 may sound like a big budget for a five-star sit-down meal for 100 people, because £2,000 may sound like a lot of money to you personally. However, if you divide £2,000 by 100 people, you'll see that the budget is only £20 per person. For a sit-down meal, this is less than you pay in most restaurants; add in all the additional costs, such as venue hire, furniture, decorations and so on, and you find that the budget is unrealistic. This is not to say you can't design an event for 100 people for this budget, but you'd need to change the criteria.

To agree with your client what his or her expectations and budget are is often a very difficult part of the process. Clients naturally want the best, but can't always afford to pay for the best.

Where there's a will there's a way to make an event work for the budget. Just be creative.

Different clients and events have different deliverables. So a sit-down meal for 100 people for one client may cost £20,000, and for another client it may cost £150,000. Both events may be great experiences for the guests, and both events may go very well, but they have wildly different budgets. More money doesn't mean a better event; it's how you spend the money that's important. Often with a larger budget, it's easy to be less creative and just throw money at solutions. Some of the most creative events I go to are planned with a tiny budget, but the organisers have thought carefully about how to make the most of the small things.

For example, at a recent conference, the event organisers couldn't afford table decorations. Instead, they designed a team-building activity during which the delegates created table decorations.

How much money needs to be spent is often dictated by the value that the client expects to get out of the event. Events are always organised for a reason, for example for fundraising, to launch a new product or to sell products. Companies aim for every corporate event to deliver a financial benefit in the long run. Even the local village fete is often a fundraising event for the local area. The only exceptions are private events such as weddings or birthday parties. I look into return on investment a little later in this chapter. The projected return on investment can often help establish your overall budget.

Building up Your Budget

There's no such thing as a typical budget for an event, because events are bespoke – designed to fit the client, objectives and budget. It wouldn't be unusual for your event to include many more areas than those noted in the following sections.

What should you include in your budget?

When you know what budget your client has allocated, the next stage is to work out whether that amount is enough money and, if it is, how you are going to spend it. Whatever type of event you're planning, the budget is likely to need to cover some key areas.

Venue

A vitally important part of any event is where the event will be hosted. There is more information in Chapter 10 on how to select a venue. As the world is becoming more commercially aware, there is now nearly always a cost associated with the venue. Sometimes a venue will give you the physical space for free but they may charge you for some of the following:

Also beware of additional costs on top of the venue fee, for:

- Extra hours that you need the venue to be open for, either for the build or for the live event
- Power
- Front-of-house crew (find out what's included and what isn't, they might provide use of the in-house lighting rig, but does it include the crew to actually use it?)
- Inflated fees at prime times

Content

What happens at your event has a cost, and you should budget for that cost. If you're planning any extra brand experiences such as games or additional interactive entertainment, there's the cost of the experiences to add in too. If it's an awards ceremony, there may be the cost of creating film montages of the entries plus the cost of the awards. For a conference, there's the cost for someone to write the presentations and for any interactive tablets on the tables.

The content is one of the most bespoke areas of the event. It's also one of the areas where you can be most creative and keep costs low.

Entertainment

Entertainment costs vary hugely. For example, you may want an A-list celebrity to generate a large amount of PR coverage around your event, or a DJ to play background music during your dinner. Celebrities who are referred to as *named talent* – those who are household names – can demand a high fee and therefore cost huge amounts; don't be surprised to receive a quote of *£25,000* an hour. Obviously this type of entertainment doesn't suit every budget.

An additional cost to be aware of when budgeting for talent is any riders; for example, a celebrity may expect certain types of drink or food, or particular furniture in the dressing room. These plus the cost of chauffeured travel can add up.

Lighting, sound and power

The costs of lighting, sound and power are often combined and referred to as technical costs. Such costs are strongly dictated by your venue and what, if anything, is included there. For example, a theatre is likely to have in-house lighting and sound facilities, so your costs ought to be minimal. At a music festival in a greenfield site, the cost of lighting and sound is high as all the trussing, lights and power cabling would need to be transported, rigged and managed especially for this event. The cost of the set and staging – the backdrop to your event – is often also included in the technical costs.

Furniture

A hotel or similar venue is likely to include furniture in your venue hire cost, or for a small addition. Other venues don't provide this facility, so you need to source some furniture from a supplier. Remember that not only do you need furniture for your guests, you also need furniture back of house for a sound desk, green room and/or production office.

Catering

Almost all events need some kind of catering. Even if this is at the very basic level of providing water, tea and coffee and biscuits, you still need to add the cost to your budget. Everything comes with a cost, even hot water and tea bags. In addition to the cost of the ingredients, consider the cost of the equipment and servers.

Most hotels and conference centres offer catering in-house, so you don't need to speak to outside caterers. They often include tea and coffee in a day delegate rate, depending on their charging model.

Catering quotes are normally based on a quote per head, for example £10 per person for lunch. This cost normally includes the food, service and equipment. It's easy, for example, if 20 more people will attend the event, for you to calculate the additional cost.

If you're running a festival in a field, you need to include a much higher cost for equipment, because an outside kitchen is needed.

Aside from catering for your guests, you also need to consider crew catering. All those lovely team members of yours who are likely to be working long hours to help make the event happen need feeding. For some events, you provide crew catering, but another approach is to pay each team member a *per diem* (PD) – basically an allowance to purchase food from a local café or restaurant. Either way, you need to include the costs in your budget.

A standard crew catering allowance is around £30 per day per person.

Security

The cost of security may be included in your venue hire, or it may be an extra. Never assume anything, and ask what exactly is included in the venue cost.

The level of security relates directly to the event that you're planning and the risks involved. If you're planning an awards ceremony at which a well-known pop band will perform, you need more security than if you're hosting a meeting for board members.

Security is covered in more detail in Chapter 12. However, as a general rule, the more people, the more security, the more alcohol, the more security, and the more press attention, the more security.

A rough average cost for security is £15 per guard per hour.

Branding

You can make a brand stand out and your employees or consumers remember what your event was for. Whether it's as simple as printed posters in clip frames in the hallway or a large stage backdrop at a festival, having your event name or logo around your event has a huge impact.

The budget for branding is often squeezed throughout the planning process, but you should hang onto it for as long as possible. Branding can make a big impact at your event and differentiate it from other similar events.

Marketing

Ensuring your audience knows the event is happening is important and deserves its own line on your budget.

Marketing may be as simple as an internal email, which just requires a designer to design a logo or email template, or it may be a multi-million-pound campaign with mixed media.

The objectives of your event help determine how much of your budget to spend on marketing. The budget for marketing often isn't included in the events budget, but is included in a different budget, because you're not necessarily the person who markets the event.

Staff

There are normally many elements to an event and more often than not, far too much for one person. Therefore it's likely that you'll hire at least one person to work with you in either the lead-up to the event or on the actual day. This person may be a photographer, a production manager or a health and safety officer.

These people have day rates. Also remember to ask about any additional charges, such as for travel to meetings, to avoid any nasty surprises when you receive their invoices.

Administration costs

Costs such as insurance and your expenses are often missed off budgets. Insurance is for the benefit of your client (as well as you), and you should be able to charge on the cost of the policy.

The number of meetings you go to and how often you have to courier something to your client affects the cost of your event. These tiny amounts add up over the course of planning your event. A few £27 train journeys here and there soon add up. Make sure you keep track of these costs, because they may be too small individually to put in your budget.

The expenses tracker in Figure 5–1 is an easy way to record your expenses as you go along. In essence, the tracker is as simple as a spreadsheet, but I often find that having a pre-made form encourages me to keep it filled in.

Location	Date	Session	Amount Spent	Amount in Budget	Difference	Payment Method
Roadshow site 1	23-May	Dinner	£81.08	£60.00	–£21.08	Petty Cash
		Breakfast	£52.50	£60.00	£7.50	Petty Cash
	24-May	Lunch	£49.22	£130.00	£80.78	Petty Cash
		Dinner	£92.97	£360.00	£267.03	Petty Cash
	27-May	Breakfast	£34.32	£70.00	£35.68	Petty Cash
		Snacks		£150.00		
Roadshow site 2	30-May	Dinner	£120.00	£60.00	–£60.00	Petty Cash
		Breakfast	£65.00	£60.00	–£5.00	Petty Cash
	31-May	Lunch	£80.00	£130.00	£50.00	Petty Cash
		Dinner	£121.18	£360.00	£238.82	Credit Card - John
	03-Jun	Breakfast	£30.00	£70.00	£40.00	Petty Cash
		Snacks	£50	£150.00	£100.00	Petty Cash
Roadshow site 3	06-Jun	Dinner	£134.90	£60.00	–£74.90	Credit Card - Sam
		Breakfast	£46.00	£60.00	£14.00	Credit Card - John
	07-Jun	Lunch	£86.53	£130.00	£43.47	Credit Card - John
		Dinner	£138.45	£360.00	£221.55	Credit Card - Sam
	10-Jun	Breakfast	£12.90	£70.00	£57.10	Petty Cash
		Snacks	£71.26	£150.00	£78.74	Credit Card - John
Roadshow site 4	13-Jun	Dinner	£61.01	£60.00	–£1.01	Credit Card - John
		Breakfast	£99.80	£60.00	–£39.80	Credit Card - Sam
	14-Jun	Lunch	£103.00	£130.00	£27.00	Petty Cash
		Dinner	£89.77	£360.00	£270.23	Credit Card - Laura
	17-Jun	Breakfast	£42.59	£70.00	£27.41	Petty Cash
		Snacks	£18.65	£150.00	£131.35	Petty Cash
Roadshow site 5	20-Jun	Dinner		£60.00		Credit Card - John
		Breakfast		£60.00		Credit Card - Sam
	21-Jun	Lunch	£106.75	£130.00	£23.25	Credit Card - John
		Dinner	£362.34	£360.00	–£2.34	Credit Card - John
	24-Jun	Breakfast		£70.00	-	-
		Snacks		£150.00	-	-
		Total Spent	£2,150.22			
				Total in Budget	£4,150.00	
				Difference	£1,999.78	

Figure 5-1: Expenses tracking form.

Your time

How will you charge for your time? You can charge a day rate. Alternatively, you may prefer to charge a fixed amount for organising the whole event; you can do this by taking a percentage of the cost of the event, such as 10 per cent of the budget, as your fee.

Making sure you have a contingency pot

You may be tempted to spend your entire budget in your efforts to make the perfect event. Make sure you spend to achieve all the objectives. You also need to remember that, in events, anything may happen, so keep some budget available. I cover contingency planning in more detail in Chapter 13. Deciding what figure to keep aside is difficult, but the amount is normally worked out as a percentage of the overall budget. For example, 5–10 per cent of the total is kept in case your printed material is ripped and needs to be replaced. Or you arrive on-site and all of your caterers are wearing T-shirts in a competitor's colour and you need to go out and buy new T-shirts at the last minute.

More often than not, your event goes to plan and you don't touch the contingency pot. You can then either reinvest the money at the last minute into something that you considered a luxury, or keep it until the next event.

What your budget should look like

As long as your budget is easy to understand and has all the appropriate information, it doesn't matter what it looks like. You can purchase many specialist budgeting programs, but just drawing up a simple spreadsheet can do the job.

As budgets constantly change, it's important to have your budget written in such a way that it's easy to update. Have clear headings with the lines totalled at the bottom.

Make sure that you version-control your budgets by labelling them, for example, V1 and V2. Otherwise you guarantee that your client will ask to go back to a version they saw a week ago and you will not know what it is.

I've spent many hours staring at a spreadsheet when the numbers don't add up as they should. Always check that every single line in a budget is as it should be. Sometimes, when you're too close to your budget, it's difficult to spot the error. Ask someone else to look over your entries, and hopefully the mistake will jump straight out.

It can be useful to have a summary sheet for your client and a more detailed version for yourself. Some clients are interested in the detail of how much the individual floral displays cost; others just want to know the total decoration cost. Ask how much detail your client is looking for. You can always create a summary sheet as part of your spreadsheet, so you don't even need to re-write it.

The example budget in Figure 5-2 is for a morning seminar for 100 people in a free-of-charge venue such as your own office. Use it as a guide, but remember you need to research your own costs to make it fit your brief.

sledge

Job No.   8453
Job Title   MHRA Paediatric Seminar
Client   MHRA

Pre-Production

Administration

Meetings, reccees etc.			45
Telephones, mobiles, etc			30
Administration Sub Total			**£ 75**

Rate Card

Account Manager	4	Days	2,200
Account Executive	2.5	Days	825
Production Manager	2	Days	960
Designer	3	Hours	330
Rate Card Sub Total			**£ 4,315**

Misc

Print - 100 x lanyards		Allow	80
Misc Sub Total			**£ 80**
Pre-Production Total			**£ 4,470**

Production

Travel and Subs

Accommodation			440
Crew travel, parking etc			290
Per Diems - £24.40 x 5, 9.30 x 2 personnel on site			141
Travel and Subs Sub Total			**£ 871**

Rate Card

Account Manager	1	Days	550
Account Executive	1	Days	330
Production Manager	1.5	Days	720
General Tech - Set & Lighting	1.5	Days	450
Video Engineer	1.5	Days	480
Sound 1	1.5	Days	480
Local Crew		Allow	260
Rate Card Sub Total			**£ 3,270**

Video

projector and backup, graphics machine and back up, 24"comfort monitor, DVD player and backup, cue light system	425
Video Sub Total	**£ 425**

Sound

4 x microphone kit to include up to 4 lav mics or 2 lav, 2 x HH mics, 2 x lecturn mic, 4 x speaker PA system suitable for 100 pax	326
Sound Sub Total	**£ 326**

Lighting

key white light stage wash, lectern and logo spots, 8 x LED tricolour LED floor cans to light set	319

Figure 5-2:
An example
budget.

Pennies Add Up to Pounds

As the proverb goes, 'Take care of the pennies and the pounds will take care of themselves.' You should probably take care of the pounds in events and let the hundreds of pounds take care of themselves, but the theory is right.

My policy is to always treat my client's budget as though it's my own personal bank account, so that I think carefully about what I spend the budget on. This approach encourages me to focus on the practical things first, and then the leftover money is spent on the luxuries or the nice-to-haves.

Understanding the power of three quotes

One of the easiest ways to buy better is to shop around. As a general rule, asking three different suppliers gives you a good indication of the price you should be paying.

Suppliers all vary in the costs they quote for different aspects of a job. Each tries to make a certain mark-up, and each tries to cover different overheads. As such, you're unlikely to get three identical quotes. The quotes do, however, allow you to find a middle ground or an average cost. This is then a good number to put in your budget, because you know that cheaper suppliers exist, so you're not likely to go over this cost.

When asking suppliers to quote for furniture or catering, for example, make sure you brief them clearly and check that their quotes cover all the aspects that you require. It's also necessary to check each quote is for the same thing. Does one supplier include delivery, but another expect you to organise it? Does one caterer include canapés as well as the three-course dinner, and the other doesn't? If you don't check what suppliers include in their quotes, you may rule out a quote from supplier who includes extra items, thinking it's too expensive.

If you have time, ask more than three suppliers for a quote – but three gives you adequate guidance.

Negotiating like a pro

Everyone likes a bargain and to believe they've got the maximum for their money. Some people are naturals and have a flair for striking a deal. Think of salesmen: They know how to convince people of their point of view and have the confidence to name a price. It's much the same when buying.

Events management is different from most other marketing disciplines, because it requires a lot of practical purchasing rather than budgets that are spent mainly on people time and creative thought development. As such, even if you're organising a small event with a budget of £5,000, you're still likely to have to talk to 10–20 suppliers. Imagine what that number can creep up to for a large event and budget.

If you can hire a production manager to help you, he or she can focus on the technical production suppliers, such as lighting and sound, and has the experience and technical knowledge to know whether you're getting a good deal.

Some tips are:

✔ **Prepare before you speak to your supplier.** Be clear about exactly what you want – your wishlist. Also consider what you're willing to negotiate (why should they give you a discount?) and who you'll speak to from their side.

✔ **Listen to what they're saying.** Epictetus, a very wise Greek philosopher, once said that we have two ears and one mouth so that we can listen twice as much as we speak. Very wise words, particularly in negotiations. Listen for little hints as to how far your supplier may be willing to go and what may be stopping him or her agreeing to what you want.

✔ **Always start by asking for more than what you would be willing to settle for.** By going in with a request for a really large discount such as 40 per cent, after negotiation, the supplier may feel that he is getting a really good deal if he agrees on a 20% discount. This way you still may end up with you want and your supplier feels like they have managed to negotiate down with you too.

Work with your suppliers

You don't have to negotiate on a project-by-project basis. If you know that you'll be doing a few events for which you'll need similar suppliers, why not chat with your suppliers and see whether you can set up a more permanent relationship? Some suppliers set up an agreement where you get larger discounts over a period for repeat orders. These discounts can then be passed on to your clients and may help with your budget.

Sorting out Contracts

You create a lot of contracts when organising events, due to the amount of purchasing you need to do. You don't need to be a legal expert to understand contracts, but you need to read them carefully. If you can afford legal advice, it's always good to have a second opinion.

Reading the contract with your venue is likely to unearth some details which you need to know for planning your event. You may find that the venue has sneaked a corkage cost or additional management fee on top of the costs you discussed.

You don't need contracts for every single supplier or element of your event. For many suppliers, simply providing a purchase order (PO) number is a good enough indication of intent. Figure 5-3 shows a typical Purchase Order.

Event management company   PURCHASE ORDER

Your name
Your address
E-mail   PAYMENT TERMS
Phone
Date

PURCHASE ORDER NO:

TO:

DESCRIPTION	COST	
Provision of 5,000 A5 leaflets	£	725.67
Doublesided on 180gsm emerald white		
Cut and packed into boxes of 500		
subtotal	£	725.67
VAT		145.13
TOTAL	**£**	**870.80**

APPROVED BY   DATE

Figure 5-3:
A purchase
order
template.

Don't be scared or embarrassed to go back to your supplier and question terms within the contract if you don't understand or don't agree. The contract is a point for negotiation, not a black and white transaction.

Keep electronic copies of all your signed contracts, but also keep printed versions in your event folder for easy access on the day of the event.

Confirming a quote

When you receive a quote that you want to go with, you need to confirm this with the supplier. Ensure that the quote is in writing, and is not just verbal. For the services detailed on the PO, you'll pay the supplier the amount agreed on the PO. Depending on the finance system in your organisation, you may be able to generate a number automatically or you may need to keep detailed records yourself of the number issued, the supplier, the amount and the detail.

When the supplier has received a PO, it then issues an invoice at an agreed time. This may be after the event on completion, or the payment may be split so that 50 per cent is invoiced up front and the remainder after the event. An invoice is the supplier's demand for the money detailed on the PO. When you receive an invoice, you need to pay the agreed amount in the agreed time frame.

If you keep a manual record of all these transactions, it can get complicated. Ensure that you create a good log of all of the PO numbers and of the invoices that you've received and paid. Figure 5-4 shows an example of an invoicing template.

Event management company   INVOICE

Your name
Your address
E-mail
Phone   **PAYMENT TERMS**
Date

PURCHASE ORDER NO:

TO:

DESCRIPTION	COST
	########
First stage payment for awards ceremony.	
Invoice 1 of 3	
subtotal	########
VAT	500.00
TOTAL	########

Figure 5-4:
A template
for
invoicing.

APPROVED BY   DATE

Non-disclosure agreements (NDAs)

An NDA is a contract that you're likely to receive from big organisations that may share confidential information with you. You may just be organising a conference for the organisation, but the fact that you have access to all the strategic plans and their results can put you in a privileged position. By signing an NDA, you agree that you won't tell anyone the details of that company. Naturally, you need to provide some information to your team. Check the details of the NDA to see whether you're signing on behalf of the company or yourself.

Templates are available online, free of charge, if you need to provide an NDA yourself.

Consider asking suppliers to sign an NDA to cover yourself legally if one of them releases confidential information.

Reading the small print

Read through every single line of a contract, even if it is a long and time- consuming process. By signing a contract, you confirm that you've read, understood and agreed its contents, so explaining that you didn't read a contract before signing it isn't an acceptable excuse.

Here are some common areas to check in contracts:

- ✔ **Entertainment:** Rider requirements and specifics with regards to type of hotel or transport.
- ✔ **Venue:** Load in and out restrictions that incur costs; corkage fees.
- ✔ **Print:** Delivery times and costs. One person's end of play is different to another person's.
- ✔ **Catering:** Last-minute costs associated with number changes; waste removal.

Payment Schedules

People in business circles talk about cash flow being at the heart of any business. Cash flow can make or break your event. By ensuring you have a good grasp on your cash flow, you can ensure you have sufficient funds to pay the many suppliers you use while planning an event. Due to the large amount of purchasing for events, it's even more important than in other marketing disciplines to make sure you agree the payment plan with your client.

Always insist on receiving some of the funds before the event date. When possible, aim to have 50 per cent of your overall budget as clear funds, available at the start of the planning to allow you to pay without going into a negative balance.

Many suppliers invoice for payment in 30 or 60 days. Some suppliers that haven't worked with you before will, however, request payment upfront to protect their businesses. If you pass these costs onto the client before the event, you are using exactly the same principle.

You are also likely to have a large number of credit card transactions. You have a month from the statement date to pay the balance, but if you haven't received cleared funds from your client, and can't pay, you incur interest charges.

Ask your client for 50 per cent on confirming the budget, 25 per cent of the budget two weeks before the event and 25 per cent when the event is complete.

In conjunction with your client, write a simple document to agree the payment schedule. Figure 5-5 shows an example that also includes the dates when you'll receive funds from the client.

Client
Event
Budget
Version/Date

Figure 5-5:
Payment
schedule.

Month invoice	Amount (exc VAT)	Item/Des	Client PO number	Invoice number	Payment terms	Notes
Feb	£ 19,960.00	1st stage payment			ASAP	
April	£ 19,960.00	2nd stage payment inc main stage			30 days	
August	£ 19,960.00	3rd stage payment post-event			30 days	
Total	£ 59,880.00					

What to Do When You're Going Over Budget

Even when you put every effort into making sure your event planning is within budget, things outside your control may incur additional costs that you hadn't budgeted for.

Your client may also ask for items that you hadn't budgeted for: Some more screens or an additional course, for example. You are quite within your rights to explain to your client why these costs weren't included in the original budget, and to either ask for the extra budget or reduce the budget in other areas.

When your client agrees additional costs, ask him or her to confirm it in writing. I use a form called a project change notice (PCN) – an additional page to your contract or PO which confirms that the client knows that there will be extra costs after the event. The PCN is also a great piece of paper to have when you're talking to procurement people and trying to justify a bigger budget for the same event next year. Figure 5-6 shows you an example of a project change notice.

PROJECT CHANGE NOTICE

Event:
Originator:
Date:
1.   Reason for Change:
2.   Description:
3.   The Price (if any) (including itemised break down):
Signed for and on behalf of Client
Signed for and on behalf of the   Event Manager

Figure 5-6:
Project
change
notice.

Finding Partnerships that Help Bring Your Event to Fruition

Your client may brief you on an event for which they don't have the budget, hoping that you can find some other method of funding. Because you can no longer barter with camels, you'll need to find someone to invest money in the event. By looking at bringing in partnerships, you may enable yourself to not only put on the event but also to make it much better than you ever imagined.

Understanding the benefits of sponsorship

There are multiple benefits to looking for sponsors or partners, but it's by no means essential to have a sponsor for your event. In essence, your client is the main sponsor by providing you with a brief and cash.

Sponsors, however, can offer:

- **Financial investment:** This is a major reason for you and your client to consider sourcing sponsorship. A sponsor who invests money into your event in exchange for either brand awareness or activation by the sponsor at your event is often the only reason why your event can happen as you planned. If a sponsor wants to have an activation at the event, it normally requires you to provide space where they can bring a unit or vehicle or brand experience that people can see and engage with.

- **Benefit in kind:** Sometimes it isn't cash that you're looking for, but someone who can provide something in return for the association with your event. Such a sponsor may provide tablet devices to all your delegates to use during the conference, or offer your guests a discount on its services with a special promotion.

- **Brand association:** Consider trying to target certain brands just because you want your event to be associated with them or to have their stamp of approval. Associations often happen with industry bodies; for example, the British Heart Foundation may support a medical products or medical company event.

Securing sponsorship

It sounds so much easier than it is: Find a partner to invest some money, and all can carry on as planned. Securing sponsorship can be very time consuming. Consider employing a sponsorship manager to help with this. You need to do the following:

- ✔ **Consider your strategy:** How much do you need and how many sponsors do you want to be involved? Also, who will find and speak to sponsors: You or an external sponsorship agent that you employ, or will you use a mixture of various approaches? What will you offer a sponsor in return for its involvement? There may be 'low-hanging fruit' – people or businesses with whom you or your client have good relationships and who won't need much convincing to get involved.

- ✔ **Create a long list of targets:** Hopefully, you can make a good start on this by going through your and your client's address books. If you need to go beyond that, consider purchasing industry-segmented contact lists.

- ✔ **Create a sponsorship pack:** First impressions do count, so put some time into thinking about how to display the information about the event and also the options open to potential sponsors. The following example, Figure 5-7, shows how many of the items don't cost you any money to implement but are valuable for your sponsor.

- ✔ **Make your approach:** Through the method you chose at the strategy stage, approach your targets and see how they react.

- ✔ **Follow-up approaches:** Don't take silence as an answer; people are often busy and plan to respond later to your email or voicemail. By politely getting in contact again, you may be able to jog the target's memory. Depending on how much investment you hope to achieve, you're likely to attend many rounds of meetings with various people to allow everyone at each particular organisation to decide whether to invest.

Consider whether you actually need additional sponsors, and whether it's worth the time that you need to invest to secure them.

1. Headline Sponsor

For sponsorship of £20,000 plus VAT we would be pleased to offer you the following benefits:

Marketing collateral
- The highest level of promotion and brand identity including your Company name included on all printed and digital event collateral
- Your Company logo on the home page of the exhibition website
- 250 word profile under the 'Sponsorship' section, including contact details, logo and hyperlink to your own website
- Full-page colour advert within the official exhibition brochure
- All official sponsors will have use of the exhibition branding to use on or in conjunction with their own corporate marketing literature
- References to your involvement in the exhibition on social media sites including a dedicated Twitter feed and Facebook

Event focused
- A premium site at the exhibition (location to be agreed with yourselves) for your own promotional space
- 20 invites for the exhibition launch party

2. Zone Sponsor

For sponsorship of £10,000 plus VAT we would be pleased to offer you the following benefits:

Marketing collateral
- Your Company logo on the sponsors page of the exhibition website
- 125 word profile under the 'Sponsorship' section, including contact details, logo and hyperlink to your own website
- Half-page colour advert within the official exhibition brochure
- All official sponsors will have use of the exhibition branding to use on or in conjunction with their own corporate marketing literature
- References to your involvement in the exhibition on social media sites including a dedicated Twitter feed and Facebook

Event focused
- A gold-ranked site at the exhibition (location to be agreed with yourselves) for your own promotional space
- 10 invites for the exhibition launch party

3. Individual Sponsor

For sponsorship of between £1,000 - £5,000 plus VAT we would be pleased to offer you a bespoke package including a selection of the following benefits:

- Your Company's branding in the Festival brochure and on the website
- All official sponsors will have use of the exhibition branding to use on their own corporate marketing literature
- References to your involvement in the exhibition on social media sites including a dedicated Twitter feed and Facebook

Figure 5-7:
Sponsor
pack
example.

Other Revenue Opportunities

You can achieve additional revenue not just through sponsorship; other options may work at your event. The options available depend on the event, and you need to consider them carefully in relation to what your audience may accept.

Remember that if you need to change your objectives to make one of the following work, it isn't a good option. Stay true to the event objectives.

Table 5-1 gives an example of revenue projection. A good-practice tip is to not just put your hoped-for figures but the minimum and maximum figures, so you can see where you're realistically going to fall and how tight it may be.

Table 5-1	Example revenue projection	
Area	*Minimum*	*Maximum*
Food concessions	£4,600	£13,100
Ticket sales (10,000 sales at £10 per adult and £5 per child)	£25,000	£75,000
Bar	£3,000	£12,000
Brand partners (sponsorship)	£0	£55,000
Merchandise	£250	£2,900
Product sales (concessions and bars)	£900	£2,745
TOTAL	£33,750	£160,745

Ticket sales

For most types of events, it's feasible to sell tickets if the event will create enough of a draw and/or provide the type of entertainment to make people want to attend. The cost of a ticket may also be referred to as the delegate rate or registration fee.

Not only are tickets a useful revenue stream, but they can also enable a dialogue with the purchaser. You may be able to add purchasers' details into a customer relationship management (CRM) system, so that after the event your client can contact them about future events. Contact details also help in generating feedback after this event.

By selling tickets to an event, you can control numbers. If your event may draw huge crowds, such as for a launch or music festival, it's worth selling tickets to encourage fewer people to just turn up on the day, which may result in crowd and security issues outside your venue.

Consider holding some tickets back to sell on the day (say 10 per cent), so you don't anger everyone who's made the journey to your venue.

Wherever possible, find a financial expert to help you.

What should you charge?

Assessing the ideal ticket cost can be difficult if you've not run a similar event previously. Charging too much and making the event too expensive means you won't sell enough tickets, and charging too little means a missed opportunity for revenue.

Research

Someone, somewhere, has run a similar enough event for you to research as a good starting point.

Once you have a rough idea what you hope to charge, don't be afraid to ask some of your target market what they'd be willing to pay. Test the market.

Psychological commitment

By selling tickets to an event, even if it doesn't provide a large revenue stream for you, you're more likely to assure attendance. People make a psychological connection between a financial transaction, however small, and the desirability of attending the event. If you're concerned that bad weather may put people off on the day, consider charging a low fee of £5–10.

Early-bird discounts

To generate a quick income and help your cash flow, you can sell 'early-bird' tickets at a slightly reduced rate. You not only receive the money sooner, but you can communicate to stakeholders, including your client, that you have some attendees already. You do need to make it clear that the lower ticket price is for a limited time, rather than just putting the cost up closer to the event.

Enhanced experience tickets

Why not create an area or an additional experience that people pay extra for? Think how many people pay extra for Speedy Boarding on easyJet; some people pay for any opportunity to make their lives more efficient.

If you can organise a 'meet and greet' with your named talent before or after the event, you can charge for this or use it as part of your marketing plan.

What costs are involved in selling tickets?

It costs money to sell tickets, but the cost doesn't normally prohibit you from selling tickets. Depending on the capacity of the event and how many tickets you intend to sell, you may be able to sell tickets through your venue or your client's website, or you may want to use a ticketing agency. All these options incur some costs, including:

- ✔ Designing and printing tickets
- ✔ Updating a website with ticketing facilities
- ✔ Paying commission to a ticketing agent.

In most cases, when securing a merchant account with your bank (which allows you to receive money), credit card fees are likely. You need to decide whether to pass these charges on to your customers or whether you want to absorb this cost.

Selecting a ticketing agent requires research. Ask ticketing agents:

- ✔ What their marketing channels are as this will impact how many people are likely to see their marketing. If they only ever use printed advertisements at train stations and no digital communications, this will impact the number and type of people that will potentially purchase tickets.
- ✔ How many people they have on their database and what percentage are of your target market
- ✔ What the commission structure is
- ✔ What other costs are included

You also need to discuss with your client how you'll transfer the money back to them. Does your client want the money as it comes in, or is your client happy to wait until the end of the event? The second option is best, because it requires less paperwork and allows you to focus on planning the event rather than arranging money transfers.

You need to charge VAT on your tickets. For events where the attendees claim the cost back through expenses from their place of work, common practice is to clearly identify the VAT cost. With events for the general public, VAT is more commonly included in the overall ticket price.

I talk more about marketing your ticketing plan in Chapter 8.

Bar sales

If you bring a mobile bar into your event – such as an event in a greenfield site – you have the opportunity to negotiate a share of the bar sales. You're unlikely to be able to negotiate a share in venues that already have a bar, but it's always worth asking the question.

Merchandise

If you're planning an event that has a strong creative identity and where guests are proud to be associated with the brand, this offers a good opportunity to generate some additional revenue. For example, you can sell T-shirts, phone covers or Oyster card holders.

If your event doesn't lend itself to a strong identity, you can consider selling books that your audience may find interesting and arranging with the publishers to receive a fee for each book sold.

The upfront costs of merchandise need to be covered in your main budget, because you can't assume that you'll sell all your merchandise to cover these costs. The revenue is then a bonus revenue stream.

Live streaming

For events where you have a limited capacity and for which you've sold all your tickets, there are other opportunities for further revenue. Consider live streaming of your event or main keynote talks and charging the viewers. Many specialist companies can come to your event and set up live streaming for you.

When considering what to charge for access to the live coverage, make sure the amount is relative to the ticket price but goes some way to covering the live streaming costs.

Economic Factors to Consider

When budgeting, you need to consider items beyond the actual event that you're planning, such as background economic factors. Areas for consideration are:

> ✔ **Exchange rates:** Remember that when you purchase from another country with a different currency, the conversion rate changes, so on one day something may cost more than on another. Always agree with your supplier what currency it invoices you in and what currency you pay in.
>
> Also bear in mind that transactions with foreign countries using a credit card may incur an additional fee from your cardholder.
>
> ✔ **Trade union industry bodies:** Some regions around the world have tough restrictions on working hours, conditions and rates. Make sure that you investigate any potential impacts before you put together your budget.

Looking at Return on Investment

As budgets get smaller and smaller, not only will you need to be able to adapt your solution to fit the budget, you are also likely to need to justify why money has been invested. This is a job that your client should do with you. If your event is customer facing, your client is likely to talk about return on investment.

Return on investment (ROI) is what the client expects to get back for the investment made. For example, if the client spends £100,000 on a pop-up experience and 2,000 people attend the event, the cost per attendee is £50. However, if the event creates a large amount of PR and is so memorable and fun that each of those 2,000 people tells two other people, the £100,000 has suddenly gone much further, because so many people have now heard about the event. If all these people then go on to buy the product that the client is promoting, the ROI can be huge, based on additional sales.

Trying to calculate ROI can be difficult and the method of calculating it has caused much debate in the industry for many years. Because events are often part of a larger campaign, it's difficult to attribute additional sales and/or success to the event; it's easier to assess based on the whole campaign.

The example in Figure 5-8 is based on a bottled drinks brand having a brand experience activation at a festival, but as part of a larger campaign. Not only does this example show the impact that an event can have on sales, but also the impact on future sales.

These templates tend to look very complicated, but spend some time looking through the numbers. Use the template as a guide to create your own and then test what may work for your clients and events.

Figure 5-8:
A return on investment (ROI) model.

ROI Calculation

		Bottles per year (based on brand serves a week)	Total Bottles	Bottle profit	Total profit	Profit less investment	ROI
Total Consumers attending	10,250						
Advocacy Rate	0.5119		Bottle Profit TBC (£)	0.250			
Total Direct Advocates	5,246						
Gold (Adorer)	1,312	30.00	39,349	0.250	9,837		
Silver (Adopter)	2,623	21.20	55,613	0.250	13,903		
Bronze (Accepter)	1,312	6.30	8,263	0.250	2,066		
Direct Advocates	5,246	20	103,224	0.250	25,806		
Indirect Consumers	4	20,986					
Of Which Become Advocates	20%	4,197					
With Purchasing Intent	50%		10				
Indirect Advocates		4,197	10	41,290	0.250	10,322	
Total Advocates		9,444	15	144,514	0.250	36,128	23,628	189%
Total consumers reached		31,236					

Event Cost

Event Name	Cost Per Event	No of consumers per event	Activity Desc.	Advocacy rate	Av cost per direct advocate	Av cost per advocate	Av cost per Total Consumers Reached
FESTIVALS	£ 12,500.00	3,015	Total footfall	1.00%			
		5,000	Sales	100.00%			
		1,450	Photos	10.00%			
		2,860	Giveaways	50.00%			
		1,400	Sample	30.00%			
	£ 12,500.00	13,725		0.511851	£ 2.38	£ 1.32	£ 0.40

Key variables driving the ROI
(1) - Number of consumers at events (and what they are doing - type of event / leisure or business etc.)
(2) - Event cost (consider mass sampling vs. brand equity building)
(3) - Number of bottles per advocate (what is a 'gold', 'silver' and 'bronze' user? Varies by brand and product)
(4) - Advocacy rate (are you more likely to recommend chocolate or Fabric conditioner? - depends on audience / saliency / cost)
(5) - Bar profit (at retail is crucial to calculate ROI)
(6) - ROI levels needed to achieve post investment (ie break even at 0% or 100%? - depends on product and where sampled)

Part II
Planning Your Event's Look and Feel

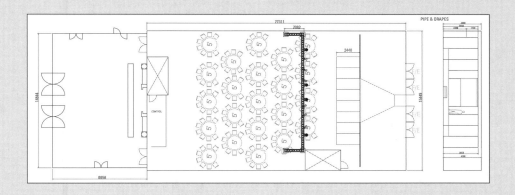

In this part . . .

- ✒ Establish who your event is talking to, and what they need to be told.

- ✒ Understand the types of content you have at your command, from slideshow presentations to firework extravaganzas.

- ✒ See the event through your customers' eyes, and understand what you need to provide to give them a great experience.

- ✒ Discover how to tell the world about your event – or at least that part of the world you want to attend it.

- ✒ Get to grips with handling the media and mastering online communications.

Chapter 6

Crafting the Message

*E*very event has a purpose, which the branding and content aim to communicate. This chapter gives you information on how to establish who you're talking to and what they need to be told, plus some methods to communicate with them across a variety of events.

If you have a clear idea of the creative brief at the start of the planning process, you can then check each idea to see whether it supports the objectives in the brief.

Building the Creative Brief

When you start work on your event, you've already established clear objectives with your client (see Chapter 1 for advice on how to write your event objectives/brief). The next step is to establish a creative brief with your client to create an event identity and provide more detail around the specific messages to communicate to the audience.

An objective for your event may be to speak to 1,000 new customers; your creative brief may have an objective that 60 per cent of the audience must understand that your brand of Internet banking is the best on the market for students. This means that you can use the event objective figure of 1,000 conversations to structure what type of event and where you should host your event. Regardless of where you host your event, the target of convincing 60 per cent of the audience to believe something will be the role of the creative and messaging that you use at your event.

The creative brief is the document against which you check all your content and experiences to make sure the event achieves its objectives. Here is an example creative brief template which you can use as a guide to answer some of the following questions. The more information you and your client can fill in on the template, the better. There is a saying that 'you get out what you put in' so try to get the best creative brief you can. Figure 6-1 shows a template for a creative brief.

creative brief

Client:	Job Name:
Job No:	Total Job Budget:

Type of execution *e.g. print 3D*	
First Review:	Final Approval:
Acc Dir:	Creative Time Allowed in Budget:

What is our task?

Who are we talking to?

What do they currently believe?

What must the communication say?
(proposition)

What do we want them to believe?

What tone of voice should the communication have?

What practical considerations should be borne in mind?

Mandatory Requirements *e.g. logo, strap-line*

Assets available and where they can be found

Figure 6-1:
A template
for a cre-
ative brief.

What does the audience know already?

Firstly you need to understand what your audience already believes. Taking the Internet banking example, do students in university cities even know that this brand exists? If they know it exists, do they know that it specialises in student banking? Ask your client for as much background information as possible to help answer these questions; if your client doesn't have all the information, try to find out for yourself by asking people you may know in the target market. It is also possible to search online and try to find forums and fan pages where you can start to get an idea of people's opinions.

From this, you can establish the biggest need for communication. You may need to focus less on brand awareness, and more on product awareness.

What do we want to tell the audience?

After understanding your target market's biggest knowledge gap, you then need to agree with your client what to tell your audience. You may agree with your client that you don't want to be as abrupt as 'Brand X is the best student bank option around.' You may decide instead to focus on the point of difference between your client's product and other Internet banking options for students. For example, if your client's brand offers all new student customers a free overdraft of £1,500 for three years, and all the competitors only offer £1,000, this may be the area to focus your messaging on.

Supporting messages

Clients are often influenced from within their organisations; corporate influence may mean they are forced to add to the messaging to include wider, strategic messages. For example, although the prime message in the example of the student bank account may be to do with the point of difference in the overdraft offer, one of the supporting messages may be that if students take out insurance at the same time as opening an account, they will receive an added cash benefit.

Supporting messages need to be identified as supporting and not as the prime message. This allows you to prioritise all activity based on the priority order of the messages.

How should we talk to them?

Once you and your client have decided the priority of messages, you need to agree what tone of voice and formats to use when talking to your target market. Students are not likely to respond well to being preached at (they have enough of that in the lecture theatre), but might accept a recommendation from their friends as a reason to interact with a student brand.

That's fine, but how can you talk to the friends of the potential new customers? Consider running a promotion that if someone brings a friend to the event experience at the student union, both are entered into a prize draw. Or ask all existing customers to recommend new customers, and offer a similar prize.

Students are socially aware and have grown up with social networking. Some older target markets may have heard of it but not interact with any of their friends on it. A promotion on a social network that uses the informal tone of that medium may resonate better with your target market than a formal piece of direct marketing through their letter-box.

Always consider what's appropriate for your audience. The way to talk to a student is totally different from how you talk to the CEOs you want to attract to your networking event.

The Event Brand

Your event needs to reflect your client's brand in the right way. Every event has a brand. If, for example, you're organising an exhibition that brings many companies and brands together, the event itself – such as Innovate UK 2013 – has its own brand identity that you need to communicate to potential guests. Take music festivals as an example. The name of the event such as Wireless isn't the same as the company that organises it; in fact, most people that attend the event won't ever know who actually organises it.

Part of your role may be to create this event identity. If this is the case, you need to recruit some designers to help you. It's not as simple as creating a name for the event and a logo; you also need to consider a theme for the event.

Conferences often have a theme that pulls all the elements together. I recently used the theme 'In Focus' for a sales and marketing conference where the team needed to clearly see the opportunities for the following year, and to focus on four key products rather than the whole range.

It's not just conferences, though, that can use a theme. Bestival, a music festival on the Isle of Wight, has a theme each year, such as space-age or underwater, to encourage visitors to dress up. The organisers support the theme by providing props around the site.

Consider the objectives, the message that you're trying to communicate, and also how to bring this to life before, during and after your event. Be realistic; don't present a theme to your client that you can't afford to activate. Branding and theming cost money.

The branding hierarchy

As with the messaging hierarchy, you often have to incorporate multiple brands in your experience messaging. You may have an event brand, a client brand, an agreement with the venue that you need to include its brand, and any sponsor brands. Lots of logos and straplines in one place can be confusing, and they are unlikely to benefit anyone.

When incorporating multiple brands:

- Organise all the brands into a hierarchy that makes sense to your audience.
- Speak to the 'guardian' of each brand to see whether that brand really needs to be included.
- Think about the primary objectives of the activity, and place greater focus on those brands that are more important to achieving the objectives or those that have paid most to be part of it.

Working within brand guidelines

Having clear brand guidelines to work from ensures a consistent brand message. It may fall upon your shoulders to create the event brand guidelines for your client. You will need to create a document (online or offline) that people can use as a set of rules around the brand – what can be done and what can't be done? The typical contents of a brand guidelines document would include the following:

- Introduction/background to the event and reason for the brand identity.
- Logo showing any variants on size and colour (for example, if your logo is coloured, you might have a black and white version too).

> ✔ The colours used and their pantone reference, CMYK and RGB references.
>
> ✔ Font info and sizes that should be used (typography).
>
> ✔ Use of imagery or photography; for example, whether or not your brand only uses stickmen or landscape photos.
>
> ✔ Examples of the event logo being used in printed and digital collateral.
>
> ✔ Integrating examples of dos and don'ts is also helpful for everyone to see.

If you're working within existing brand guidelines set out by your client, check every piece of branding or content against these guidelines to ensure they adhere.

What is Content?

All the information and messages that you want to communicate on the day of your event comprise what is called *content*. This may be the detail of your conference agenda and who is presenting what slides, or it may be the experiences of a guest at a music festival when watching the main stage or at other smaller stages or stands. Content can cross all senses and is not slides in a presentation, as is often thought. In fact, the more types of content you can have at an event, the better.

Deciding who produces the content

Designing, producing and co-ordinating content is a job in itself and can be time consuming, depending on how much support your client gives you. If you have a producer in your team (see Chapter 4 for more on roles and responsibilities), this person's main role is to produce the content. In small teams, however, it often falls on your shoulders to organise this.

Work closely with your client and your client's team to extract a clear brief describing what guests will experience before, during and after your event.

Achieving a consistent look and message

You may decide to split the content across a few team members, to give it the attention it needs. If this is the case, it is even more important to have clear brand and messaging guidelines. All branding or content that is being created should always be cross-referenced against the brand guidelines which should be used as a checklist to ensure consistency.

It is often useful to nominate a 'Brand Guardian' within your team who will be responsible for making sure that the brand is always correctly represented and that they get final sign-off before anything is produced.

Common Types of Content

The type of content that you choose needs to be appropriate for the audience you're speaking to and for the venue that you're using. Most corporate events rely heavily on a similar, familiar, format for guests that involve slides, video content, interactive sessions and often a hand-out. Events that speak to consumers rather than employees follow a less rigid format and can incorporate many types of content to distribute messages.

If you're responsible for creating the content and aren't able to hire a producer to support you in this role, I suggest sticking to the more common types of content because they're common for a reason: They work and are easy to manage.

Slides

Slides on a screen are an easy way to communicate information, and act as a prompt for speakers on stage to use. PowerPoint and Keynote are the most common programs used.

If you have speakers who are bringing their own slides, tell them what format to create them in. Ask to see the slides before the event, so that you can check that they work and that they fit the brand guidelines.

Find out what screen sizes you have at the venue and match your slides to that screen size. Common screen sizes for content are 16:9 and 4:3.

Slides that are being displayed on screens around your venue should be succinct and easy to understand. Whilst a speaker should be able to embellish the points, the meaning of each slide should be clear to any reader.

When creating slides:

- ✔ Try to limit bullet points to four or five per slide.
- ✔ Make each bullet point less than a sentence.
- ✔ Limit the number of slides to no more than one every two minutes.
- ✔ Use images and charts to break up information on slides.

Video content

As video is becoming more accessible to everyone through the rise in smartphones and the reduced cost of video recorders, video is becoming more and more common in events.

Videos can be a creative way of making information more memorable, and can even be used to inject humour into an event. At a recent conference, the sales director used a video to show tongue-in-cheek examples of bad and good techniques, to reinforce his point about personalised service for potential customers. This was a much more memorable and light-hearted approach than going through a list of dos and don'ts with his team.

As with slides, find out the screen size and orientation to make sure that your videos will play well at the event; don't record all your footage in a vertical format if all the screens are landscape.

As with anything, don't use video for the sake of it. Make sure your videos convey a message in an efficient and memorable way.

Hand-outs and other printed material

To help remind your visitors what they have seen at your event, it is often worthwhile providing them with handouts that they can take home with them. Depending on how much information you wish to provide, this can take a significant amount of time to pull together. Whereas you may be changing slides up until a minute before a speaker goes on stage, with printed materials, you will need to have it designed, approved, printed and delivered prior to your event.

Using printed maps and agendas will also ensure your visitors know where they are going on the day.

Consider whether you intend to distribute the printed information before, during or after your event.

 ✔ By providing it on entry, you can guarantee that everyone will have a copy and will also allow your visitors time to read it in between sessions or over lunch.

 ✔ If you distribute during the event, then think carefully about how logistically that will work and how best to do it when moving people from one space to another.

> ✔ Another option is to give a summary of all the information provided during the day in printed form on exit so they can refer back to it when they head back to the office. The only thing to consider here is that often at events, some people will sneak out early so you will need to make it clear that there is information available.

At more public facing, experiential events, you could consider providing your visitors with discount vouchers for the product you are promoting with details on URLs and social networking links. (See information on giveaways in Chapter 3). If you are planning a family event, such as a family festival, consider having printed games such as treasure hunts to help the children explore the whole event.

Interactive experiences

Sometimes slides are not the most appropriate form of content and actually you are looking for more interactivity and are not as focused on providing structured information in a linear way. The use of slides is used extensively in corporate events but events targeting consumers and the general public, rarely use this format. There are other options for this.

Interactivity is important. People often need to be encouraged to listen in the first place. You and your team need to be as creative as possible and come up with ways of communicating with your audience and encouraging them to get involved.

Recently, augmented reality has become a popular method of achieving inter-activity between the brand and customers. Rather than the event providing lots of information and detail to consumers, the brand inspired people to find out more because of what they had seen during the experience.

CASE STUDY

Bringing it to life: Virtual reality

A *National Geographic* augmented reality show touring around Hungary brought the opportunity for shoppers to interact with everything from *T. Rex* to an astronaut walking around in a space suit. A large digital screen and a high-powered camera were placed in front of a marker on the floor for the augmented reality interaction.

When shoppers stepped on the marker on the floor, the content came alive on the screen in front of them. To help shoppers interact with the experience, a brand ambassador dressed as a park ranger showed them what to do and answered questions about the concept.

Interactive content doesn't need to be very technically advanced, though, if you're trying to create an experience to help children understand more about the world they live in. Colouring in a variety of flags and dressing up in clothes from various cultures has much more impact than looking at a screen with slides on it and listening to someone speaking.

The opportunities for interactive content are endless. The best way to generate ideas is to run brainstorming sessions with your team and mini focus groups of your target market, if possible.

More Than Just a Presentation Slide

Slides are easy to pull together and amend right up until the final hour. If you're looking for something with a little more impact and have the budget to support it, then check out my suggestions in the following sections for some good alternative forms of messaging. All of them, however, require longer lead times and rely heavily on the quality of technology that you invest in at your event.

Radio Frequency Identification (RFID)

This great technique is just starting to become popular at events. RFID is a way of identifying, tracking and improving a guest's experience at your event. Small chips are inserted into each individual's event pass, which the guest then carries around the event.

If you have interactive screens at your event, a sensor can detect each guest's chip to give your guests access to more information that's relevant to them.

By encouraging your visitors to scan in and out of each of your experiences, you can see their journey. You can use this information to make further recommendations to your visitors, or for yourself when planning your next event. Think of the event pass as being like a Tesco Clubcard, where you receive recommendations when you log on for online shopping.

When budgeting for RFID, consider not just the cost of the software, but also all the additional hardware you need, plus the time for bespoke content to be designed.

Projections

Projections are very impressive. Slides are often projected onto a stage. Rear and front projections are the two basic types to be aware of.

> ✔ **Rear projection:** An image is projected onto a screen from behind the screen. (Additional space is therefore needed behind the screen for the projector.)
>
> ✔ **Front projection:** This is a standard way of projecting. A projector in front of the screen presents across the audience. This projector should be mounted on the ceiling so guests don't block the projection.

Projectors are becoming much more powerful than previously, and there are other opportunities for creative content at events. Consider adding a sound track to the following types of projection, because it can enhance the mood and the guests' experience.

3D holographic video projections

Do you remember watching *Star Wars* and seeing the projection of Princess Leia's plea for help from Obi-Wan Kenobi? This was an early version of 3D holographic video projection. The appearance is of an object or person appearing and moving in front of you, all through the power of projectors and clever lighting.

The technology has advanced significantly in the last 30 years. Whilst such projections are costly to implement, they can add another dimension to the content used in events.

Fog screen projections

Another form of projection is to project onto a wall of fog or mist. This can't be used for highly detailed images such as photos, but works well for colours and shapes plus some basic words. The experience for your guest of seeing content on such an unusual surface can often have more impact than the actual content being projected.

Video mapping

Video mapping is the process of projecting video onto any surface (rather than just a screen) and using the content creatively to make the surface look 3D.

This great technique is often used in publicity stunts, but is also effective in a conference or festival environment. To have the greatest impact, the technique requires space.

You need to work carefully with your supplier to establish what content is likely to work best.

There are some great examples of publicity stunts during which video has been projected onto buildings such as castles and made it look like the building is falling down. Such effects need to be seen to be understood and believed!

Pyrotechnics

Pyrotechnics are, in basic terms, fireworks. They can add drama to your event and are a great way to support an announcement or finish an event in style.

Organising pyrotechnics is a specialist role, and you need a qualified supplier if you want to include them in your event. Pyrotechnics can be costly. You need permission from your venue and also the local council, so obtain this before going too far down the planning process.

Chapter 7

Designing the Experience

- -

- -

*T*his chapter talks you through the basic elements of the visitor journey. It covers what every event is likely to have, but also some other options which you may want to consider. The best events are those where the event manager has gone beyond meeting just the basic requirements and has put extra thought into making everyone's day better than they hoped.

Understanding the Visitor Journey

The *visitor journey* is the experience your visitor has during your event. If you work in marketing, you're probably familiar with the phrase customer journey. The visitor journey is pretty much the same concept but for events, where not only 'customers' attend; for example, for internal events the audience comprises employees.

Event management is more than just making sure there's sufficient lighting, food and seating; it's about making sure that your visitors have a memorable and inspiring experience. That requires a little more thought than just dealing with the production basics: Consider the details that make each visitor's day that bit easier. Regardless of what type of event you're hosting, some fundamental aspects of the visitor journey are relevant to most events. These are some of the first interactions that visitors have with your event, so aim to execute them well.

Guest registration and accreditation

Identification may be needed for you and your team, and what about your visitors: Do any of them need to be identifiable? In events, this identification is generally called accreditation. Everyone feels a sense of importance when they have an accreditation lanyard or a wristband on; everyone pretends it's got AAA (access all areas) on it. The very nature of feeling part of something inspires a positive feeling!

Some starter questions are:

✔ **Do you have VIPs?** If so, do you intend to provide them with a different experience than the majority of your visitors? You may consider sending a volunteer to meet the VIPs and escort them to a reserved area, so they don't need to queue and they get the best seats in the house. How about giving them a different-coloured lanyard – the cord their accreditation badge hangs from – so staff throughout your event can easily identify them and provide special service?

✔ **Are only certain people allowed to enter some areas?** By having different colours or codes on items such as lanyards or wristbands, you can identify different access levels. Explain your system to any on-site security personnel, so they know what to look for when allowing guests into different areas of your event. The number of delegates you expect will dictate whether you will require a logistics company to help you with delegate/visitor management or if you will be able to do this yourself. My recommendation would be that a group of over approximately 50 people would be too much for you to deal with on the morning of your event whilst managing everything else. (See Chapters 9 and 11 for more information on your on-site roles during the build and show day.)

✔ **Are you doing an activity where only certain people are involved and therefore need an easy way to group people?** Sometimes at a conference, you may want to split your entire audience into three or four groups for a team-building or ice-breaker activity (see Chapter 3 for more information on these). Rather than running through everyone's names or hoping that people won't sit next to their colleagues, you can pre-plan the groups of people. If you provide different-coloured wristbands, you can then ask all people with a particular colour of wristband to go to a different room.

The entry process can be even more technological than using a basic lanyard, though. Why not send your visitors a confirmation email with a barcode embedded in it and encourage them to scan their smartphone under your barcode reader when they arrive? Using technology sets the tone of your event as more innovative and in tune with how your visitors often interact using their phones. However always ensure that you have a back-up option for those visitors that don't have smartphones or who have lost the email with the barcode.

The basic lanyard is also a handy place to store additional information such as a site plan or agenda in a clear plastic slip attached to the lanyard cord. But nowadays lanyards can be even more advanced than that. By having a unique barcode or using RFID technology, you can give each visitor a truly bespoke experience. I talk more about RFID in Chapter 6.

Don't forget the basics: Think through where to put your accreditation/ registration desk. The desk needs to be manned by the hosts who are the face of your event. It needs to be easy for your guests to find, so is generally at the entrance of the event.

Don't put the registration table right in front of the door: The queue of people will stretch out of the door and potentially into the rain. It's always best to position it just to the side of the door, inside the venue, with the cloakroom just beyond.

Wherever I hang my hat . . .

Particularly at corporate events, where everyone has a laptop bag, and for events in the winter when everyone has a coat, the piles of bags and coats in corners of the room can be a health and safety risk.

It's much better to invest in a couple of rails, some hangers and some raffle tickets, and create a cloakroom. The solution can be as simple as that or another opportunity for showing your attention to detail; for example, you could design branded coat tickets with a little message or fact on them. Venues that host events sometimes have a dedicated cloakroom area and offer their venue staff to help man this element of the event.

Any time you design a piece of printed collateral such as an agenda or floor-plan to give to a visitor, think how it may be branded.

If your event has a fixed start and end time, a large number of people will want to check in and collect their belongings, at the same time. Ensure that enough people are available to manage this to make it as smooth as possible. If you know how long you expect it to take to collect each item in the cloakroom, you can work out how many attendants you need to clear your event. For example, if you have 100 guests, of whom 75 per cent leave something in the cloakroom, based on 15 seconds per item, it will take just under 20 minutes to find everyone their coat. Are you happy for your guests to wait 20 minutes, or can you find another volunteer to reduce the time by half? Ten minutes to wait for your coat is a lot more appealing than 20.

Lost property

Some events are more likely to have lost property than others. Parties and family events are notorious for lost property, whereas it's less of a concern at conferences and exhibitions. Business people seem to be a lot more responsible when it comes to their belongings!

Assign a place for lost property. This doesn't need to be identifiable to your guests, but make any of your team who are interacting with your guests aware of the process. If your event has an event controller, as quite often large, outdoor events will, lost property is usually taken to the event control office and recorded in the event log. Event control is the hub of all radio communications on site and will make it easier for items to be tracked down quickly by a radio call. If a guest has lost an item, take a basic description and then ensure the guest signs for the item. Agree a process with the venue for returning lost property once you have de-rigged the event.

Signage

Basic signage such as information telling your guests where the toilets are can make a huge difference to everyone's experience during the event. Whether your event has 25 people or 2,500 people, your life is much easier if every single one of those people doesn't ask you for directions.

Many approaches can be taken; assess your event and budget to decide which is most appropriate. There are options that suit a basic budget, so every event can be clearly signposted. The two main categories are to provide human or printed directions, but digital signage is also a popular choice when the budget allows.

Human signage

It sounds like a funny name, but human signage is just what it is: Humans directing people, as a sign would. Rather than always relying on a printed board or prop to direct people around an event, sometimes the more human touch is required. Human signage is also useful when it's not physically possible to have a printed board with your message.

Think of London 2012 and the Games Makers; one of their main roles was to show people the way and to make sure thousands of people didn't get lost and turn up late for the events. Imagine if the organisers had replaced all those people with posters – it wouldn't have had quite the same impact.

Human signage is definitely more expensive than printed signage, but it's important to think about your visitors' journey through the site and whether at different times of day they may need different directions. Can the printed signage be changed quickly enough?

Giving it up for the Games Makers

Games Makers – the volunteer helpers, stewards and attendants – were some of the biggest stars of the London 2012 Olympics. McDonald's helped train 70,000 volunteers before the London Olympics. These volunteers weren't just given a T-shirt on the day and pointed in the direction of a queue; intense training programmes were set up months before the event. But before that, they had to get through the application process, which saw over 240,000 people ask to take part.

Three months before the Games, all volunteers attended general training courses at Wembley. The London Organising Committee of the Olympic and Paralympic Games (LOCOG) then provided role-specific training during which job roles were explained in detail and role-play scenarios followed.

McDonald's wanted to help create a legacy of exceptional customer service for the hospitality and volunteering sectors for years to come.

It should also act as an inspiration to event managers that if you can put together the perfect team of volunteers, you then have your own set of brand ambassadors who will do a lot of your promotion for you.

The Games Makers were the heroes of the Olympics and were thanked in nearly every speech given; they were even honoured by the Royal Mail, which produced a special limited-edition stamp.

Providing directions is the perfect role for volunteers, so remember to recruit, brief and train your own team of 'games makers'.

Printed signage

There are many different options for printed signage at an event and you should always aim to include branding in each sign. Base the decision about what to use on the:

- ✓ **Chosen venue:** If you are using an outdoor venue, you will need to use waterproof signage that has a good wind rating so it doesn't blow over. If you have a large site, make sure your signage is large enough that it stands out around the site. If you are using an indoor venue, you will need to discuss with the venue what type of signage will be suitable and how it can be attached to walls or the floor.

- ✓ **Type of event:** The type of event will dictate the type of person that attends and what information and signage they might need. At a conference with business delegates, you may need to consider printed information with floorplans, an agenda and even wireless access codes. At a music festival, the signage could be made up by large flags that will also act as decoration around the site.

- ✓ **Budget:** Individual pieces of signage don't cost a huge amount but when you have a large event, they quickly add up. Look carefully at your budget and speak to your print supplier to assess the best use of your budget. It may be worth investing in a couple of large pieces of print that have impact or it may be that you can rely more heavily on in-house digital signage at a hotel or conference centre.

✔ **Requirement for re-use:** Clients will often want to re-use signage as they will have invested money in it. However, this is not always possible, depending on how it is fixed. If you do need to re-use signage, assess with the printer and the venue the best ways to design and attach it so it can be removed and stored easily after. It will also be worth considering how specific you make the messaging on the signage if it may be re-used – it may be better to use the client's company brand rather than the event brand in case the event brand gets updated at each event.

The reasons why you may need printed signage include to provide branding opportunities, for directional signage (to point people in the right direction for toilets and so on) and even for use during parts of an activity. The kind of signage you should consider is:

✔ Entrance/Exit/Emergency Exit/Fire Exit/Fire meeting point/Registration

✔ Toilets/Male/Female/Disabled/Baby Changing

✔ Meeting Point (for lost children, although it cannot be advertised as such)

✔ First Aid (needs to have a green background with white lettering)

✔ DDA Viewing Platform (disabled viewing platform)

✔ Information Point

✔ Backstage Access – Event Crew and Personnel Only

✔ Event Control/Production Office/Green Room (for any performers)

Depending on the budget you have available and the level of printing that you need to do, you may want to hire a scheduler, who will work with your designer and printer to instruct the designer on all the specification that the printer requires and ensures that the printer is matching the correct colours. More often that not, though, this job is one you can do yourself. Create a spreadsheet with details on all the printed collateral that is required and the dimensions that the artwork is required. Figure 7-1 shows a standard schedule for producing signage.

Digital signage

Digital signage consists of screens around a venue which can have information relayed onto them. This could be plain text, graphics or event photos. For example, on the London Underground, digital screens are used more and more for advertising; imagine having this type of screen and functionality around your event site. Conference centres and hotels are increasingly investing in digital signage to offer onto their customers. Beware as sometimes they can charge extra to use the digital signage, so don't assume that if it's there you can use it.

Signage Schedule

EVENT ENTRANCE	Item	Artwork	Branding	Quantity	Dims	Deadline	Unit price	Total £	Notes
Flags	Large power flag + water base	Event Manager	**Event logo + 'Welcome' on both**	2		14-May	£268.5	£537	Covered in budget
Boards	Disclamer board	Event Manager	Copy provided by Client	2	A0	14-May	£100	£200	Addition
Inflatables	Gantry	Client	tbc	2	Printer to provide dimensions	9-May	£1,037	£2,074	Covered in budget

GENERAL SITE	Item	Artwork	Branding	Quantity	Dims	Deadline	Unit price	Total £	Notes
Flags	Large power flag + water base	Event Manager	Zone logo	2		14-May	268.5	537	Covered in budget
Boards	Clip frames + A3 print	Client		5	A3	14-May	£85	£425	Addition
Boards	A4 estate agent boards and stakes	Client	Treasure Hunt	26	A4	14-May	7.48	194.5	Addition
Fencing	Branded heras scrim	Client	Event logo	87m/ 25 panels	3.37m x 1.78m	14-May		£3,241	Covered in budget
Fencing	Unbranded heras	N/A	Blue/white	30 panels	3.37m x 1.78m	14-May	Included in above cost	Included in above cost	Covered in budget
Generic	Large power flag + water base	Event Manager	Toilet	2		14-May	268.5	537	Covered in budget
Generic	Large power flag + water base	Event Manager	First Aid	1		14-May	268.5	268.5	Covered in budget
Generic	Large power flag + water base	Event Manager	Information Tent	1		14-May	268.5	268.5	Covered in budget

MAIN	Item	Artwork	Branding	Quantity	Dims	Deadline	Unit price	Total £	Notes
	PA Scrims	Client	tbc	2	3.05m x 3.5m (50mm bleed)	14-May	684	684	Covered in budget
	Stage backdrop	Client	tbc	1	9m x 4m (50mm bleed)	14-May	756	756	Covered in budget
	Hanging banners	John	N/A	3	3000mm x 100mm	To be sent directly to AV supplier	N/A	N/A	Provided by Client
	Crowd Barrier	Client	tbc	3	10.2m x 0.91m	14-May	£160	£480	Addition

Figure 7-1:
A standard signage schedule

By using screens you are also able to incorporate other elements such as having a ticker tape of tweets or even the next part of the agenda flashing up.

Types of digital signage include an event app that provides your guests with floorplans, and even one that uses GPS to show where they are in your venue. See the next section for more information on event apps.

Making use of event apps

According to some bold predictions, by the end of 2016 there may be 10 billion smartphones – that's 1.4 for every person on the planet. It's not surprising, then, that this area needs to be considered in all communications, and particularly for events. An event-specific app is a commonly requested element of the event planning, particularly when the audience is so tech savvy. Apps are a great networking tool, but they're also used at music festivals to help visitors plan their day.

Apps are a great way to:

✔ Send last-minute announcements, such as 'the weather is hot, so bring some suntan lotion' or 'a speaker is unfortunately unwell, so is not able to attend'.

✔ Ease the entry system and combine the app and use of barcodes for entry.

✔ Allow conversation during plenary sessions, when the room should be quiet, for example by encouraging updates to a dedicated Twitter hashtag.

✔ Make sure that visitors know where they're going, by including floor plans.

✔ Enable targeted networking. By visitors filling in a mini profile on the app, it can save the need for business cards to be passed around, with contact details being stored directly on visitors' phones. (See Chapter 3 for more information on networking.)

✔ Offer additional opportunities to attract revenue from sponsors and exhibitors, by selling space in the app. (See Chapter 5 for more information on sponsorship revenue generation.)

✔ Capture real-time data and information, which will help in making any necessary adjustments and also help improve the ROI of the event.

✔ Save money on costly print runs of event programmes and signage. Most apps have a content management system, so you can update information quickly from a laptop.

✔ Reduce the volume of printing for an event and thus also reduce your carbon footprint – everyone wins!

As with all technology-based solutions, you can go as basic or as complex as your budget will allow.

Some great websites such as www.yapp.us and www.twoppy.com allow you to create a free app for your event.

Home time

Your event has gone swimmingly well, you have hundreds of happy guests and now you need to get them all out of your venue so you and your team can help dismantle the set and furniture and go home. Some basic thinking and signage makes this process a lot simpler:

- ✔ Alert your team 15 minutes before your event finishes and then again 2 minutes before.
- ✔ Ensure that the cloakroom is adequately manned.
- ✔ Make sure the toilets have been cleaned and are ready for the influx of people who will probably make use of the facilities before going home.
- ✔ Ensure any goody bags or printed collateral is ready for collection by your guests.
- ✔ Ensure any transport that you are providing is ready and waiting and clearly identified.
- ✔ If your guests are departing by road, check the local travel situation and alert those who may be affected by any incidents, so they can navigate a different route home.
- ✔ If you have any VIPs on site, make sure someone is on hand to escort them to a different exit if they need to make a quick getaway.

The Best Environment for Your Content

The way in which content is presented, and the type of environment it's delivered in, has an impact on how memorable your event is. Once you've picked your venue, you need to work out how your event will fit into it. Conduct brainstorming sessions with team members and do lots of research online to see what's available to help make your vision a reality.

Think about your visitor journey around the space and how to make it most efficient. You also need space for those added extras, which will be like the magic dust on top of your event.

How to visualise your event space

An event designer can transform your scribbles on a sticky note into a plan to use for production and to help your client understand your vision.

Depending on how easy your client finds it to interpret floor plans, it's often worthwhile asking a designer to draw a computer-aided design (CAD) plan and add the client's branding. For the client, the plan then looks like a vision of the room on show day.

Figure 7-2 is a basic CAD plan of a conference room. You can use computer programs to create this type of plan (and you can work towards qualifications if you want to advance in this area). Alternatively, specialists can be found on the Internet.

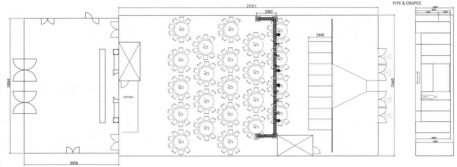

Figure 7-2:
A computer-aided design venue plan

Photo-like visuals can cost a few thousand pounds to create, so it's worth discussing with your client whether they are needed.

Room layouts and seating plans

How you decide to use a room can totally transform a space. Designing the layouts is your opportunity to focus the audience's attention where you want; consider the rooms at your venue as blank canvases wherever possible. Certain production restrictions will affect your design, such as the location of pillars and fire exits, but in essence you can put anything you want in the space.

Designers are specialists in understanding how to best use a room, so it's helpful to involve one when designing your event spaces.

Consider the props, stage, seating requirements or any floor entertainment that you want when deciding the layout of your room.

You may be restricted to using the same room at a venue for your conference and for the awards dinner in the evening. Try altering the layout while your guests are getting changed, so that it feels like a new room in the evening.

Theatre seating

Theatre seating comprises lines of seats facing towards the stage. As the name suggests, it's like being in a theatre or a cinema. This type of seating is common in conferences and encourages the audience to focus on the messages being given out on the stage, rather than have conversations with other delegates. It's also the best use of space, in that you can fit more people into a room than with other forms of seating plan.

Banquet seating

A banquet seating design has many round tables in a room, with normally eight or ten people at each table. It's a common style for awards dinners and events where conversations between delegates are encouraged.

Crescent seating

This is a mixture between theatre and banquet seating, where everyone faces the stage but sits around halves of large tables. This gives the benefits of both types of seating plan, but does take up more space.

Classroom seating

Classroom seating is used only for small groups, and is exactly how you remember it from school. The room contains a number of tables of different sizes. Classroom seating is used when delegates are expected to do a lot of table work – when problem solving, for example – in breakout sessions.

Exhibition layouts

Putting on an exhibition can be a big job, depending on how many exhibitors will attend. (See Chapter 3 for information on how to find your exhibitors.)

Be aware when planning the design of an exhibition to consider the visitor journey (see the section 'Understanding the Visitor Journey' earlier in this chapter).

A common approach is to split the exhibition into zones and group similar companies, departments and so on by themes. You can identify these zones through branding or by using basic techniques such as changing the colour of the carpet for each new zone.

Most exhibitions use a mixture of shell-scheme stands and space-only stands.

- ✔ **Shell schemes:** These are those uniform-looking structures (normally white panels), to which businesses attach their own posters, and within which they lay out their wares on a trestle table, maybe with a few extra props to the side. Whilst exhibitors pay a fee to use this facility, it's often a much cheaper way of having a presence at an exhibition than designing and creating an entire stand from scratch.

> ✔ **Space only:** With space-only approaches, exhibitors purchase an area of space in square feet or square metres, generally at a lower rate than for a shell scheme stand, but are responsible for everything in that space: The structure, branding and even often the flooring. This is a much more expensive space but it allows exhibitors complete control over the environment and how the brand and message are communicated (assuming the venue approves, of course).

With either style stand, it's important to consider what happens on the stand. Consider the following questions:

> ✔ Will products be sold and, if so, how will exhibitors take payment?
>
> ✔ Where will stock be stored?
>
> ✔ How will customers carry their purchases around for the rest of the day?
>
> ✔ If the product is food, how will exhibitors prepare it?
>
> ✔ How will exhibitors manage queues?

As with anything in events, ask yourself lots of questions and work through the potential answers one at a time.

The trick is to not put the most appealing things at the front of an exhibition; put them at the back to encourage visitors to tour the whole venue and hopefully find more things of interest to them.

Setting the stage

If your event requires a stage for speakers, presenters or performers, you need a stage designed. If you know who your speakers or performers are, ask them what kind of set they prefer. Do they prefer to stand behind a lectern or do they like to walk around? This affects the stage design but also what microphones the people on stage need. Also think about what kind of surface the stage should have. Carpet is good to keep noise down, but a dancer, if you plan to have one, may need a hard surface.

A stage can be designed to cater for a couple of different speaking styles. A stage manager can bring chairs and lecterns on and off in between speakers if required, but ideally there should be minimal furniture movement during the live event.

The late Steve Jobs of Apple had a world-renowned stage set and speaking approach. Because Steve Jobs wanted the focus to be on the benefits of the product that he was launching, the stage was empty and plain, and all the light was on him.

Depending on what is being presented on stage, you may need to incorporate screens into the stage design to display content. Base the size of the screen on the size of the room and what can be seen from the back of the room.

If you intend people to sit down on the stage, maybe for a panel session interview, you need to source and hire furniture that fits on your stage. Ask your designer to plot the furniture on the stage plan to make sure there's plenty of space for your guests to move around easily without the risk of a fall on stage.

Dressing a venue

'Dressing a venue' is a strange phrase; it refers to adding the finishing touches to the rooms to add the final bits of theming. Often you add floral decorations or props or even additional branding.

When planning the timings for the build of your event, make sure you include adequate time and resource for this stage, which has a huge impact on how finished your venue looks.

Consider whether or not the following would add to your event and if you have available budget for these finishing touches:

- Chair covers
- Table centrepieces
- Floral decorations
- Candelabras or dramatic lighting
- Carpet rolls (for a red-carpet type entrance)
- Bubble or dry ice machines
- Framed art

Sweet Music and Other Entertainment

Many events, even the most serious conferences and exhibitions, benefit from entertainment. As I always say, it needs to be appropriate, but music has a habit of relaxing people at events and lightens the mood slightly. At music festivals or in the evenings at a gala dinner or drinks reception, people expect different entertainment. To identify suitable options, consult your creative brief and find out who your audience will be.

Host or master of ceremonies (MC)

Having a host to pull together all the content throughout the day is often an excellent investment. The host doesn't always have to be someone famous; many professional hosts who are not known by the public are expert at linking content and keeping an audience entertained. For a non-named host, you need to budget of around £1,500 plus expenses.

Ask whether anyone in your client's organisation – someone who's a bit of a clown or show-off – would be happy to stand on stage all day. This saves some money.

Provide your host with information about the schedule for the day but also about any in jokes with your audience. The host can then entwine the jokes into the performance and gain the trust of the guests.

Famous talent

'Talent' in the events industry means anyone who is paid for his or her services, and who other people have heard of. Consider famous comedians, dance acts, musicians, and so on. Having a famous face at your event will surprise and delight your audience, and if the person is happy to have his or her photo taken, and give autographs, it gives your guests another memento of their day.

Many talent agencies can make this type of booking for you. You can brief some agencies on the type of person you're looking for, and they will make suggestions. This saves you trying to scour all the newspapers to see who may be relevant.

Talent can be more expensive than you may think: Paying £20,000–25,000 for one evening's work from one person is not unheard of.

If you convince your client that talent is a good investment, you then need to consider who will take the role of 'talent manager' on site. The famous person is likely to make demands, such as for chauffeur-driven transport and special requirements (also known as riders) for the dressing room. The talent manager answers every request of your talent to ensure he or she is happy and has everything needed before going on stage. Not all famous people are divas, but it's important to expect that they may be! Depending on the number of performers/the amount of talent you have, this may be a role that can be combined with a runner's role or might need a separate talent manager.

Musical entertainment

Your musical entertainment may be a famous face, in which case look at the section 'Famous talent' above. Either way, musicians require looking after.

Your producer, if you have one, often ensures that the musicians have everything they need for their performance.

If the artists play musical instruments, they're likely to have some kind of backline requirement for instruments and amp equipment. The act will provide some equipment, the venue may provide other elements, and you need to hire in everything else.

Allow any musicians time to rehearse on stage and to carry out sound checks before the show. I talk more about running orders and sound checks in Chapter 9.

Catering that's Worth Remembering

Catering is almost always a big part of event planning. Food and drink is important not only to meet basic needs, but it can also offer opportunities for networking and refresh your audience so they are more alert.

As with all elements of planning an event, you need to think carefully about what's appropriate for your audience and what answers the creative brief. If your event focuses on networking, offering a sit-down meal is counter-productive – a more fluid opportunity for catering and networking fits the brief better.

Theming your food

One of the easiest ways of ensuring that your event theme or identity is present in your catering is to theme your food. Here are some examples of themes and associated catering options:

- **Winning races:** Foods you'd expect to see at the races, such as champagne and strawberries for Ladies' Day at Ascot, or chips and gravy for an evening at the greyhound races
- **1950s:** Hot dogs, fries, candy floss, diner-style food and milkshakes
- **Global growth:** Foods from around the world
- **Las Vegas:** Large buffets with what feels like an endless supply of food
- **Scotland:** Haggis and whisky (themed with kilts, thistles and bagpipers)
- **Children's party for adults:** Sandwiches, sausage rolls, cheese and pineapple hedgehogs, jelly and ice-cream

You can think beyond just the food; consider naming foods and designing foods to be displayed in something that is on-theme.

It's also possible to theme the drinks, too. For an event in summer, serve Pimms on arrival, or in the winter, serve mulled wine or cider. As long as you provide more standard options on request, everyone will appreciate the attention to detail at the event.

Catering for dietary requirements

Remember that not everyone eats what you can eat or want to eat. Consider the impacts of various religious and health conditions when devising your food menu.

If guests register for the event, ask about any dietary requirements such as nut allergies. Pass this information on to your caterer, who can then plan accordingly. You then need to identify your guests on arrival and inform the caterer as to who requires different dishes. It's worth asking your guests whether they have any of the following common dietary requirements:

- Vegetarian
- Vegan
- Dairy free
- Gluten free
- Nut free

If you are not able to ask guests about their dietary requirements, it is a good idea to advise people prior to the event what food will be on offer. You will generally find that anyone with dietary requirements makes them known to you.

Types of service

The type of catering service you offer can be just as important as the food itself. When choosing, ask your caterer for advice. The following sections cover some examples of types of service.

If you expect the majority of guests to arrive hungry, consider carefully when the food will be available. I suggest not bringing out food until half an hour after the planned opening or start time, to allow for late arrivals.

Conversely, if you have only half an hour in which to feed 100 delegates, make sure that the food is there and ready a few minutes before everyone descends on your catering area.

Canapés

Canapés are small, bite-size portions of food, served on trays by waiters around a venue. They are often available at drinks receptions. Canapés aren't expected to fill your guests up, so can be used for early-evening events when you expect guests to leave your event and go on to dinner.

Cater for approximately five canapés per guest.

Bowl food

This food – also referred to as fork food – is slightly more filling than canapés. The bowls normally provide a couple of mouthfuls of food, which requires an eating utensil. Good caterers incorporate the implement into the design of the food so the waiter doesn't need to carry around a supply of forks. Mini fish and chips is a popular option.

Provide plenty of plinths or similar on which guests can put down bowls when they have finished eating.

Cater for approximately two to three bowls per guest.

Buffet

Buffets options range in style and cost. Your guests have the opportunity to select the food they want and the amount they want.

Although you may want wastage to be low, unfortunately this is the service that results in the most food wastage.

If you plan to offer a buffet, think about the queues that will develop around the buffet table. You also need to offer seating and tables for your guests to use.

Try to offer the same food on both sides of the room to reduce queuing.

Plated service

Traditional sit-down meals are quite common at award ceremonies. They are a good type of service when you want to spoil your guests and bring everything to them. Guests can sit down, chat with others on the table and have a few drinks. When you're also providing entertainment during dinner, you can position tables and seats to face in the direction of the stage.

Whether you ask guests to choose from a menu before sitting down, or you offer your guests a choice between two or three dishes, or everyone has the same depends on the number of guests, the catering facilities on site and the time frame for the meal.

Street food

Street food is a great option for more relaxed events such as festivals or sports events, and when you want to show off a multi-cultural approach to food. By having three or four food units (depending on the number of people – the suppliers will advise how many they can cater for) you allow people a choice and reduce queues concentrating in one area of your site. Guests still stand to eat their food, as for bowl food, but they get to be proactive rather than waiting for food to be delivered.

Responsible drinking

People sometimes expect alcohol at an event, and sometimes it's nice to have. You, as the event organiser, and your client have a duty of care for individuals who come to your event. This is especially true when you provide alcohol.

Chapter 10 gives more details on applying for Temporary Event Notices (TEN notices), which you will require if you are planning on selling alcohol at an event in a non-licensed venue for fewer than 500 people. If your event is for more than 500 people, you will need to inform the local council of your intentions and you will need to provide the details of the Personal Licence holder from your bar supplier/caterer.

As with food, think carefully about what is appropriate for your event. Having a bar at a family festival is fine, but it isn't appropriate to have a person walking around offering shots.

The Event Safety Guide, known in the business as the Purple Guide, and published by the Health and Safety Executive, sets out clear guidelines on what you need to do when offering alcohol at events.

Alcohol comes under the definition of food and should meet the requirements of the relevant food safety legislation, associated industry guides and codes of practice. Ensure that:

- The structure used for the sale of alcohol, usually marquees or tents, complies with the structural requirements (see Chapter 12).

- The operation is designed to allow the free flow of people to and from the bar areas to prevent congestion and crushing hazards (this may involve the use of suitable barriers, providing consideration has been given to the barriers becoming a hazard in themselves).

- The electrical installation complies with the requirements (see Chapter 12)

- Suitable and sufficient lighting is provided.

- Alcohol storage tanks are positioned on stable, even ground allowing suitable access for delivery vehicles, particularly in bad weather.

- Risk assessments for both food and health and safety, have been carried out.

- Carbon dioxide cylinders are suitably secured.

- Chemicals to clean pipelines are properly handled and stored.

✔ The type of containers that drinks are served in conform to any site/event specifications, e.g. no glass policy.

✔ There is a suitable means of disposal for glass bottles, used to decant drinks before serving.

✔ Bar areas are kept free of litter and the floors are cleared of spillages.

✔ If a 'token system' is used instead of cash, the 'change areas' are separate from the bar service area.

Allowances

The amount of alcohol you provide your guests depends on both the budget and how much is considered a responsible amount.

Your client may be happy to provide guests with drinks on arrival, free of charge to the guests, but may not be able to afford a free bar all night. Other clients know that their target market expect a free bar.

One option is to provide drink tokens to your guests when they arrive, which shows generosity but sets a cap on the number of free drinks; after this number, guests have to purchase drinks themselves. Some guests will share drinks tokens, because some may drive to your event. Providing a limited number of free drinks proves you to be a responsible event organiser, plus you and your client know the maximum budget needed for the bar.

It is standard to offer four drinks tokens per guest.

Safe travel

When offering alcohol, think about how your guests are likely to arrive and therefore leave the venue. Consider providing free shuttle buses back to hotels or to local transport hubs to encourage fewer people to drive. When you budget for the costs of providing transport, it's sometimes cheaper to find hotels for some or all of your guests.

For the show of it – catering additions

Remember that catering should be part of your guests' experience at your event. You may be planning to provide guests with basic food and endless bottles of water, but also think about incorporating some of the following options to make the catering side of your event more of a focal point.

✔ **Cocktail bars:** A good mixologist – as professional cocktail makers are called – can add real theatre to your event. Where sometimes standing at a bar can be boring, you suddenly turn the wait at the bar into a spectacle, because people want to see the mixologist make their drinks.

Mixologists are more expensive than standard barmen, and you also need to consider the increase in spirit consumption in your budget.

✔ **Champagne fountains:** If you want to set a theme of extravagance or provide a focal point in a large reception room, you may consider a champagne fountain. I recommend using a cheaper alternative to champagne for the main fountain, so as not to throw money away, but to pour from more expensive bottles of champagne when serving in front of guests, to keep the illusion going.

✔ **Chocolate fountains:** Traditionally used a lot at weddings, you can also use a chocolate fountain at more corporate events. Useful when large amounts of alcohol are served, a chocolate fountain can offer a good late-night snack option to soak up some alcohol before the hangovers kick in the following day.

✔ **Special effects (dry ice):** Dry ice (a solid form of carbon dioxide), or Cardice as it's known, can create a great atmosphere at events. You can use dry ice for futuristic sets or even spooky churches and cathedrals. Many venues have restrictions around using dry ice, so check with your venue before suggesting it to your client.

Documenting the Event

After months of planning the perfect event, how frustrating would it be if there was no evidence that it had even happened! It's worth thinking about what the content will be used for afterwards. Will you show it to sponsors or partners to explain what you did with their investment or to help plan the event the following year? Your event may even be part of a larger marketing campaign, and your client will use the content in a TV or online campaign.

Your plan will affect what methods you use, but as a guide, I explore some options in the following sections.

Photography

Photography is the cheapest and most popular method of documentation. At a basic level, most people can take photos on their phones. You may want to see whether a local university has a photography course, and whether a student would like to use your event in their coursework. Alternatively, hire a professional photographer.

However you source your photographer, ensure that you brief the person properly. Find out whether your client has any special requirements, and then provide guidelines of the type of photos you want the photographer to take.

The photography brief below shows a simple way to lay out the information. If the event has a set agenda, tell your photographer that and what you need as a minimum at each point. Figure 7-3 shows part of a typical photography brief.

Don't underestimate the importance of a good photo; a picture is worth a thousand words and can capture the emotions at your event.

Whilst there are many cheap ways to take a photo, you should try to ensure that the photographer knows what he or she is doing. Just taking photos of your stage straight on isn't going to capture the content or the reaction of your audience. You may use these photos to help apply for sponsorship the following year or to promote your company and the services you offer; the photos need to look as perfect as possible.

Video recording

With most past events, you had to be there to understand exactly what it was like. Words and photos don't do justice to events. Video is a good medium to use if you want people who didn't attend your event to understand it. Your client is likely to want to record the event, and should be prepared to pay to create a recording.

Ideally, a professional should make the video, but if your budget won't stretch that far, then most smartphones now have video capabilities. A video can give benefits by:

✔ Reaching a wider audience

✔ Helping viewers gain a greater understanding of the event

✔ Promoting future events

✔ Selling your skills as an event manager

✔ Working as a nice thank you to those involved, so they have something to remember it with

Social networking

An event is not an isolated activity anymore; events have become a part of a larger campaign. Whether you have planned this campaign or your visitors create it, your event will feature on social networking sites. Whether it's photos taken at the drunken Christmas party and tagged during the embarrassing morning after, or tweets referencing a new product you've just launched, everyone has social networking at their fingertips.

Launch of Exhibition

Stakeholder Launch - Photography Brief

Date:

Time:

Contact:

Address:

Photographer:

Background

On Tuesday 15 November, Business Secretary Vince Cable and Minister for Business and Enterprise Mark Prisk will be hosting a stakeholder reception to launch "Make it in Great Britain" – a campaign to transform the image of modern manufacturing.

As well as this being an opportunity for BIS to unveil plans for the campaign to key stakeholders and press, there will also be students from a local school and a local college present. They have come to learn more about manufacturing and careers in the industry from apprentices from companies such as Ford and Intelligent Energy, who will be bringing interactive stands to showcase manufacturing innovation.

Objective

We are looking for a set of photographs that can be used for both media and marketing purposes. The shots will be used to promote Make it in Great Britain in the press, as well as through stakeholder comms channels such as Twitter and Facebook and newsletters/e - bulletins. All will be uploaded to the BIS Flickr site, and many of the shots, in particular those of the Ministers and the activity at the stands will be used on the Make it in Great Britain website and for future campaign activity.

Event details

You will be met in BIS reception at 11am for a walk-around of the area and a verbal briefing by your contact. Attendees will arrive for registration from 11:30am, and the event will continue as follows:

Figure 7-3:
Part of a typical photography brief

Time	Activity	Images required
12noon	Event opens in conference centre with a two minute video	–
12:02pm	Keynote speech from Secretary of State Vince Cable	Vince Cable addressing room
12:10pm	Campaign overview from Minister for Business and Enterprise Mark Prisk	Mark Pris k addressing room
12:20pm	Mark Prisk MP joined on stage by Ian Blatchford (Director, Science Museum) and other industry colleagues for panel session Q&A	Group shots of panel, individual shots of panel, pictures of questions coming from the floor
12:35pm	Mark Prisk invites attendees to sign the 'Pledge board'/stage backdrop	Shots of Ministers interacting with those signing the board
12:45pm	All depart conference centre to view interactive showcase in foyer	–
12:45pm	Opportunity for students to be photographed with Prisk/Cable	Posed shots of student groups with Ministers–these should take place by the pledge board if possible, otherwise by the stands
12:50pm	Students and other guests invited to view showcase, try some of the activities and engage withapprentices	Images of interactions at stands
	Opportunity for press interviews with Ministers	If the Ministers do not have any press engagements, we would like you to stay with them and capture them interacting with the stands. If they have press engagements, we would like you to capture general stand activity, particularly involving students
1pm	Ministers depart	–
1 – 1:30pm	Showcase activity continues, winds down, attendees depart	Opportunity to capture any organisations/students/stakeholdersmissed in previous shots

---

Agency requirements

- Photos should be sent via email (Jpeg format) to your contact
- As discussed, we would ideally like up to five photos for media purposes to be sent back to us by 4pm on Tuesday, with the rest delivered via an FTP site or on a disk by 12 noon the following day. The five photos will ideally include:
    - A shot of Vince Cable addressing the audience
    - A shot of Mark Prisk and the panel Q&A session
    - Shots of the students interacting with the Ministers and the display
- They should be of high resolution for use by print media titles – versions which are emailable size and are suitable for print use should also be provided – i.e. 1MB

What we need to do is harness everyone's use of social networking and make it a tool in the marketing plan of your event. (Pre- and post-event marketing are covered in Chapters 8, 14 and 15.)

The # symbol, called a *hashtag,* is used to mark keywords or topics in a Tweet. It was created organically by Twitter users as a way to categorise messages.

A hashtag doesn't need to be set up officially but as people use the same common phrase or word, it might even 'trend' which is when large amounts of people use the hashtag in their tweets. For example #RoyalWedding was used by over a million people in their tweets during the Royal Wedding in 2011.

On Twitter it is possible to search all the tweets in the world by entering a particular hashtag. Therefore if you encourage people to use a particular hashtag when tweeting about your event, you will be able to search these tweets and see all the feedback that will help in the evaluation of the event.

Live streaming

For events where you have a limited capacity due to venue restrictions or where you want to create more of a buzz, streaming content from your event online is a great way to extend the reach of your event. If you create an on-demand function, visitors who did attend can also catch up on speakers or acts that they didn't see when they get home.

The players can either be embedded in your own website or can be on a hosted site that you link to. Access to the live streaming can be made secure to restrict who can see any confidential information: Online visitors can be asked to log in before they can view the content.

Less expensive than you may think, live streaming is a great addition for your visitor and non-visitor audience and a great excuse to send a post-event email and continue your communication with visitors.

There are numerous suppliers around and it's best to see if there is one that has worked with your other AV suppliers first, but some options include www.ddslimited.co.uk and www.streamingtank.com.

Guest video and photo content

Video booths are a great invention. The booths look a little like those you obtain passport photos from. If video booths are in a foyer area, your guests may give their honest opinions. As the night progresses, guests may feel comfortable enough to sing a little song!

You can hire these booths for a day, and most companies let you brand them and even provide prompt questions for people to answer. Watching the video back the next day can be amusing and insightful if guests comment in more depth than on a feedback form.

Similar booths can also be provided for taking photos; these often provide props and a fun branded backdrop. Guests can take branded photos away as a memento of the event, and you can create a disk with all the photos taken. Whilst you'll gain no insights through this, a photo booth does add to the experience and gives some great photos for follow-up marketing.

There are companies around that will supply video and photo booths so if you intend to have both at your event, it is normally cheaper to get them through the same supplier to reduce transport costs. Check out www.video diarybooth.co.uk and www.just-pose.com. Flip books are also a good option if you want to provide something back to your visitors then and there. Take a look at Funflip (www.funflip.co.uk).

Live voting

You have a great opportunity at your event to ask your audience questions. Whether it's an internal communication event with employees or it's for members of the public, by asking your audience questions, you can get some real-time customer feedback. For example, at a conference, by providing a tablet device on the desks, you can offer live voting, enabling you to gauge the temperature of people's opinions at the very moment when they hear information.

As with all aspects of events, however, you need to consider whether live voting is appropriate. Will it aid the visitor experience and also, importantly, will you gather useful information that you can pass on to your client? Customers and employees find it incredibly frustrating if they've taken the time to give their feedback but feel like their opinions have disappeared into a black hole.

Many companies offer specific applications and can set up all elements required, such as the tablet devices and software, and will even provide all the information afterwards.

At a basic level, though, consider using a Twitter hashtag to gather feedback. This can be a little less easy to monitor though than using a voting application. (See Chapter 8 for more information on social networking and event management.)

Chapter 8

Making Sure People Know about Your Event

*E*vents are a people business, and you need people at your event to make it all worthwhile. This chapter provides guidance on how you can attract delegates or guests to your event. It also explores how you can have conversations and interaction with people after they've purchased or confirmed a ticket. I show how integrating social media into a plan with more traditional marketing methods ensures you reach your entire target market.

Why Market Your Event?

Depending on the type of event you're planning, you may already have a predetermined guest list comprising, for example, the senior leaders of an organisation or the sales force. Alternatively, you may be opening your event up to the general public or representatives of a particular industry.

Marketing the event – communicating with people about your event – is a vital part of event planning. Whilst this isn't always part of your job, it's an activity you should be aware of. Ask your client whether he or she has considered the marketing plan for the event, and whether anyone has been asked to look after requirements such as digital, PR and social media. If your client hasn't asked someone to do this, it's a great opportunity for you to be involved in the whole event campaign. But beware that you need to manage your time very carefully before you take on too much.

It's much better to do a few things well rather than lots of things less well.

Marketing your event can help communicate the following, so ask your client how he or she would like to communicate this information:

- ✔ The date, timings and location
- ✔ Any associated costs
- ✔ The agenda (what the event consists of)
- ✔ Any actions attendees should complete prior to arrival at the event
- ✔ General event and brand awareness for those who are not attending

A clear plan for how you will communicate with people is beneficial right from the start of your event planning. The plan dictates the success of the event: If no-one knows about it and therefore no-one turns up, it isn't a good event. Even with a small budget for marketing, it's possible to create a big impact.

Any marketing plan tends to have three phases:

- ✔ **Before the event:** To promote the purpose of the event and to attract the audience you want.
- ✔ **During the event:** To extend the reach of your event from those who are there to people beyond.
- ✔ **After the event:** To use the event as the basis for a brand-building campaign, to amplify the impact and achieve greater marketing return on investment, or simply to continue a relationship with attendees and encourage them to attend your next event through a customer relationship marketing (CRM) tool.

I mainly cover pre-event marketing in this chapter, so look at Chapters 14 and 15 for information on opportunities during and after the event.

Developing Your Communication Plan

A marketing strategy can be simple or complex. It's also often referred to as a marketing plan or communications plan, although theoretically the strategy is part of the marketing plan. The structure and format of the plan relates to the type of event, the time available until your event, and the available budget.

A communications plan needs to contain the following:

✔ Executive summary (you may be proud of your communications plan, but some people in your client's business won't have time to read it all).

✔ Information on your target market (summary information on who you are trying to target and what they currently believe – see Chapter 2 for more information on identifying your target market).

✔ Description of the event. (Is your event a conference or an exhibition? Is it for 50 people or 500 people? Is it a 1-day event or 1-week event? Give some basic information about what your event consists of.)

✔ Event objectives. (Include a list of your objectives to show what you are trying to achieve with your event. See Chapter 1 for more information on working with your client to set your objectives.)

✔ Marketing strategy. (This is what we discuss in this chapter. How are you going to reach out to your potential visitors or guests to make sure they know about your event?)

✔ Key performance indicators against which you will assess the success of the marketing.

Or, in basic terms, your plan should cover:

✔ Who?

✔ What?

✔ Why?

✔ Where?

✔ When?

✔ How?

Who? Identifying your audience

In reality, market research is always a nice-to-have in event planning but is often the first thing that you and your client remove due to budget and timing constraints. You can contract companies to run detailed groups and report back on their findings. I find that even a quick brainstorm in the office or in a pub with some friends is of use.

Market research is a way of finding out what your target market thinks and testing the impact of some of your marketing messages.

Key questions to ask yourself and your client are:

✔ Who do you want to come to your event?

✔ Are they the people most likely to want to come?

✔ What are their needs?

✔ Why won't they come?

✔ Are there any competing events at the same time?

What and why? Developing your marketing messages

Think of marketing messages as the elements that make up the story of your event – how you describe your event so that people understand what it's all about and why they should want to attend. Marketing messages are short and snappy and offer people an incentive to find out more.

Think about what's important to your target market and what makes them take notice. Are they price sensitive or are they more interested in networking? Are they looking for an easy life or do they have time to spend on making decisions?

So to start with, describe your event. Use the following broad headings:

✔ What's the event all about?

✔ The programme:

- Performers, speakers

- Topics, the show

- Entertainment

✔ Added-value items:

- Any cool technology

- Special effects

✔ The practicalities:

- Venue and location

- Date and times

- Food and drink

- Getting there

✔ Pricing:

- Ticket costs

- Any deals

✔ Box office:

- How to register or where to buy tickets

- How people will be identified on site (lanyards or wristbands, for example)

Then, even more importantly, answer the question: 'Why should I come to your event?' One possibility is that the event is the cheapest or offers the best deals, but if it's not, you need to identify the strongest area or motivation for your audience. For example:

✔ An original or unique experience

✔ The best line-up – speakers, performers

✔ The best place to meet new people

✔ A special atmosphere

✔ The best location or venue

These combined messages then form the basis of any communications you create.

In Chapter 6, I talk more around creating a brief for the event and understanding the creative requirements, decisions about which then feed into your marketing strategy. However, whilst you will have a base of marketing messages, you may choose to vary which message you focus on depending on your marketing tool.

As with the event's creative communication and any brand or company communication, consistency is needed to make the approach professional and uniform.

Where? Deciding a media strategy

Once upon a time, media was the same as advertising. But with the advent of the Internet, and now social media, a slightly more complex picture has emerged. In order to develop a strategy that works best for your event, it helps to understand the concepts of owned, earned and paid media.

✔ **Owned media:** These are the channels that you create and control yourself. This means your website, any social media channels such as your Facebook page and Twitter feed, and direct marketing media such as emails. Creating engaging content is the key, so is closely linked to content strategy and content marketing.

✔ **Earned media:** This is a slightly less clear-cut area, because it's all about getting other people to tell your story. Earned media covers word of mouth, and is a good definition of PR. It's also the objective of a social media strategy, where you're looking for people to share your content, link to your website or reply to your online posts.

✔ **Paid media:** This is what most people think of as marketing, and is your traditional advertising: Everything from TV, radio and newspapers to outdoor posters, web banners and Google pay-per-click ads. And as the name suggests, it costs you money.

Given that paid advertising can become very expensive very quickly, it's best to build your plan around owned media and developing content that drives earned media. For some events, this may be enough, especially if you have good PR. Once this is in place, you can overlay your plan with paid media, which enables you to achieve maximum value from your budgets. I follow this approach here.

Owned media, part one: Creating an identity for your event

The three stages in using owned media to market your event involve creating a brand identity, designing a website and optimising the language used on that website to make maximum use of search engines.

Creating a brand identity

Key considerations in developing a brand identity are:

✔ **Name:** This is important – it needs to be relevant, appropriate and memorable. If you have a lot of information to convey in the name, and you have an audience that are within the industry, potentially use acronyms to shorten the name of the event.

✔ **Look and feel:** The kind of environment that you want to create will have an impact on how people experience the event. If you make your branding very formal but are trying to tell your audience how relaxed and fun your client's company/brand is, it will confuse people.

✔ **Core positioning – potentially a strapline:** If you are struggling to convey all the information about your event in a name, maybe add a strapline to provide further information that can be used across some of your branding.

(I discuss brand identity further in Chapter 6.)

Designing a website

For this one activity you need content for everything that's relevant to your audience. Start by developing your content architecture based on the messaging structure described earlier in this chapter.

If budget allows, consolidate all your information on an event website or even just a page on your client's company website. The many options for creating a website include hiring a specialist company or having a go yourself using a program like WordPress.

Again, remember to consider the role of your website: Is it a hub for social interaction or just a source of information?

If you are setting up a website, purchase a URL (web address) that's easy to remember.

Purchasing a URL is easy; there are hundreds of websites online that you can find through your search engine by typing 'purchasing a url' such as www.123-reg.co.uk or uk.godaddy.com. Type in your ideal url and it will tell you if it is available and how much it will cost.

If you want or need to set up a website yourself, a number of online suppliers exist who can help you. I've categorised them here by level of complexity.

- ✔ **Easiest:** Use Eventbrite (www.eventbrite.co.uk). You can set up an event website in a few hours, with no technical skills required. The tool also has ticketing and plenty of useful marketing tools built in.

- ✔ **Simple:** Use WordPress (http://wordpress.com) and search for event themes. These are off-the-shelf template websites designed for specific uses. Many are free, although the best ones usually cost between £50 and £100. You may need to do a bit of searching, but often you can find a theme that's right for you. Your final website may then be equivalent to a bespoke designed site costing several thousand pounds. Some technical ability is useful here, but most people can set up their own site with limited or no help. If you need help, many agencies specialise in WordPress sites and can often set one up for less than £1,000.

- ✔ **More advanced:** Have a fully bespoke site designed by a specialist company with a more complex content management system than that provided by WordPress. This enables you to have much greater control over the templates and design of the site, but you and your client pay more for the privilege.

Using search engine optimisation (SEO)

If you are not inviting guests to your event and people are able to choose to attend, you need to make sure that they can find your website if they are searching for events in that industry or genre. Search engine optimization (SEO) is the process of making sure that your event website comes as high up the Google list as possible, ideally on page 1.

Good SEO is mostly about good content. Have copy and imagery on your site that people will be interested in, as this will help with ensuring people spend time visiting your site and keep coming back; the more visits you get, the higher up the rankings you go. Use the types of words that your audience will be using, and don't make it too technical, particularly if they may only have basic knowledge on a subject.

Get a good URL and give your site good titles. If your URL includes words that people would often search for, the more likely it is to come higher up the search pages. If you can and it doesn't make it too long, use the word event or festival or expo in the URL. Search engines will pick up on the words in your website so think carefully about the titles that you give your pages.

Build plenty of links. The more links between your site and others, the higher the SEO ranking. Put links to your partners on the site, such as the venue or caterer, but make sure that they link back to your site too. Having links to your social media identities will help as well.

Owned media, part two: Using social channels

With the growth of the Internet, everyone's lives are completely different now to how they were 20 years ago. Over a third of the world's population are Internet users. You can be sure that a large proportion of the audience for your event are online. In fact, there are more devices on the Internet than people on Earth.

Social marketing has such a huge role in people's lives that it's often forgotten that there was a world online before social media. I cover social media marketing options too, but also consider in your marketing plan the more traditional digital routes such as websites and email marketing.

The power of social media continues to increase, and social media is becoming more integral in everyone's life. Most adults who go online use social media regularly, so it's a great tool and can be an inexpensive way to create a huge buzz and generate interest in your event. Make social media a part of every communications plan.

Few groups of people don't interact with social media in one way or another, so you're likely to find a social media tool that's important to your target market. The trick is identifying which tool works best for you and your event.

Social marketing works best when used in conjunction with other marketing tools.

Many specialist companies offer help with social-media marketing (as with most areas of marketing). If your client can't afford to employ a company directly, you can consider taking some basic steps yourself to help.

Which of the following you decide to set up depends on the type of event:

- ✔ **Facebook:** Best for consumer audiences, but not usually suitable for business audiences.
- ✔ **LinkedIn:** Best for business events.
- ✔ **YouTube and Twitter:** Work with both consumer and business audiences.

Pre-event marketing through Facebook

According to Wikipedia, Facebook is a social networking website with over 1 billion active users, more than half of them using Facebook on a mobile device.

Users register before using the site, after which they can create a personal profile, add other users as friends, and exchange messages, including automatic notifications when they update their profile.

As simple as it sounds, Facebook has such appeal that 10 per cent of all web traffic in 2011 went to this one site, which means it's an ideal tool to include in your marketing strategy.

The number of 'likes', for example, is often used to measure the success of a campaign, so can be added to the return-on-investment analysis after your event. Pre-marketing activity you can carry out through Facebook includes:

- ✔ **Status updates and posts:** Status updates are a method similar to tweeting that can give those connected with you instant information about your event. Maybe it's the last day of an early-bird offer or a new speaker has just agreed to present.

  The more regularly you post information, the more interaction you encourage. This is a great way for people to ask a question and for you to answer everyone at the same time.

- ✔ **Facebook events:** Facebook events are a good tool, are easy to set up, plus create an instant space for people to interact before and after your event. Facebook also reminds people that your event is approaching, and so helps with the marketing.

  Remember those stories about teenagers putting a message on Facebook about having a party while their parents are away and thousands of people turning up and ransacking the house Think about who can see the details of your event, and make sure it's only those people who you want to attend.

- ✔ **Pictures and videos on Facebook:** Images on Facebook are more likely to be of use after an event, but you can also use them sparingly in pre-event promotion. After the event, you can encourage guests to tag themselves and publish photos on their walls; however, before the event, you can upload photos of confirmed guests or speakers and of the venue.

Pre-event marketing through LinkedIn

Linkedin (uk.linkedin.com) is a great tool when you're reaching out to a specific business audience. Marketing through LinkedIn can work well when you want to extend invitations to the right guests after, effectively, vetting them on the site. You can share links to your event in your LinkedIn profile and even post links in relevant groups.

Try to encourage some of your early adopters to post on their LinkedIn profiles, too, to create awareness among their connections.

Pre-event marketing through Twitter

Twitter is an online social networking service, connecting users to the ideas, opinions and news of other people and organisations with an online presence. On Twitter you communicate using *tweets*, text-based messages with a maximum length of 140 characters. You can also embed photographs and videos in a tweet. Users can register to follow particular individuals and organisations, thus being able to see any of their tweets.

More than half of active Twitter users follow companies and brands. Twitter therefore offers a great opportunity for you to promote your event to people who are interested in hearing and sharing news.

Because any tweet is a maximum of 140 characters long, you need to word your tweets succinctly to create snappy bits of information for followers to pick up.

In the world of Twitter-speak, RT means 're-tweet': In other words, pass the message on. If you use the phrase 'Please RT', it normally encourages some of your followers to re-tweet your messages, thus sharing them with their followers too. There's no harm in asking.

#eventprofs is a well-known and well-used hashtag for the event industry. By including this in your tweets, you can reach out to the wider event industry. See Chapter 7 for more on hashtags.

Pre-event marketing you can carry out using Twitter includes:

- ✔ **Hashtagging your way to hype:** Set up a hashtag such as #InnovateUK. There's no complicated method for setting up a hashtag; simply use it and ask other people to use it too. During the event, those who want to tweet about what they've seen or experienced can then use this hashtag too. People can search for a hashtag to see all tweets; this is an easy way for you to measure successful uptake after the event too.

- ✔ **Creating an event Twitter account:** If your client wants the event to have a clear brand identity, consider setting up an event Twitter account. Bear in mind that this can be time consuming, because it's not just about tweeting information: You need to respond to people's questions too. A name could be, for example: @ThinkBigO2event.

Hashtags can't have spaces in them.

Tweeting during your event and encouraging others to tweet too encourages interaction with those in the room, but also beyond. Think of it as blogging on a small scale.

For example, I was recently in a conference where everyone was getting cold in the middle of the keynote speech, but no one felt comfortable about asking a member of staff to do something about it. Someone tweeted the event organisers and asked them to turn the air con off. The temperature increased, and no one interrupted the keynote speech.

Earned media: Getting people talking

PR and social media can help convince others of the worth of your event. You need to ensure that you have:

- ✔ Content that people want to share
- ✔ Conversations that people want to join in with

Be proactive and find conversations and people that are relevant.

If you're planning an event for an audience inside an organisation, such as a sales conference, you don't need to worry about PR.

But, for any event that members of the public, other business or the media can attend, you need to consider PR; it's a great tool for spreading news to the big wide world and helping to increase your audience size and interest in the event. You can achieve your PR through the media but also through influencers such as bloggers.

Unless you're a celebrity with lots of money, you can't control what the press says about your event. You can, however, influence the press by building positive relationships with journalists, spending time talking to them and proactively providing them with information.

Some other ideas for earning media attention effectively include:

- ✔ **Setting up Google Alerts:** This enables Google to feed you daily information on topics that may influence your event. Visit `www.google.co.uk/alerts` and add in the words that are of particular interest to you.

- ✔ **Finding out the deadlines for relevant publications:** Either for advertising opportunities or for publishing interesting content and facts from your event planning that may be of interest to their readers.

- ✔ **Trying to establish a hook for your event:** To make it interesting to the media. For example, is it the first event at the venue in a long time?

Keep a file of press clippings or PDFs, if possible, for your client after the event to help with evaluation post-event.

Planning the perfect press launch

Discuss with your client the value of hosting a press launch. Such an activity is normally one of the most cost-effective ways of generating positive media coverage. If you can, hold the launch the night or morning before your event. Any immediate coverage to encourage interest and last-minute ticket sales is invaluable.

Coverage is what you're trying to achieve with all of your marketing efforts. Coverage is any time your event, company or brand is mentioned in marketing, whether that be, for example, in a magazine or newspaper, or on the radio.

Make sure you prepare a press pack ready for the launch. A press pack contains the following types of information:

- ✔ A fact sheet with a list of 'points of interest' or 'notes to the editor'
- ✔ A list of all the artists, entertainers and speakers involved in an event, with biographies
- ✔ Short profiles of your client's business and any partners involved
- ✔ Photos of any key personnel or speakers/entertainers – if you are using an interesting or historic venue, include a photo of that and if your event is a repeat of a previous event, use photos from previous years.
- ✔ A brief history of the project

Follow up with all attendees in case they need further information and also to ask whether, and if so, when, any coverage will be published.

You can evaluate the equivalent advertising value (EAV) of any features published off the back of the press launch. The EAV measures press activities against the cost to buy the equivalent space in advertising. (See Chapter 14 for more information on measurement.)

Press releases

A press release sounds like a very daunting and formal thing to write, but it isn't. You can definitely draft an initial version. Then liaise with your client's PR team, if it has one, about any comments or additions.

A press release is one of the most basic and cheapest tools to communicate information about your event to the media and hopefully the public too.

Press releases should be no longer than about a page. The first 30 per cent of the information is the most important: It's vital that you catch people's attention at this point to encourage them to read further. Journalists receive many similar releases, so think about what you're trying to achieve.

O$_2$ Priority Moments press launch

For the launch of its new Priority Moments application, O$_2$ wanted a press launch event as exciting and innovative as the product. The end result was a piece of promenade theatre consisting of a series of immersive, exciting brand 'zone' experiences that thrilled and surprised members of the press. The evening saw a space transformed into an exclusive VIP party with entertainment from Latitude Festival headliners, The National, and celebrity guest DJ Nicola Roberts.

O$_2$'s Priority Moments application is an innovative service informing O$_2$ customers about a range of personalised retail deals and experiences in their local area, direct to their handset. The press launch aimed to create a buzz around this service, and emphasised that every customer counts – each and every attendee getting their own personalised Priority Moment experience courtesy of O$_2$.

O$_2$ transformed the newly opened OXO2 venue into four brand experiential zones, one for each of the Gold Tier brand partners. Led by O$_2$'s Guru Jack, unwitting journalists first entered the Harvey Nichols zone, brought to life with a glamorous catwalk show previewing the autumn/winter collection and accompanied by a cocktail designed specifically for O$_2$ customers.

With a complete change of tempo, the next surprise was an intimate book reading by international bestselling author Ken Follett in the informal WH Smith zone – a comfortable, contemporary lounge area.

Journalists were then ushered into a bustling Zizzi restaurant, to sit down to signature Zizzi prosecco and a mouthwatering board of antipasti served by an elite team of knowledgeable waiters.

For the final wow factor, journalists were treated to popcorn and sweets in a pop-up Odeon cinema, where they settled back in authentic Odeon chairs to watch a series of high-impact new trailers.

Finally, the space transformed into a sleek party environment for the evening, with Latitude Festival headliners The National playing a media-grabbing acoustic set, followed by celebrity guest DJ Nicola Roberts.

An exclusive guest list ensured ample online, PR and newspaper coverage the following day. This coverage will drive online word of mouth, interest from other potential brand partners, and mainstream consumer awareness.

Here's a checklist to use when writing the perfect press release. Always ask someone who doesn't know anything about the event to read the press release to check it makes sense:

- ❑ Have a catchy title of no more than eight words.
- ❑ Include a date, so the information makes sense when read with future press releases.
- ❑ Answer who, what, when, where and why in the opening paragraph.

❑ Keep to around 250 words.

❑ Avoid jargon and acronyms that other people won't understand.

❑ Put the most topical information at the top, because the press release is likely to be shortened by journalists.

❑ Try to include a quote from an interesting and relevant person about why the event is happening or is important to the industry.

❑ Provide contact details for those who want further information.

❑ Always write ENDS at the end.

❑ If you're sending your press release by email, copy and paste the attachment into the main body of the email in case journalists read it on a smartphone that can't download attachments.

Figure 8-1 shows an example of a well-written press release.

Making use of bloggers

You have two options here: Creating a blog yourself or identifying a relevant and recognised blogger on your subject matter.

You can also have someone blogging live from your event. For this, identify and contact an appropriate blogger by researching on the Internet who is talking about subjects that are important to your event and your client. Your client may be able to help with this and it should also be identified through your initial market research.

PR disaster management

It's not just social media that can help you in disaster recovery; traditional PR has a big job to do too. The reaction to a situation and the way the information is communicated can turn a disaster into something that's forgotten a week later.

Having contingency press statements ready for potential scenarios is of use. Sometimes, though, the things that go wrong are the ones you never imagined happening. In such a situation, good old quick thinking can save the day.

Bad press comes in two main types: Truths and untruths. If you have to either manage a story that paints your event in a bad light, or help a PR agency to manage it, you can take a couple of different approaches:

✔ **When the story's not true:** If the source is referencing incorrect information, then you need to correct the source and public/guests. The key is to reach out quickly and professionally for that correction to happen. There's an old saying 'Bad stories happen on A1. Corrections run on A5.' A1 paper is 16 times the size of A5 paper, the point being that the damage is already done if someone sees something incorrect in the first place.

✔ **When the story's true:** If the story is true, you need to focus on damage control rather than a cover-up. In the world we live in, people have so much information at their fingertips that it's difficult to hide anything. Be honest and have a clear plan to solve the situation. If a serious incident occurred at your event, people would want to hear how you'll ensure the same thing doesn't happen again.

As @ 22nd November 2011

Department for Business, Innovation and Skills hires Sledge and Kindred to help boost British manufacturing

The Department for Business, Innovation and Skills has called in a team of experts, including brand experience agency Sledge and communications consultancy Kindred, to support a new initiative for British manufacturing.

The 'Make it in Great Britain' campaign, which has been developed by the agencies, aims to transform the image of modern manufacturing amongst the general public, investors and in particular young people, many of whom are missing out on career opportunities in the industry.

Kindred will deliver a national PR programme which will focus on stakeholder relations, consumer and B2B communications, with Sledge creating a six-week exhibition of the best of modern British manufacturing, which will take place at the Science Museum during Games time next summer.

[Department spokesperson] commented: "We were very impressed with the overall vision that Sledge and Kindred created for this campaign. The Make it in Great Britain campaign encompasses multiple opportunities to engage people working within the manufacturing industry, as well as the general public and young people, who are a key focus for us. Initiatives like this only work with the full backing of the sector, and the agencies have made this a key consideration from day one."

The campaign will be led by Client Services Director Laura Capell from Sledge and Kindred Director Anastasia Scott.

Laura/Anastasia said: "We're all very excited about this project; it's a real opportunity to work collaboratively with agencies who can bring different expertise to the table and deliver something with tangible results that we feel will ultimately benefit our economy. We're working with some great companies and finding out first hand just how cutting-edge manufacturing in this country can be, and we're looking forward to demonstrating this to a wider national and international audience."

ends

1. Background to the British Manufacturing sector:
   a. The UK is one of the world's largest manufacturers. The sector contributes £140bn pa to the UK economy (11.1% of GDP in 2009 – similar to France and US, but well below Germany at over 20%).
   b. Manufacturing is responsible for 55% of UK exports and over 2.5m workforce jobs.
   c. Manufacturing accounts for 74% of all business expenditure on UK R&D.
   d. Around a third of the 1,600 new inward foreign direct investment projects in 2009 were in the areas of advanced manufacturing, life sciences, ICT and environmental technology.
2. The Business Secretary and Mark Prisk launched the Make it in Great Britain campaign at a stakeholder event in Central London attended by 150 of Britain's manufacturers and trade associations. Photos are now available on the BIS Flickr site www.flickr.com/photos/bisgovuk

Figure 8-1:
An example press release.

Listing sites

You can submit details of your event to any of a range of online calendars, directories and event listing sites that are usually free. These include time-out.com, visitbritain.com or any local/national newspaper. These sites are simple to use and allow you to increase awareness, and potentially increase ticket sales. Also, the multiple links across sites can improve your digital search engine optimisation (SEO) rating; even if not directly, listing sites can therefore indirectly help drive more traffic to your event website.

Paid media: Driving awareness and sales

You're unlikely to need to pay for advertising. If you do, using a few well-chosen paid media is better than spreading yourself thinly across many. Paid media fall into two main varieties: Online media and traditional media.

Online paid media

The two most effective options here are Facebook advertising and Google pay-per-click both of which are small boxes or blocks of text that are on the right-hand side of your screen when viewing Facebook or Google:

- ✔ **Facebook advertising:** This is excellent for targeting a specific audience in a specific location. Check out `www.facebook.com/business/connect`, which gives a step-by-step guide on how to set up a Facebook ad and focus on your target market amongst the billion people on Facebook.

- ✔ **Google pay per click:** Useful if you are competing with other similar events. `www.google.co.uk/ads/adwords` is easy to use with a simple step-by-step guide.

Traditional paid media

Traditional media is the name that covers all the ways of getting your message to the world that existed before the Internet was invented (there really was such a time). They can still be very effective. The ones you need to be aware of are:

- ✔ **Radio:** Much cheaper than TV advertising, radio advertising can be tailored to local audiences. Radio stations are looking for content, and so by being a bit more creative, such as by devising a competition that the radio station can repeat over a few days with a decent prize (probably more than just tickets to your event), you provide content and a draw for the radio station's listeners.

  You may also be able to persuade the local radio station to attend your event, if appropriate, and broadcast live from it. This approach is used quite often for festivals and sporting events.

✔ **Outdoor:** Outdoor media such as 48-sheet posters, bus advertising and even adverts on the side of buildings, are powerful ways of telling people about an event. They can, however, be expensive, because whilst the design and printing of the poster may not cost that much, huge costs are often involved in hiring the space for it. In general, for most events, outdoor advertising is too expensive an option.

✔ **Mobile marketing:** Various forms of mobile marketing are available to you when planning an event.

- **Mass messaging (often called spam):** I don't recommend this; it's the equivalent of junk email but viewed as more offensive and invasive, because individuals see their mobile phones as personal tools. However easily you can access a list of mobile numbers through your client, this form of marketing is likely to do more harm than good.

- **Phone marketing (telesales):** Not often used for event marketing , but useful if you are targeting a very specific group of delegates for an exclusive networking event or seminar. Remember to do your research before you or someone in your team speak to them. Make sure you have confirmed that the person you are trying to contact is the person most suitable for your event, you don't want to find that out after the event.

- **Voucher sites:** With the rise and rise of voucher sites such as Voucher Cloud, Groupon and O2 Priority Moments, there is the opportunity to offer any last-minute tickets to your event at a discounted rate if it is appropriate for the general public.

✔ **TV advertising:** This form of marketing is likely to be beyond your budget. Few events use television advertising, because it's so expensive. If your client is a brand with a big budget, it may be possible to tag details of the event onto the end of one of the client's adverts. This is unlikely to be something that you're involved in directly, but you may need to liaise with an advertising agency and provide the logo for the event or check details.

✔ **Press advertising:** The press is going through a lot of changes, so beware of offers unless you're certain of reaching your target audience. Specialist magazines are becoming more effective, for example targeting business audiences or families in specific areas.

But press ads are not dead; if you choose the right publication for your target market, press ads can still have a huge impact on awareness and ticket sales, especially if they offer a tailored discount package.

Some publications offer advertising space for free if they still have space unfilled just before going to print.

✔ **Local advertising:** Local advertising can help add to the turnout for your public-facing events. Contact the local council or tourist board, who can put you in contact with the relevant organisations, such as the local papers.

Invite local journalists to attend the event; they may not be communicating with your main target market but may appreciate being asked, which will help acceptance of the event in the local area. Ask if they would consider running an advertorial rather than an advert, which will allow you to include a lot more information than is possible on an advert.

You can also get creative and design posters and pin them up in local businesses. Keep in mind who you're targeting: You may have a varied demographic of potential attendees, and it's important that you target everyone.

✔ **Direct mail and email:** Everyone receives so much digital information every day that sometimes it's worth going back to more traditional marketing methods to get cut-through. Well thought-out and designed direct mail can be an effective (but expensive) marketing approach to support your event.

Only use direct mail if you have an existing database of previous customers, because the effectiveness of using 'cold' lists is low.

Creative media

Depending on how conventional you need to act (which will depend on your client and target market), you could look at some other options that will have mass stand out for relatively low budgets but won't have as much impact as other media.

✔ **Graffiti:** When used correctly and legally, graffiti is a great tool for promotional activity. Writing messages in public places that lead people to your event or encourage a group of people to interact is a cost-effective method of branding.

One of the most popular and acceptable methods is reverse graffiti, which is the process of temporarily cleaning a surface of dirt to show your message.

Think how many times you've been stuck in traffic behind a dirty white van with a message such as 'wash me' on it. Now think how you can use this type of messaging in events, particularly to help create intrigue or promote a brand message.

✔ **Road signs (from the AA):** Road signs are excellent for increasing awareness and can help when you are liaising with local councils on traffic and crowd management. The AA can even attend planning meetings with you and liaise with the local highways authority. You pay for the signs, but the cost is often worthwhile.

When? So many jobs, so little time . . .

Write a timings plan that covers each marketing tool that you intend to use. If you're marketing as well as producing your event, you need to be keenly aware of timings and how the marketing plan timings integrate with your event-planning timings. For example, try not to plan to launch your website at the same time as you need to send your health and safety documentation to the venue; remember that there are only 24 hours in a day.

Plot what else is happening in your target market's world at the same time as your event. If other major events are happening, can you change your messaging to account for this or do you need to change the timing of the marketing?

Ideally give yourself three to four months before the event, for your promotional plan to have an impact. Figure 8-2 gives you the rundown.

The amount of time you give yourself for live marketing activity will be purely dictated by how much budget you have available to support it. It is always best to focus the main push of the marketing activity in the six weeks or so leading up to your event as people are planning their diaries. Unless it is a very large, exclusive or well-established event, if you promote it nine months in advance, potential delegates won't action it or remember it when needed. However there may be certain events leading up to yours that are good opportunities that it's not worth missing. If you know that your target market will be gathering at a similar event three months prior to yours, see if you can do some promotional activity at that point in time too. A targeted approach is more beneficial than trying to do a little bit of everything.

	Jun-12				Jul-12					Aug-12				Sep-12			
	4-Jun	11-Jun	18-Jun	25-Jun	2-Jul	9-Jul	16-Jul	23-Jul	30-Jul	6-Aug	13-Aug	20-Aug	27-Aug	3-Sep	10-Sep	17-Sep	24-Sep
Press launch																	
Press listings *								24-Jul									
Press releases**																	
Marketing within the venue																	
Table talkers																	
Toilet posters																	
Feature in venue map					may be earlier dependent on print run												
External advertising																	
Posters in local tube tunnel																	
Local marketing																	
Digital																	
Social media (twitter, facebook and G+)	(Will increase as we have more to say around launch)																
Inclusion in PPC keywords																	
Venue homepage presence ***																	
E newsletters																	
Blogs (dependent on content)																	

Figure 8-2:
An example timings plan.

This is an example of how you can create a basic plan that quickly highlights any crossovers. Sometimes it's good to just write down what you're thinking and ask others to check it. No one expects you to be a marketing expert, but you need to know in what order tasks should happen in order to maximise the impact of the event.

It's not just about establishing what to do and when; you also need to make sure that everything integrates properly to achieve a cohesive campaign. The nearby sidebar is a great example of an integrated multi-channel strategy.

Falling with style: Taking a sponsored stunt to a new level

Felix Baumgartner's freefall parachute record attempt is a fantastic example of how a brand (Red Bull) maximised the value of the event way beyond the 30 seconds that it took for Baumgartner to fall the 23 miles from space.

Over 8 million people watched the live video stream, according to YouTube; the previous record for a live stream was half a million. People will remember for years where they watched the jump.

Referring to this as a sponsored event doesn't do it justice; this was an example of a well thought-out and considered partnership. In a true value exchange the audience, partner and rights holder became completely interdependent over a sustained period.

Whilst this event had a much larger budget and was on a much larger scale than any event you're likely to come across, you can learn from it.

Had Red Bull not ensured that people knew about the event prior to the jump, who would have cared or known? So many people watched the jump because the marketing started weeks before the day to make sure as many people had heard and talked about it as possible.

The jump was followed with a series of programmes showing the coming together of the experience, which continued the conversations and story even further – pre- and post-event marketing at its best.

This is one of the best examples in history of creating a campaign around an event. Anyone trying to compete with this is going to have to go a long way!

Part III

When, Where and Who: The Devil's in the Detail

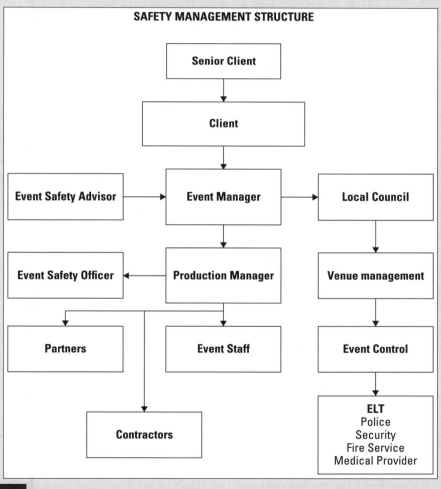

SAFETY MANAGEMENT STRUCTURE

- Senior Client
- Client
- Event Safety Advisor → Event Manager → Local Council
- Event Safety Officer ← Production Manager
- Venue management
- Partners
- Event Staff
- Event Control
- Contractors
- **ELT**
  Police
  Security
  Fire Service
  Medical Provider

In this part . . .

✔ Learn about the crucial role played by accurate scheduling, from deciding when your event should take place through to the minute-by-minute running order.

✔ Grasp the importance of where to hold your event to maximise interest and reach the people you need to.

✔ Establish your criteria for a knockout venue – and get it booked.

✔ Understand and learn to manage the special requirements of outdoor events.

✔ Deal with the detail of who does what on the big day –or days. Learn to handle the nitty gritty of back of house, front of house, and dealing with your team on site.

Chapter 9

Timings, Timings, Timings

Many people believe that to be a good event manager you need to be a good organiser; this reflects the importance of logistics in planning your event. Good organisation skills definitely help you; however, I do know event planners who are not naturally good at organising. Organisational skills can be learnt and practised.

The time of year you schedule your event has a big impact on its success. The amount of time spent picking venues and booking talent or guest presenters is often greater than the time spent thinking about the exact date of the event. Even when the client gives a date in a brief, it's your responsibility to make sure it's the best date possible. This chapter details some of the things that affect what date you choose.

How you get to this date also takes some good organisation and decision-making skills. You can use various documents to help in this process, all of which have various names depending on what industry you work in. In this chapter, I look into what critical time paths can do to keep the milestones on track during the planning process. The production schedule shows you how to turn a blank venue into your event space in the time allowed, and the running order demonstrates how it all comes together on the day.

Deciding the Date of Your Event

A good client brief tells you roughly when to hold the event. The date may relate directly to a product launch or the release of company figures. Always link a business objective to the decision-making process. However, other factors may influence your decision.

Certain events are suited to particular times of year. Corporate events such as conferences and meetings are more likely to happen during the school year. Business people may take their annual leave during school holidays, so fewer are able to attend during those periods. A popular time to hold a conference, for example, is from September to November, while children are at school.

Events for the general public, such as brand experiences or public exhibitions, are best held at weekends and during school holidays. During such times, members of your target market are with their families and not at work.

When deciding the date of your event, the main questions to consider are:

- What type of event is it?
- Who is your audience?

Objectives analysis

You plan your event for a particular set of reasons – to meet a set of objectives – that your client has agreed. The event may, for example, aim to raise brand awareness or update a team about a set of results, or it may be a celebratory event.

Consider the objectives when you and your client agree the duration of the event. If you have enough to talk about (that is, you have enough content) for only one day, why put on an event for three days?

If the event is to launch a new product to the press, ensure that it's scheduled for the product launch day or as close to it as possible. The press that you invite can then amplify your message. There's no point launching a new product in store but then holding the press launch after that date.

If your objective revolves around capturing the spirit of Christmas, it needs to be in the run-up to Christmas to make sure the messaging is well timed. By January, everyone is bored of Christmas messaging and less receptive to a Christmas-themed event.

Competitor activity

Carefully consider whether and, if so, when your competitors are hosting events by looking online for any press releases they may have released. To put your event on during the same weekend as a direct competitor is a high-risk strategy.

Consider two types of event: Those that compete for the time of your customer, but which are not directly related, and those that your competitors are putting on.

External influences

Factors such as the weather and dates of public holidays and international sporting fixtures may affect whether your potential attendees are interested in and available to attend your event. If an election is happening on the day of your event, whilst it may not initially seem like a competing event, it takes attention away from your event.

Research the dates of the following to see whether they clash:

- Public holidays
- Sporting events
- Religious holidays
- School holidays
- Political events

Also consider whether your preferred date is in a peak season, for example requiring Christmas theming the week before Christmas. In this instance could the event be moved to the first week in December when requirements will be less stressful? Peak seasons may affect the costs that you have to pay and the availability of certain items. For example, before the London 2012 Olympics, event organisers were concerned about how much technical kit was available. There was a rumour that the reason why another big event, Glastonbury, was not going to happen in 2012 was a shortage of portaloos caused by the Olympics. In fact, it was to allow the ground to rest. On a slightly smaller, local scale, items may be in short supply, so it's worth considering likely demand for the kit your event may require.

When planning to host an event abroad, consider other influences that may have an impact on your event. Identify any public holidays and local events that are important in that. Try to speak to the local tourist board or destination management company (DMC) to understand the impacts.

Another consideration when you're deciding when to hold your event is the weather. When you've picked a location, research the previous weather patterns for that time of year and time of day. Whilst you can't accurately predict the weather, previous experience is a good starting point. You can then ascertain whether the climatic conditions are an issue and whether you can work around them. For example, whilst not an issue in the UK, in some locations it's too hot at certain times of year to hold an event outside in the middle of the day.

The financial situation

Your client may be completely certain it needs to host an event and that you're the person to organise it. If, however, there are financial pressures on your client, the event may be delayed until more money is available. There's only so much that you can debate with your client, because if there's not the money to pay for the event, then the event can't happen.

Not only should you consider the financial situation of your client, but also that of your audience. If potential attendees will need to make a financial investment themselves, such as purchasing a ticket, consider the time of the month you organise the event. Think when people's paydays may be, how much you ask for deposits and full payments, and when.

What day and what time of day?

When you've established the month, or even the week, in which to host your event, think about the day of the week on which to hold it. Consider what members of your potential audience do each day; for example, do they visit customers on a Tuesday? If so, holding an event on the Tuesday would not be advisable, but also on the Wednesday they may follow up on requests from their visits. As such, your event may be best on the Thursday.

For corporate events, avoid Friday – the day when people plan their weekends and want to get home in good time after their week at work.

For events that engage with the general public, consider when people have free time. Most people's free time is before and after work during the week, and at the weekend. Although more and more people work shifts or work from home, a large proportion of the working population still work a traditional nine-to-five day. As such, events between these hours are likely to miss the target market.

The weekend is a popular time to speak to members of the general public.

Also consider the effect of the time of day you hold your event. For example, consider the catering: Will it be appropriate to provide breakfast or dinner, or even have a drinks bar? Such decisions also affect the cost of your event, so consider them carefully.

Deciding the Duration of Your Event

Before releasing a film, studios release trailers to leave you wanting more so that you go to watch the full film. You need to make sure your event doesn't feel too much like a trailer in that it is long enough for everyone to discover all that they want to, but not so long that people get bored hearing the same message over and over again – like the 2nd and 3rd parts of a trilogy.

Considering your audience

Everyone is different and everyone has different interests, which affects their attention span. You can retain your audience's attention by splitting up the content with little breaks such as energisers.

Contrary to popular belief, there is no average attention span; it can range from 10 to 90 minutes.

Also consider whether the people you expect to attend your event will do so in their free time or when they'd normally be working.

Understanding how type dictates time

The type of the event you're organising often decides the duration of your event. Table 9-1 gives the average duration of various types of event.

Table 9-1	Typical event durations
Type of Event	*Average Duration*
Meetings	1–4 hours
Conference	1–5 days
Networking	1–4 hours
Product launch	1–4 hours
Awards Ceremony	1–5 hours
Sporting event	1 hour to 1 month
Festival	1–3 days

(continued)

Table 9-1 (continued)

Type of Event	Average Duration
Brand Experience	15 mins to 10 days
Pop-up experiences	1–30 days
Exhibition	4 hours to 1 month depending on if it is part of another event, such as a part of the day at a conference, or a stand-alone exhibition.

Table 9-1 gives approximate guidelines for the duration of events. Duration does, however, depend on many factors. In the following sections I give a few examples of types of events and the factors that may have an impact on the duration. Sporting tournaments can go on for weeks and the Olympics, one of the greatest sporting events, lasts for over a month, but guests do not all stay for the whole duration.

Conferences

A conference can last from half a day to five days, generally. The trick is to make sure that your delegates are not clock watching and that the time is broken up into varied bite-sized chunks. Few conferences can be completed in a short period, so consider how to break your event into different sections. You can schedule plenary sessions, breakout sessions, networking and energisers. (See Chapter 3 for types of event.)

Product launches and awards ceremonies

Depending on the product being launched, you either want a quick, high-impact launch during which you reveal the new look of something, or a slightly more engaging event with time for visitors to experience the product or service. You're likely to want the press to attend your product launch, along with some high-level, important guests to help add credibility to the event. Their time is also limited, so the shorter the better is often true for this type of event.

Similarly, for awards ceremonies, if VIPs are presenting your awards, their time is limited and therefore you should keep your ceremony short. Consider adding a networking element to the event if you want to extend the time.

Pop-up experiences

The location of these can be anything from shops and exhibitions to more immersive and interactive experiential spaces. Generally they are live for at least a day and normally at least a week. They can take a large amount of organising as the focus is heavily focused on making a big impact in as short a time frame as possible. They rarely involve celebrities or named talent and have more of an underground phenomenon approach. Pop-up restaurants have become really popular over the last few years where a Michelin star chef may create a restaurant that is more affordable for people to try.

Exhibitions

Exhibitions tend to be longer events than others, because of the high level of content for visitors to engage with. Exhibitors invest time and money to attend this type of event, and achieve a higher value from it if the audience that flows through the event is larger. As such, often exhibitions tend to maximise the investment from all those involved.

The general rule is that the longer your event, the more time you need in which to plan it.

Scheduling Your Event

Event management is all about good scheduling and communication. You schedule the event with your client, with your suppliers, with your audience and sometimes even with the press. Unlike with other forms of marketing, it's difficult to change the date once it's been decided. For example, if you're launching an offer for barbeques on a website, and rain is predicted for the next two weeks, you can relatively easily postpone the launch of the offer online until an appropriate time. It's not easy to do the same with a launch event for barbeques; you have to pick a date and commit to it. I give some options for weather management in Chapter 13.

You can use various tools and templates to help with the scheduling process. Critical time paths help with long-term planning, production schedules help with supplier management during the build and de-rig (when you take everything down and pack away; also called a *load out*), and your technical running order helps make it all go smoothly on the day.

Always work backwards when planning timelines and schedules. The event date is normally the one that you can't change.

Creating critical time paths

Everything coming together on time is an event manager's dream and primary goal. Unfortunately, success doesn't just come down to luck; the amount of preparation you've done and the focus you've put on timings and communication of these within your team influence the outcome. A great tool, which other industries use too, is a *critical time path*. It shows the dates (milestones) in the planning which you can't miss or move; if these dates change, it has a huge impact on the delivery date and, as is known in events, the delivery date can never be changed.

Everything always takes longer than you think it will.

It's good practice to write a critical time path right at the beginning of the project. You can establish whether you have enough time by doing this, or whether you should try to review the time available.

The format you use for your critical time path is entirely up to you. The most basic approach is to use a spreadsheet or word-processed document, but electronic project management programs exist; look online for specific packages. Figures 9-1 and 9-2 present two approaches for creating the same document; decide which works best for you.

Event Title

Week	Action	Who	Complete
	w.c 13.08.2012		
15	Initial Themes Presented	Event Manager	Y
	w.c 20.08.2012		
14	Feedback	Client	Y
	w.c 27.08.2012		
13	Site visit to the venue	Event Manager	Y
	Critical timeline document presented	Event Manager	Y
	Initial draft of Creative identity to be provided by Event Manager	Client	Y
	Discussions regarding Event Manager involvements in identity, video stings & additional video requirements	All	Y
	Pre-Comms discussions commence - information regarding dates for live experience	Event Manager	Y
	Host availability & cost info requested	Event Manager	Not available
	Opening number discussions commence	Event Manager	Y
	Additional experiences researched and costed	Event Manager	Y
	w.c 03.09.2012		
12	Pre-Comms discussions commence	Event Manager	Y
	Event Manager to commence Event identity creation	Event Manager	Y
	Event Manager to present initial identity concepts	Event Manager	Y
	Roles & Responsibilities finalised	Event Manager	Y

Figure 9-1: Critical time path template 1.

Build in contingency time on everything. If the printers have told you that a piece of artwork must go to print on Tuesday afternoon, tell others that it must go to print on Monday morning. You know the critical time path – the dates that you can't move – but you've given yourself some contingency time for your client to eat into.

Write a version of the critical time path at the start of any project, as a date-focused project plan. Update this document throughout the project-planning process, as things change, but it's a document that needs to be taken seriously.

JOB DETAILS

COMPANY	
PROJECT	
CLIENT CONTACT	
CLIENT CONTACT DETAILS	
EVENT RIG DATE	
EVENT DATE	
EVENT DE-RIG DATE	
VENUE	

EVENT MANAGER PRODUCTION CREW		
DEPARTMENT	**CONTACT NAME**	**TEL NO**
ACCOUNT DIRECTOR		
ACCOUNT MANAGER		
ACCOUNT EXECUTIVE		
PRODUCTION MANAGER		
PRODUCER		
SHOW CALLER		
PHOTOGRAPHER		

Figure 9-2:
Critical time
path
template 2.

To give you an idea of the types of actions to add into your time path, see the suggestions below. These are for guidance only; each event is different, and your duration for planning will be different, too, but the list is a good starting point.

Six months before the event:

- ✔ Agree your objectives with your client – see Chapter 1 for information on making sure your objectives are SMART.
- ✔ Pick a date.
- ✔ Agree your budget and write a basic budget breakdown to ensure that it's realistic – see Chapter 5 for all you need to know on writing and managing budgets.
- ✔ Shortlist venue options by having a look at Chapter 10.

- ✔ Visit potential venue options and see Chapter 10 for information on what to look at and ask on a site visit.

- ✔ Choose your venue and pencil in a date.

- ✔ Write a basic timeline.

- ✔ Establish your creative theming or approach – have a look at Chapters 6 and 7 for ideas on how to make sure you get the right messages across and make it memorable at the same time.

- ✔ Create a team around you that can help plan your event – see Chapters 4 and 11 for ideas on who you may need to help make your event a success.

- ✔ Design the creative identity of your event by looking at Chapter 6 for advice on how to use an event brand in conjunction with your client's own brand.

- ✔ Draft a marketing plan – refer to Chapter 8 where each step of a possible marketing plan is detailed.

Four months before the event:

- ✔ Write a basic timeline.

- ✔ Start a marketing and PR plan.

- ✔ Research suitable suppliers.

- ✔ Refine the budget breakdown that you wrote at the start of the event planning.

- ✔ Request contracts for your venue and any major kit purchases and kit hire – see Chapter 10 on the importance of contracting your venue.

- ✔ Design any brand collateral.

- ✔ Design the floor plan (layout).

- ✔ Source all hotel accommodation required for crew.

- ✔ If required, send a 'save the date' to guests for the event.

- ✔ Write the first draft of the running order.

- ✔ Apply for any required permits.

Two months before the event:

- ✔ Confirm all suppliers.

- ✔ Write the health and safety documentation – use Chapter 12 for some guidance on the common misconceptions.

- ✔ Refine the budget, always checking that you don't overspend.

✔ Write staffing briefs and details of roles and responsibilities on site – Chapter 11 gives you support on this.

✔ Collate a signage list for things such as toilets, cloakrooms and so on.

✔ Send out invites if required.

✔ Brief the security firm.

✔ Book tastings for any catering requirements – see Chapter 7 for some ideas of how to maximise the impact of your catering.

One month before the event:

✔ Write the first draft of your production schedule.

Two weeks before the event:

✔ Distribute the final production schedule to all suppliers.

✔ Brief the photographer – see Chapter 7 for help on this.

✔ Collate the final guest list, if required.

One week before the event:

✔ Cross-check that all deliveries have arrived, including any collateral or goody bags.

✔ Refine the budget.

✔ Ensure you have petty cash available for on-the-day last-minute purchases.

✔ Phone all suppliers to confirm arrangements.

A critical time path is important for any type of event that you organise, however big or small. If used properly, it can be a useful document to refer to and keep everyone in your team on track. Areas to include in this type of document are the task, the date by which it must be actioned, and the name of the person who will take the action.

I recommend that you have regular status meetings with your client, during which you run through your status report and the critical time path document. Use the documents together to ensure that the two sets of information don't contradict each other. (See Chapter 4 for information on status reports.)

Preparing production schedules

One of the most important documents that you compile when planning your event is the production schedule. If you're working on a large event with a production manager, he or she can support you on this. Your critical time path and status report are invaluable tools for working with your client, but the production schedule is your bible and that of your suppliers.

The production schedule outlines every time and task required during the period from the build through to the de-rig of your event. As such, the detail of this document varies from event to event, but covers some key areas. Figure 9-3 shows you a standard example.

Name of event

Deliveries Master Document

Contact name:
Address:
Phone number:

Date	Item	Delivery Time	Lead Contact	Received

Figure 9-3: Example production schedule.

The production schedule is a document for you and your team to use, so tailor it to work for you. Generally, however, aim to include the following information:

- ✔ Dates of the build, event and de-rig
- ✔ Address details, and how to get there
- ✔ Contact details of all team members, clients, stakeholders, venue staff and suppliers
- ✔ Briefing times and locations
- ✔ Deliveries and pick-ups
- ✔ Crew catering

✔ Floor plans

✔ Rehearsals

✔ Show times

The schedule should be detailed and clear enough that if you're suddenly unavailable, another event manager can use it to step into your shoes.

As with all documents that you may need to refer to during the actual event, printed copies are better than relying on an electronic copy. It may seem old-fashioned in the world of digital technology and smart phones, but knowing that the piece of paper will remain with you, regardless of how many hours (and therefore battery hours) you've used it for, is a big reassurance.

It's also useful to have some paper on which you can write notes and numbers as you are running around.

The last day in the office

Whilst the last day in the office before the event doesn't necessarily need to be included in your schedule, it may be important if deliveries are being picked up. The last day in the office should be a calm day; it should be the day when you do your filing, catch up on emails about other projects, and double-check everything before the hectic pace of the next few days.

When you've planned your event as thoroughly as you can, the hours before the build starts should be calm. Everything's been organised and communicated; at your start time, everything will happen to plan. You may be nervous, but this just means you have lots of adrenalin going around your body, and you can just be excited about seeing the event come to life.

✔ Re-read your production schedule; make sure you remember exactly what happens when.

✔ Phone all your suppliers to ensure they understand what's expected of them during the build and show day.

✔ Print spare copies of all of your documents for your team, and in case you lose your copy.

✔ Phone your client to check he or she is happy and confident about all the plans for the event.

✔ Choose what to wear during the build and the event day. Outfit choices are not going to be a high priority, so it's best to decide this kind of thing before the event.

I recommend always wearing a black outfit with comfy shoes. You are on your feet for a large portion of the build and on show day, so you want to be comfortable. Match how smart your outfit is to the occasion.

Oh, and get a good night's sleep. Depending on the duration of your event, you may not get much sleep.

The event build

Also known as *rigging the event* or *load in*, this is the process of bringing all your suppliers into your venue to create your event. The build can take anything from an hour to weeks, and it gives the first indication of whether your planning has been successful. The second indication is a successful show day. Most of your production schedule is made up of the details of this period.

To plan your build, you need to speak to your venue staff and your suppliers.

The first questions for the venue are:

- ✔ At what time are you allowed into the venue?
- ✔ When does your event need to start?

The difference between these two times is how much time you have for your build. For example, if your event starts at 6 p.m. and you can get the keys for the venue from 9 a.m., you have nine hours in which to build your event and complete the technical checks and rehearsals. For larger events, you may have many more hours, days or even weeks.

If you book the venue yourself, you need to state how many days you want to hire it for. Venues are familiar with the phrases 'build days', 'live days' and 'days for de-rig'. The venue will want to know how the time is allocated between these stages, rather than just that you need the venue for a particular number of days. It can be difficult to estimate how much time you need. Event management relies heavily on communication with others and on their skills and knowledge.

Speak to suppliers and ask the venue staff how it normally works in their venue.

It's best to work back from the start time of your event, because this point can't change, whereas you may be able to convince the venue to let you in slightly earlier, or you can bring more team members to help you finish in time.

Scheduling time for sign-off by your client and venue and for rehearsals is important but often forgotten. If you work out your schedule backwards, these are the first two things that you need to make time for. Then consider the physical process of bringing in any lights, staging, decorations, and so on, that you require.

The sign-off

The final moments before your event goes live are when you should walk around the event patting yourself on the back for how fantastic you are at planning events. Walk around with your schedule and your designs, and make sure everything is as it should be.

Also build some time into your schedule to take your client and the venue manager around the site to check that they're happy with everything. Walk around the event as if you were a visitor, checking that every single detail is as expected.

This should be done with your client and normally takes half an hour to an hour, depending on the complexity of your event.

For some larger events, you also need a health and safety sign-off, too. Your venue manager or health and safety office can advise whether this is necessary. If time permits, do a sign-off walk round with each of your main suppliers.

The rehearsals

Practice makes perfect. You can rehearse some parts of events, such as a plenary session at a conference or an awards ceremony. Build rehearsal time into your production schedule, because it's part of the planning process.

Make time for rehearsals whenever possible.

In an ideal situation, the build of your event finishes with a few hours to spare before the show starts (or before you go to bed the night before).

Your speakers can then practise on the actual stage set that they'll be using. Whilst everyone participating on stage should be encouraged to practise in their own time, it's invaluable for them to experience the environment in which they'll be performing or presenting. Whilst you (or your producer) will have briefed all the team, it may be the first time you see the presenters' slides with the words they plan on speaking. Watching the rehearsal is your way of not assuming anything.

Some people are naturally gifted on stage, and others need a little more encouragement. Be there to offer practical support, such as about standing positions, smiling more, and so on, but also try to build the presenters' confidence so they don't panic just before the show day. If you have a producer helping, he or she may be able to help support the speakers and give them full feedback on techniques to improve their delivery.

As a guide, allow for 30 minutes of rehearsal time for every hour of show time for presentations or performances. If it's a one-hour event, why not schedule in two hours if you can and run the whole event a couple of times?

If your event is in a public place or is secret, you need to think carefully about when your rehearsals can happen. Consider hiring a warehouse space close to the venue, where rehearsals can take place with fewer time restrictions. It's always better to rehearse in the actual environment of the show, but practice still gets you as close to perfect as a live show day can be.

The environment build

The easiest way to approach the environment build is to write a comprehensive list of everything that you'll bring into the venue, everything that needs to be taken out, and anything that needs to be done after elements have been brought in and taken out, such as laying out tablecloths. The build is the part of the event that takes the longest to plan; spend some time scheduling it thoroughly.

Here I take the example build time of nine hours for an awards ceremony:

✔ **Give yourself some breathing space just before the event starts.** Think of it as contingency time in case anything goes wrong. For example, allow half an hour; therefore your venue needs to be ready for 5:30 p.m. This may also be when you do the sign-off with your client.

✔ **Consider how much time you want for rehearsals.** You may have two sets of entertainment for your awards show, so you may need to allow for an hour of sound-checking and rehearsals, which brings you back to 4:30 p.m.

The time between 9 a.m. and 4:30 p.m. is therefore available in which to build the environment of the event – that is, 7.5 hours.

The type of event that you are planning affects how many suppliers there are and the actions needed within this time.

Scheduling vehicle deliveries

Speak to your suppliers in order to understand what and how many trucks or other vehicles they plan to bring to the site. (See Chapter 10 for more information on vehicle movement.) Check that this number of vehicles fits in the venue's loading bay. If only one vehicle can fit in at one time, discuss with your suppliers how long each vehicle needs, and schedule the vehicles consecutively to arrive and use the loading bay. Allow adequate time for each supplier to use the loading bay without crossing over with other suppliers.

If your venue has multiple loading bays, this can make your life easier, by enabling multiple deliveries at the same time. However, you need to allocate team members to monitor these loading bays and sign off (accept) the deliveries. When accepting deliveries, check that what arrives is what you expected; have a clear delivery list and tick this off as deliveries arrive.

When planning your event, discuss with your suppliers where their remit lies. Are they installing your kit or just delivering it? You don't want something to be delivered without knowing who will install it. Communication is important; this is the type of conversation that a production manager can help you with. (See Chapter 4 for more information on production managers.)

Even if you think you're asking basic, silly questions, your supplier has, no doubt, been asked a sillier question by someone else.

The order in which suppliers access the site is also important; for example, aim to bring all of the large elements into the venue first, and then deliveries of smaller things such as flowers later. If you've set all the tables up with decorations and cutlery and then try to bring in the stage set, you'll struggle to get it into the venue without knocking everything over.

Scheduling the practical production elements

Also consider how long the actions required for a certain element will take. For example, initially it may seem to make sense to bring all the large elements in first, but if it will take your team four hours to organise the marketing collateral into individual packs, you may need the individual printed components delivered earlier in the day.

It's difficult to balance all the different deliveries. Communication with your suppliers is important; they can advise on timings.

A typical build schedule is something like this:

- Power distribution
- False floor if required
- Set/staging
- Lighting
- Sound
- Prop layout
- Branding

Printed branding, which includes items such as posters, signs or any bespoke props, is always one of the last things you install, and this branding adds the finishing touch to your event space. It's also one of the things that can get damaged in the rush. Even though you may be rushing around, take your time (or instruct your team to take their time) to ensure nothing gets broken.

Research which printing company is closest to the venue in case of any last-minute emergencies. You should also ensure that you have some volunteers to call upon or other team members who can help with all the small elements.

During this time you need to keep calm and practise your good communication skills.

Planning your exit strategy

When your event is live and going to plan, your client is likely to be busy with guests. You may have some spare time. Use this time to check your plans for the load out/de-rig. You're likely to have arranged for some suppliers to arrive before the event ends and wait outside so they can start the de-rig as quickly as possible.

You may be surprised how much quicker the de-rig is than the rigging of the event. An eight-hour build can take just 90 minutes to dismantle and remove from the venue. All your suppliers know that the quicker they finish, the quicker they go home.

Communication during this process is important. Everyone's keen to get their kit out of the venue and head home, but you need to ensure that everything is done in the order you planned. Just one truck not turning up on time can have an impact on the rest of the de-rig process. While your event is live (and if you find the time, the day before too), phone all your suppliers to double-check that they know and are happy with your production schedule.

Book a meeting with your venue manager to hand the venue back over. Walk around the site with the venue manager to make sure that everything is how it was before your event. You don't want, when you return to the office, to receive an unexpected bill because you left rubbish on site.

The day after show day

You've done it – congratulations! Depending on the details of your de-rig, you can, hopefully, relax for a moment and enjoy the successful outcome due to your event management skills. It's not the end of your event management duties though: 95 per cent of event management is in the planning, 4 per cent is the live event and 1 per cent is the post-event tasks.

After the event:

- Phone your client to check that he or she is happy with how the event went.
- Write thank-you emails to all your crew and team members.
- Reconcile your petty cash and any final costs that came in during the event.
- Send your client a final version of the budget, to inform of any reasons for increases in costs.
- Send in your final invoice.
- Plan a de-brief meeting with your internal team and your client (ideally separate meetings) – these help with planning for any further events for your client.
- File the final show files of presentations and such like on your server for easy reference in the future.
- Consider your post-event marketing plan (see Chapter 15 for further information).
- Evaluate your event (see Chapter 14 for more about measurement).
- Pat yourself on the back!

Technical Running Orders

Scheduling everything while planning your event results in a smooth-running day. The critical time path gets you to the day, the production schedule gets you through the build, and the technical running order keeps your event day on track.

For events where timings on the day are critical, such as conferences, award ceremonies and launch events, the precision of delivery on the day makes or breaks it. A technical running order gives the instructions that your technical production team need during the show. It provides the exact times at which the lighting design needs to change, walk-in music needs to go on, microphones need to be turned off, and so on.

Your critical time path is accurate to the day, the production schedule is accurate to the hour, but your technical running order needs to be accurate to the minute. Figure 9-4 shows a sample technical running order. You will see how detailed it needs to be so that it is clear for all lighting, sound and any other backstage crew. Stage management is often something that gets missed off running orders but is important to the smooth running of the show.

If you're organising an event with a producer and production manager, they write and own the technical running order, because they are the primary users.

Learning the lingo of a technical running order

Here's a handy glossary of terms to help you navigate the complexities of your technical running order:

✔ **Autocue:** A screen that shows a presenter or host the words to speak or details of what is coming up next.

✔ **Disk jockey (DJ):** A person who plays recorded music for an audience.

✔ **Dry ice:** An effect that looks like a gentle fog.

✔ **Handheld (HH):** A microphone held in the hand and used to pick up human speech.

✔ **Lighting effects (LX):** Different lights and lighting patterns used to alter the mood and appearance of the environment.

✔ **PowerPoint (PPT):** A computer program for presentations.

✔ **Sting:** A short snip of video that introduces content or a break in the proceedings

✔ **Voice of God (VOG):** An announcer who makes tannoy announcements (see Chapter 11).

Figure 9-4:
A sample-technical running order.

Time	Duration	Item	Sound	LX	Main Screen	Side Screens	Stage Management
19:00	0:30	Guests arrive - Pre dinner drinks	Escala: Marquee VOG		window PPT	window PPT	
19:30	0:10	Guests called to dinner & seated in main room	Escala music/ VOG	Room	window PPT	As main screen	
					1. window PPT (Live Camera TBC) 2. Window Animation - on cue 3. Logo PPT		
19:40	0:04	Dance performance	Keeley Pineapple	Dry Ice, Stage		As main screen	
19:44	0:16	Host performance (VOG to introduce host)	HH #1	Stage	Live Camera/ window PPT	As main screen	
20:00	0:20	Starters served	DJ	Room	window PPT	As main screen	Lectern & auto cue set
20:20	0:40	Main course served	DJ, VOG's	Room	window PPT	As main screen	
21:00	0:25	Awards part 1 (1 to 4)					
		Host - Opening	VOG, Walk on sting HH #1, Lectern Mics	Stage	window PPT/ Live Camera	As main screen	
		Research directors	Start of awards sting	moving everywhere	window PPT	As main screen	

Sticking to the Plan

There's a reason why you've spent weeks and probably months writing schedule version after schedule version, so don't throw the schedule out of the window on the day!

The proof of a well-written schedule is your ability to stick to it during show day.

To stick to the schedule, you need a watch. Sounds basic, but if you don't normally wear a watch, how will you know whether your deliveryman is late? You won't have time to be in front of your laptop constantly, and let me tell you, however good your smartphone is, your battery is unlikely to stand up to the hours of constant calls, email checking, Internet access and emergency downloading of music.

Make sure someone is responsible for keeping each element of the schedule to time. If you're working in a small team, this person may be you. Clear and concise roles and responsibilities are beneficial. For example, if those Portacabins don't arrive on your greenfield site on time, you'll have a lot of jumpy crew members until they arrive, and it will affect productivity.

Things happen; it's a live event, and even the best planning and contingency planning can't take into account all the potential scenarios that can happen when there's no second chance to get it right. That's the best and the worst side of event management.

However, there must be some general guidelines as to how events are likely to pan out. If something does happen that has an impact on your timing schedule, make sure you immediately look at the impact that will have on every single line.

Many situations don't need explaining in detail to your client or boss if you can find a solution, but managing expectations is important.

One small problem may become a bigger problem if it is not assessed quickly. But don't worry: There's always a solution!

Chapter 10

Deciding Where to Hold Your Event

. . . .

In This Chapter

▶ Finding the perfect venue

▶ Eating, sleeping and holding the event in the same place

▶ Using the history of the building to your advantage

▶ Arranging for a spot of shopping with your event

▶ Ensuring no nasty surprises when you get on site

▶ Where do you think you are storing that?

. . . .

*W*here you host your event is one of the most important decisions that you make. Whether you host it in the gardens of a palace or in the conference room of the local hotel, your choice of venue is a big influence on what your audience think of the event.

Deciding where, geographically, to host your event can be a difficult or simple process. If your entire team of 250 people is based in one city, organising your event in the surrounding area saves a lot on accommodation. You may, however, have more scope than that. Maybe your event is for 50 people and you want them to be immersed in a new product or message. You may consider taking them somewhere unexpected where they can truly focus on your event – maybe even somewhere with no Internet access!

If your target audience is consumers who may be based anywhere in the country, delve deeper into your client's target market figures. Your client generally has a priority area to focus on. London, for example, may be your client's biggest market, but it may be trying to grow its business in Manchester. Do an event in Manchester, therefore, to increase brand awareness.

The BBC famously takes a grass-roots approach to its live events, always trying to visit areas other than the big cities, so everyone feels included. Often companies naturally gravitate towards major cities due to the large number of people likely to be attracted to the event. This isn't a bad plan, but why not think about focusing your activity on the suburbs? You suddenly have a potential audience who are impressed that you've come out of town to be close to them – potentially increasing loyalty and attendance.

You can follow a set of criteria to help select the most appropriate place, but appropriate is the key word. If you're holding a conference to explain how a company is being restructured and how redundancies will occur due to lack of profit, it's probably not appropriate to host the conference in a five-star hotel. You don't want to be seen as hypocritical when spending money on your venue. Similarly, if you're trying to attract the media industry's finest, a local pub is less likely to succeed than a new bar or space they've never seen before.

Establishing Your Criteria and Getting Started

In an ideal world, you base your choice on a set of pre-agreed criteria. Often, however, you're told where to host the event, and thus need to make all your plans fit around the venue.

You ideally choose your venue after deciding on the capacity, theme and type of event to organise, rather than the other way around, but often you have little choice.

Selecting your venue requires a similar level of groundwork as when buying a car. The three steps to choosing the perfect venue are:

1. **Create a shortlist that matches your criteria**

2. **Go on site visits and ask the right questions**

3. **Select and contract your perfect venue**

Creating a Shortlist of Venues

The first step is to create a shortlist of venues. The Internet has revolutionised this stage of event planning. Search engines have opened up a world of new venue options and are a great way to gather a long list of possibilities.

A variety of websites are specifically designed for sourcing venues. Don't be afraid to ask for help or for recommendations. You can even ask your audience where the perfect event would be. You can make the venue-selection process part of the event marketing.

A website called www.funkyvenues.co.uk is a really good resource when considering more unusual venues. Or visit www.venuesforevents.co.uk for some slightly more corporate venues.

To develop a shortlist, you first need to put in some work to develop a long list, from which the shortlist evolves. Creating your long list may feel like a really lengthy process, but the groundwork you put in at this first stage is invaluable when you start to visit the venues. The best scenario is that you shortlist such good venues that you have too many suitable options. Then you know you've put in the right amount of groundwork.

When looking at multiple venues, don't think that you have to decide straight away. If you want to shortlist, site visit and then deliberate, that's fine. You can ask the venues to pencil in your event. Most venues can pencil you in and contact you for first refusal if someone asks to host an event on the same day. However, money always wins: If another company offers more money for the event and is happy to sign the contract that day, it is likely to secure the venue. You need to act as fast as you can.

You can ask venues to pencil you in, to give yourself more time to consider, but don't forget to confirm and decline the other venues as soon as you can.

Permanent venue options

You can choose from thousands upon thousands of event spaces in which to put on your event. The trick is finding the one that's right for you!

Permanent venues give a great opportunity to use existing infrastructure, and offer the expertise of the in-house events team. They are also a more sustainable option than creating a venue specifically for your event. Permanent venues are generally cheaper than creating new venues but naturally limit your opportunities – only slightly, though, because you have so many venue options that you shouldn't find it too difficult to find the right one for your event.

I include information on some of the most common types of event venue, but essentially any building is a potential event space. Table 10-1 gives you a rundown on which sorts of venue are suitable for particular types of event.

Table 10-1	Suitable events venues			
Type of venue	**Type of event**			
	Meetings	**Conferences**	**Networking**	**Exhibitions**
Conference Centres	No	Yes	Yes	Yes
Hotels	Yes	Yes	Yes	Yes
Historic venues and galleries	Yes	Yes	Yes	No
Shopping centres	No	No	No	No
Sports and leisure	Yes	Yes	Yes	Yes
Temporary structures	Yes	Yes	Yes	Yes

Conference centres

According to Wikipedia: A conference centre (also known as a convention centre) is a large building that is designed to hold a conference, where individuals and groups gather to promote and share common interests.

Conference centres typically offer sufficient floor area to accommodate several thousand attendees. Very large venues, suitable for major trade shows, are sometimes known as exhibition centres. A conference centre typically has at least one auditorium and may also contain concert halls, lecture halls, meeting rooms and breakout rooms.

A conference centre is great for a large-scale event, but can often be intimidating for a gathering of fewer than a thousand people.

Because their main function is putting on events, conference centres are geared up for events and are likely to have all the basic requirements in house. If you need advice about a specific situation, ask the staff how they handled it in the past.

In multi-room sites such as convention centres and hotels, ask the venue manager what other events are happening there on the same day. For example, if you're planning an internal sales and marketing conference for Cadbury's, you don't want to be in the same venue as Mars in case confidential information is publicised. The same applies to consumer-facing events: If you've put lots of effort into getting your consumers there, you don't want them attracted by the entrance to another event. Most venues can give you exclusivity of sector or type of event, but it's worth asking the question and having the agreement put in your contract just in case.

Hotels

Most hotels have conference rooms and facilities. They generally have large rooms that can seat 100 or more people, and they offer wireless Internet (wi-fi) plus, potentially, some basic audiovisual kit (microphone, lights and screens).

The benefit of using a hotel as a conference venue is that it can provide many other elements of your event in house. You don't need to worry about:

- ✔ **Where your delegates can sleep:** They can pop upstairs.
- ✔ **Where delegates will park:** They can park in the dedicated car park.
- ✔ **Catering:** Delegates can eat in the restaurant and drink in the bar.
- ✔ **Furniture:** The hotel can provide tables and chairs.

(All of the above are provided for an additional fee, of course.)

If you plan to organise lots of conferences, it may be sensible to consider developing an official relationship with a hotel or chain of hotels. By committing to use a certain venue multiple times a year, you are in a much better position to negotiate a better deal.

The only real downside to using a hotel is that often hotels provide only plain and uninspiring rooms. This is deliberate, of course, so that anyone can go in and use the rooms as a blank canvas. If you want your venue to look the part, you may need to set aside lots of money for branding or decoration.

As always, your decision depends on what's appropriate for your event. Hotels are great for conferences but not good for experiential marketing, due to the low passing traffic.

Historic venues and galleries

Stunning venues, often with a great story behind them, can make great event spaces. If selected carefully, the story can become part of or complement your event theming and creative activity.

These types of venue are in high demand and the venue managers are able to decide who they want their venue to be associated with. You may have to prove that your event can benefit the venue rather than the other way around.

As you can imagine, what you can do in some of these venues is restricted. Often event organisers have to bring freestanding lighting, and so on, as there may be no hanging points for lighting. These things are generally easy to work around.

Often this type of venue has preferred suppliers who know how to work quickly and efficiently in what can be quite a quick turnaround for rigging events.

Shopping centres

Shopping centres are *high-footfall areas* (that is, lots of people go there) where customers are in a spending-money kind of mood. If you are organising an experiential event or a brand awareness campaign for a customer product, shopping centres make great event spaces. Every shopping centre has at least one event space, and many larger shopping centres have multiple spaces of various sizes.

Finding the WOW factor

The Hampton Court Palace Flower Show, which the Royal Horticultural Society (RHS) runs annually in early July, is the biggest flower show in the world. The RHS holds it at Hampton Court Palace in south-west London. The show has a huge range of attractions, from specially designed gardens to floral marquees, and also has a wide range of lectures and demonstrations.

When considering a venue such as this, take time to understand the impact of the backdrop on your event. It's likely to minimise your costs for branding and props as you're able to make use of features such as fountains, gardens and statues.

The London 2012 Olympics showed that shopping centres play a major part in our lives. Every person who watched the Olympics in Stratford had to pass through the Westfield shopping centre; that's over 200,000 people going through a shopping centre over one summer.

The benefits of using a shopping centre as a venue are that:

- You're close to a point of purchase; someone who likes your client's product can buy it that day.
- Customers go to the shopping centre to spend money, so are in a frame of mind to consider new purchases.
- Most sites have a power connection.
- They are family-friendly venues.

Most shopping centre sites are internal, but a shopping centre may have an outdoor space if you want to promote a car, for example.

When planning your event at a shopping centre, bear in mind that its opening hours are often long. Some of the big super shopping centres such as Westfield Shepherd's Bush, are open until 10 p.m. during the week and until midnight just before Christmas.

The opening hours can have an impact on your experience in two ways:

- Rigging your event in a shopping centre can be tricky. You can't start building your event in a main space until after the centre has closed and all personnel have left the building. This may be very late at night. Bear this in mind when planning your build schedule.
- You need to staff your stand for longer each day, which has a cost implication. However, the longer opening hours are likely to mean higher returns, so hopefully pay for themself.

Ask about any height restrictions; you often can't build a stand higher than 2.1 metres due to sight lines for shop units.

You don't have to use shopping centres only for brand awareness or experience campaigns; they make great venues for longer-term activity too. Due to changes in shopping patterns and rate charges, more and more shop units in shopping centres or high streets are empty. These make great event spaces when you want to create a more immersive experience to last longer than a few days – something like a potential pop-up shop, where you take over an empty unit and make a temporary shop. Check out *Pop-Up Business For Dummies*, by Dan Thompson (Wiley) for more on these.

Experiencing the brand

When Toyota launched the new Auris in 2007, it wanted something spectacular and memorable but didn't want to invest in a large-scale advertising campaign. Instead, Toyota used brand experience marketing to drive awareness and interest in the product.

For two weeks prior to the launch of the car, Toyota installed six hoardings over shop units in shopping centres around the country. They also installed clocks on the hoardings to count down to the launch, with interactive touch screens through which passers-by could submit their contact details to receive further information.

On the day of the car launch, the hoardings were removed and mini 'shops' were revealed with welcome desks, sound booths, a 3D holographic show and the Toyota Auris in the centre. These shops were open for two weeks for customers to come and discover the Auris.

This is a great example of bringing an experience to the customer; in this case, vendors normally expect customers to travel to attend a car showroom. The marketing activity made the vehicle more approachable and also greatly increased brand awareness.

Consider spaces beyond the traditional event spaces, and consider other options such as empty shop units and the car parks of the shopping centres.

Sports and leisure

If you're putting on a sports event, sports grounds and leisure centres are perfect venue options to start with. Because these venues cater for large numbers of people, the infrastructure is already in place and therefore additional technical costs are limited.

Thousands of local council sports grounds are available around the country. These spaces aren't often available to rent like other spaces, but if you can incorporate in your offer benefits for the council, it may be open to allowing you to put on an event. Consider how you can provide funding back into the community or create something of long-term use to the venue.

Sports grounds don't have to be just for sports events, though; they're often used for conferences and gala dinners, where you can consider offering an additional piece of theatre such as walking onto the pitch or going into the changing rooms. Often hotels are connected to the grounds.

Due to the nature of sports grounds, for large parts of the year they are not available. Check sporting schedules before you phone to enquire about availability.

Another option is to hold your event when a sporting event is on and you can communicate with the audience in a piece of experiential activity. For example, if rugby players from the London area are your target market, capitalise on all these people being in one place.

O2 has had a relationship with English Rugby for many years and extends this to its customers on match days. O2 created the 'O2 Blueroom' in the car park of Twickenham rugby ground, in which fans can enjoy pre-match entertainment and have a free pie and pint with players after the game. This provides a tailored experience and ensures that the customers O2 is speaking to are genuinely interested in sports. Had O2 placed this event in a city centre, large numbers of people wouldn't have been interested in the offering.

It's always important to consider the appropriateness of your venue. If you want to connect with sports fans, find a sporting venue to host your event. In the case of O2, they want to speak to their customers and some of them are sports fans.

Temporary venues

Whilst there are thousands of venues in the UK, if you feel ambitious, you may consider creating your own venue. Maybe the perfect venue for your complex brief doesn't exist, in which case you need to take a can-do attitude and make that perfect venue.

Temporary structures require a large amount of work to manage, more than an existing event venue, but they do give you complete flexibility to create something that works perfectly for what you need. Yes, they also cost a lot more, which often rules them out, but they are an option to consider when the budget is available.

Dry hire

You may hear the phrase 'dry hire' when talking to venue staff. A *dry hire* is when you hire the venue but nothing within it; the venue therefore has no furniture, operatives or additional kit.

A dry hire can be a really good opportunity to bring your own kit and crew into an event and make it truly bespoke. Your things-to-do-list is a little longer, but if you have the budget and capacity to dry hire, your event can feel different from any other event in the same venue.

Ask the staff at any venues that you are considering using what the cost difference is between dry and inclusive hire. (Some venues don't offer dry hire, though, because of the effort involved in removing their furniture and lighting rigs.) Always ask the question up front.

A temporary venue can be as simple as a marquee in a garden or a semi-permanent structure like those in the Frieze Art Fair in Regent's Park.

Temporary event notices (TENs)

Permanent venues have the necessary permissions to run events according to their regulations. When planning an event in a venue that's not normally an event space, slightly more paperwork is involved.

If you're organising an event at which you want to serve or sell alcohol, provide late night refreshments or put on entertainment, you need to apply for a temporary event notice. You can find full details of the restrictions around what qualifies for a TEN on the Home Office website (www.homeoffice.gov.uk). Briefly, they are as follows:

- A temporary event is classed as a relatively small-scale event attracting fewer than 500 people.

- The event must last no more than 168 hours and can be held either outdoors or indoors.

- Any premises can only be used for 12 temporary events per year, up to a total maximum of 21 days.

- You must be over 18 in order to hold a temporary event.

- Temporary events organised by the same person or an associate, in relation to the same premises, must be at least 24 hours apart.

- Once the police or environmental health officers receive your TEN, they have three working days to make any objections to it on the grounds of any of the four licensing objectives: prevention of crime and disorder; prevention of public nuisance; public safety; protection of children from harm.

- If the police or environmental health officers object, the council organises a hearing to consider the evidence, and may decide that your event can't proceed. If there's an objection to a late TEN, the event is not allowed to proceed. Otherwise, the event can go ahead as planned.

It's important that you find out from the venue how many temporary events it has hosted already that year. Finding out from the local council that it has rejected your application means you have wasted a lot of time. It can take 2–3 months to obtain a TEN licence and it will very much depend on the council you are approaching, as each council will have their own internal processes and resourcing that will affect the speed of your response. There is, however, the option of an emergency TEN but generally always try to give as much notice as possible.

Following on from a TEN application, you need to further involve the local authorities in planning your event. This is covered more in Chapter 12.

Using outdoor sites

A music festival outside can be an appealing proposition. Outdoors, there's plenty of space to do what you want, and you're not restricted by the décor and style of an existing venue.

Working outdoors can be tricky, though, and requires more thorough planning than when using an existing venue, because of the lack of any infrastructure in place.

When deciding on an external site, consider what's appropriate for your event. Assess the following, if relevant for your event type:

- Ground conditions
- Access routes
- Environmental constraints such as noise restrictions
- Site hazards such as bodies of water or changes in gradient of the ground
- Provision of mains power and water
- Fencing or boundary identification of the area

Ownership of land

When looking at using an outdoor site, first work out who owns the land. If it's privately owned, you need to ask the relevant person or company whether you can rent the space for your event.

Most greenfield sites, however, are owned and run by local councils or, if in London, by the Royal Parks. Contact the council to ask for permission to use the site. Local council sites tend to be low cost, because councils try to maximise the use of their spaces. However, you may need to go through a long process of completing paper-based applications. The process is:

- The council is likely to ask you to provide a basic proposal and fill in an application form.
- The council will review your proposal to see whether it fits the type of event that it wants to be associated with.
- The request may go to local residents of the space or a local committee, depending on the details and impact that the event may have on them.
- You're asked to attend a Safety Advisory Group (SAG) meeting. (More on this in Chapter 12.)
- You then receive formal permission to use the site.

This process can often take 3–4 months, so build plenty of time into your timelines for this process (advice on how to build your timing plan can be found in Chapter 9); there's no hurrying a local council!

Outdoor infrastructure

Infrastructure is the term used when talking about the physical structures and facilities needed to operate the event. The infrastructure varies depending on the type of event, but covers all the things that have to be there no matter what to make your event work. Things like screens in different tents and the branding around the site aren't classed as infrastructure, because they're not essential.

I deal with toilets and waste management further on in this chapter, but other areas to consider when hosting an event outside are:

✔ Fencing

✔ Health and safety

✔ Providing water

✔ Power

✔ Structures such as tents and stages

Fencing

The site you select may not have any natural boundaries, for example your event may be taking place in the corner of a large playing field, and you therefore need to identify the space. Fencing may be a large cost, depending on the event.

Consider what's appropriate for your event and audience, but bear in mind the associated financial and security implications.

Event planners often debate whether the site needs to be fenced. I recommend that you have fencing, and that you should only exclude it in exceptional circumstances.

The benefits of having a fenced event mainly fall into two themes: On the one hand safety and security, and on the other financial:

✔ **Safety and security reasons:** The safety and security benefits of fencing are:

   • You can control numbers, so can tell your client how many people attended your event.

   • You have control if a child or other person goes missing.

   • You can stop people drinking and smoking at your event if it's not appropriate.

- You can control who attends the event; you can exclude people who are not desirable for your event.

- You limit your responsibility to only the people within your event space. If you don't fence the event, you're responsible for everyone in the vicinity.

✔ **Financial reasons:** The financial benefits of fencing are:

- You can limit the number of stewards and security staff to an appropriate number for the size of site.

- You can limit the number of overnight security staff needed to keep your kit secure.

If you don't fence the event and are therefore responsible for everyone in the vicinity (say a whole park, for example), you need to increase:

✔ The number of toilets

✔ The number of food and beverage outlets

✔ The number of crowd control barriers around the experiences and the main stage, to reduce the risk of crushing

✔ Catering facilities for crew (to include security staff and stewards).

Health and safety

I cover health and safety in more detail in Chapter 12. If you're producing an outdoor event in a temporary space, consider this area carefully to make sure your event is safe and fun; you don't want it to be memorable for the wrong reasons. Below are just a few of the areas you will need to consider:

✔ Ensure the local authorities know of your event and have approved the access routes for their vehicles

✔ Provide on-site first aid support

✔ Ensure your space is big enough for the number of people you expect and you have a way to stop people entering if too many do arrive

✔ Provide safety barriers to block off back of house areas or areas where there is technical kit such as generators

✔ Be sure that you have the appropriate fire safety equipment and signage on site

Providing water

Drinking water is often taken for granted, especially in permanent venues. Everyone expects to be able to find a tap, go to a bar and ask for a glass of water, or go to the toilet and wash their hands. At outdoor events, however, you're unlikely to have an easily available water supply.

When visiting the site, you need to look at and ask about any water supplies such as mains taps. You then need to hire a plumber to distribute the water to the required locations on your site – the catering area, the toilet area and any areas with higher fire safety risks. This is not a difficult or even expensive job, but you do need to plan it in advance. On completion of the work, ask your plumber to provide a water-testing certificate to show whether the water is suitable for drinking.

If you are unable to re-route an existing water supply, you can use water bowsers, which are large containers. If you use water containers, consider how to fill and move these (large containers are heavy). Also consider providing cups for people to use to drink the water.

Power

A permanent venue has a power supply; a field is not likely to have. This isn't a problem, though; it's just something that you need to add to your things-to-do list. You may not have a stage on your event space, or even lighting, but you're still likely to need some kind of power. How will you use your computer? Where will you charge your phone? How will you provide a hot catering service for the crew without power?

You can hire a basic generator for a small amount, and I strongly recommend that it's connected to the power distribution (power sockets), too. Have an electrician on site; power's not something you want to deal with on your own if you're not trained.

Consider carefully what type of generator to hire and where to position it. Generators are often noisy and need to be fenced off properly so that no one can touch them.

Your production manager, if you have one in your event team, can advise on all aspects of the power supply.

Structures

If you decide to plan an event outdoors, consider what structures you require. Structures include those often referred to as 'tents', but more besides. Go online to find suppliers of structures; there are thousands.

Your production manager can assist with this. Your choice has a great impact on the cost of your event. The costs are affected by the:

- Cost of the actual structure
- Number of crew required to erect the structure
- Number of days of site hire that are required to erect and strike (rig and de-rig) the structure
- Quantity of furniture and/or branding required to fill the space

Many different structures are available; plenty of flexible solutions can make your site into a temporary event venue.

If you have covered structures at an outside event, the impact of weather is reduced (although not removed): A structure offers shelter from rain or sun.

Consider the customer journey for the day and how visitors will use the structure.

Some structures have poles in the middle to make peaks (like a circus big top) and others are pole free using an aluminium frame. Both options make great event spaces. Maybe think about other events that you've been to and which structures impressed you the most.

You may be looking for a structure for the main event site or potentially as a back-of-house area, such as a press room or catering unit. The structure supplier can advise from its experience what structure may be most suitable. Insist that your structure supplier visits your event space before you sign a contract, so that both parties are confident that there will be no surprises.

When deciding how big a structure to choose for your event, use the basic calculation of 1–2 square metres per person, 1.5 is a good figure to aim for but you have flexibility if your venue is bigger or smaller

Inflatable structures are great options and can be really quick to erect. Bear in mind that they require power, and so you need a generator or power supply on site before the structure can go up. This is helpful to know when planning your production schedule.

Span structures are often used for festivals as stage structures and music venues. They are striking and offer an impactful branding solution.

You might look into using slightly more unusual structures such as shipping containers. They are solid structures that can easily be transported. In the last couple of years they have become popular due to their low cost. By using multiple containers, you can create different rooms at your event. Bear in mind that they are shipping containers and need basic infrastructure such as lighting and heating. If you intend to stack them on top of each other, you need to provide an access route to the top unit – in other words, stairs.

You can buy or hire structures. Consider whether you're likely to repeat the same event regularly in the same site. If so, whilst the initial investment is large, you may find it more cost-effective in the long run to purchase the kit and rent it out to your client, as if you use it regularly, you will make your money back: You can charge higher than proportionate costs for rental.

Structures are a great branding opportunity, although bear in mind that this adds costs your budget. If you purchase the structure, you can have branding printed directly onto the material. If you hire the structure, you can ask for your branding to be printed on fabric panels that you then attach to the structure using either Velcro or hooks.

As with an internal venue, you need to consider basic infrastructure such as lighting, heating and sound. Trussing creates hanging points, and any large event space needs a full wooden floor. A hard floor is not only beneficial to your guests, who will find it much easier to walk on; it also allows you to run unsightly wires and cables under the flooring to keep the space as clear as possible. Flooring also makes it a lot easier to keep your tables level, too.

Depending on the type of structure and the supplier, you may have to hire your own crew to erect it or the supplier may send trained crew to erect it as part of the service. When the service is available, I advise asking your supplier to install the structure, so that the company takes full responsibility. A badly erected or secured structure can have serious implications.

Structures should not be erected in extreme weather conditions. Always seek professional advice about the wind speed, to make sure the structure doesn't blow away. Check that your supplier has public liability insurance and the relevant fire and wind rating certificates for the structure.

Weather

People often ask me, 'Well, what if it rains?' The weather is one of the few things that you can't control in event management, but you can manage around it.

As well as 'bad' weather such as rain or snow that can affect your event, a hot, sunny day can also do so if you're not prepared. Ensure you have shelters available to protect people from the high temperatures, and consider offering additional water points and even suntan lotion.

Also, don't forget to consider your team, because they are on site in any extreme weather conditions for a lot longer than your guests. A happy team is an efficient team.

Because of the nature of the climate in Europe, it's difficult to be certain of anything. Your contingency planning needs to reach a new level. See Chapter 13 for more information on contingency planning.

More-unusual venues

Plenty of more-unusual venues are available too. You may be trying to bring a particular theme to life, or you may want to do something really memorable. Don't let typical event spaces restrict you, because so many other options are out there. Also, don't be shy to ask those running a venue whether they'll consider hosting an event, even if they've never done so before.

Venues such as the following all work as event spaces but offer a rather more unusual option:

- ✔ Those at height, such as the London Eye
- ✔ Building sites
- ✔ Barges and boats, for example, the Silver Sturgeon
- ✔ Nightclubs
- ✔ Themed venues, for example Ice Bar or Madame Tussauds
- ✔ Schools
- ✔ Car parks

These, plus many others, all offer their own positives and negatives. Hosting an event at height, for example, automatically excludes those people who have a fear of heights. If you host an event on a building site, your guests need to wear hard hats. An event in a school can only take place at certain times. All such venues, however, tend to be slightly cheaper than more-traditional event spaces. When organising events, try to see a problem as a challenge that you can overcome. There's always a solution.

With any venue, if you intend to take over the whole of a venue that normally other people visit, make sure the venue has a plan in place to communicate with existing patrons. Although the venue should take responsibility for this, as a sign of goodwill you can offer assistance. For example, if the buy-in of local residents to a venue is important to you and your client, maybe offer them free tickets to your event.

Looking abroad

After reviewing your brief, you may decide that the best option is to find a venue abroad. There are challenges involved when working abroad, but nothing that a good bit of planning can't make easier.

Consider partnering with a destination management company (DMC), because this can be valuable when planning an event abroad. A DMC can help you organise your event from within the destination country, rather than from another country like the one you are in.

The advantages of using a DMC include:

- ✔ A local DMC may be able to save you some money by negotiating the best deals.
- ✔ The DMC's staff speak the local language – invaluable when sourcing venues, suppliers and staff.

> ✔ The DMC's staff are experts in their country; if you need suggestions and advice, ask them.
>
> ✔ You can focus on looking after your client rather than on organising the details of the event.

You need to consider many additional areas if you plan to host your event abroad:

> ✔ Research the permits or visas that your team require.
>
> ✔ Consider shipping options or local suppliers.
>
> ✔ Check the currency of suppliers' quotes.
>
> ✔ Locate the local embassy.
>
> ✔ Check all your insurance documents to ensure that your team and kit are covered for working abroad.
>
> ✔ Speak to local suppliers and the embassy to understand any working restrictions in your chosen country – some countries have specific trade union restrictions.
>
> ✔ Check whether any local customs or public holidays are specific to the region.

Check the season in the country you intend to visit, for the time of your event.

The weather is different around the world, and you need to consider this when planning an event abroad. Are you asking your guests to visit a hot destination when it's cold at home? If so, is this a positive, or an inconvenience if they don't have appropriate clothes available?

When Not Just One Event or Venue Will Do

If you can't decide one location as your audience is based across the country, consider a roadshow (multi-location) approach. Rather than assuming that everyone will travel for four hours to your event, put on smaller events that are more accessible for your target audience. Often internal communications events and consumer shopping-centre-based events follow this pattern.

Consider where your audience is based. If you're organising an event for your national sales team, then maybe the Midlands is an easy place for everyone to get to, as an alternative to a regional roadshow.

You can tweak your event slightly at each site, so it's more bespoke to the venue and audience. For example, if you're hosting events in Manchester, London and Edinburgh, consider changing your host to be a local person with the local regional accent. Similarly, if your retail team is doing really well in the north compared to the west, you can change the messaging at each event to make it more focused.

Roadshows are, realistically, more time-intensive to organise; they are, in essence, multiple mini events. You can often reduce the scale of the event and therefore the amount of organisation required by reducing the number of attendees.

Logistics are really important for you when organising a roadshow, less so for your client. Your client may need to send out five sets of invitations, but you need to plan how to move your kit to five different parts of the country.

The considerations for a multi-location event, or roadshow, are:

✔ How does your kit move from event to event?

✔ How is your kit stored in between the events?

✔ Is the route around the country sensible? Try, for example, not to go from Plymouth to Birmingham to Brighton to Glasgow.

✔ Do you have enough time in between each event to have one team and one kit, or do you need more than one of each?

✔ If you have only one kit, can you build time into your schedule to do maintenance on the kit if required?

Asking the Venue the Right Questions

When creating an event, you're likely to want to bring in some elements yourself. However much is included with the venue, you're still likely to bring in branding, giveaways and/or other documentation. Consider how you'll take these items to the venue.

Find out whether the venue only allows you to use its suppliers – sometimes venues only allow you to bring in pre-approved suppliers.

The importance of site visits

You and your team and/or client will visit the site of your event before the event day. Ideally, you visit a few different sites or venues when choosing one. Then, when you've chosen a venue, you return for a technical site visit.

On your first set of site visits, consider basics such as:

✔ Is the venue big enough for what you require?

✔ Does it have the right look and style?

- ✔ Is it easy for your audience to get to?
- ✔ Is the site affordable in your budget?

When you decide on your venue and head back to the site, try to set up a meeting with the venue manager, who can give you some further information. Look at and discuss the following in more detail:

- ✔ Vehicle and audience access
- ✔ Facilities on site
- ✔ Marketing support
- ✔ Branding opportunities
- ✔ Measuring exact sizes of the rooms and/or spaces
- ✔ Local transport options
- ✔ Impact on local area and residents
- ✔ Hanging points on the ceiling
- ✔ Wireless Internet access

Consider using a scorecard or reminder sheet when on a site visit. See Figure 10-1 for an example.

I can't overstate the importance of a site visit. However many plans, photos and video fly-throughs you watch, you still don't gather as much information than when you walk around the site yourself. Travelling miles to go to see a venue when you've already seen plans may seem like a big inconvenience, but no excuses: Do a site visit.

No one would buy a car or house without looking at it first. You want to know that your possible purchase works for your purposes, looks how you expect it to look and that you can deal with the current owners. A photo in a magazine or online and a chat over the phone never give you the level of detail you need.

The precise team that you take on the site visit depends on the event you're planning. In an ideal situation, you take the entire team so that everyone can easily imagine how the event will flow on the day.

You and your team (plus your client) need a lot of imagination when going to look at these venues. It can sometimes be a challenge to look at an empty room and imagine what 25 tables and chairs plus a stage and drinks reception may look like.

Try scribbling out a plan of how your guests will move around the venue through the event, and walk it yourself as though you were a guest to get a good idea of the guest experience.

site visit template

Client	Event date: Build date:

Venue	**Date of report**

		YES	NO
1.	**Venue layout** • Can they provide you with site plans/CAD plans? • Can any of the rooms be changed in shape or size? • How many rooms are included in the hire price? • If required - do they have a dance floor that they can bring in and are there additional costs attached?		
2.	**Outside the venue** • Do they have a preferred list of suppliers that you have to use? • Are the walls soundproofed? • Do they have venue personnel that will be included in the hire costs? • Do they have wireless internet? Can it be used by your team and your guests? • Do they have any plant (forklifts, cranes etc) that you can use and do they have a trained operator?		
3.	**Internal facilities** • Do they have a supply of drinking water that your crew and your guests can have access to? • How many toilets do they have and where are they positioned? • What is the signage like around the venue and can it be replaced with your own branded signage? • Where could your catering preparation area be positioned? • What are the waste disposal and recycling facilities? • What are the power levels and distribution points?		

Figure 10-1:
A site visit
template

Loading bays

When you go on your site visit, look for the loading bays. If you're not sure what they look like, or you can't find one, ask in the venue. The loading bays are where suppliers unload items.

Check for any restrictions on the times when you can use these bays. The venue may have regular deliveries booked in, which you need to work around when planning your delivery schedules.

Also establish on your site visit whether any restrictions affect what size vehicle you can use. Is there enough space for your large truck to get into the loading bay, and just as importantly, is there enough space for the truck to get out? With practice, you can estimate this yourself; in the meantime, ask your truck driver to pop down to the venue, too, to do a site visit. Your truck driver is likely to be happy to be involved in the planning stage, rather than just receiving a brief.

Weight, width and height restrictions

Before I started working in events, I'd never considered that structures have weight restrictions. In my head, if cars go on a road, and I don't intend to have anything heavier than a car, why do I need to worry about weight restrictions?

Well, I was once putting on a car event at a shopping centre, and the access point was through a ramped car park. My crew arrived on site in the middle of the night and tried to move the cars into the building. What I hadn't checked was that there was a weight restriction on the ramp, and whilst the car would have been fine, the truck that was carrying the car was too heavy. Thankfully, through the power of making friends quickly (you need to be able to do this in events), I managed to convince the maintenance man at the shopping centre to help us push in the car from around the corner.

It was a small thing that I should have checked. Had I known before I got on site, I could have asked for a different size truck. It was lucky the maintenance man helped, otherwise I'd have needed a very awkward and costly conversation with my client to explain that the event had to be cancelled.

Always check weight restrictions.

Hanging points

Lighting and sound can make or break an event. Often, lighting is rigged on the ceiling so it can point down to the stage. There are two ways to do this:

- Hanging points
- Trussing

Hanging points are hooks off the ceiling that have enough load-bearing capacity that you can hang heavy objects off them. *Trussing* is like scaffolding, which creates a metal framework to hang technical kit off.

The venue should test the hanging points; you can extract more specific information about the results of these tests. If you have large, heavy items that you need to suspend, you may want to consider running additional tests, so that you have fully up-to-date details of the load-bearing capacity of the hanging points.

If hanging points are not available, you may still be able to create a similar experience by using a truss to create an internal structure with hanging points. This reduces the space available within the venue and also increases the costs, because you need to bring in the trussing and the crew to erect it.

Transportation issues

When planning your event and deciding on your venue, also consider how you will physically create your event. Do you plan to dress the venue with vast amounts of props and new furniture, or are you using it as it is?

If, for example, you want to hold an event on the top floor of a building that only has a small door to access the space, you may need to reconsider your plan to bring in a 10-foot fountain. If the fountain can be broken down and fitted into a lift, or if you have some strong crew, you can still make your plan work. You need, however, to consider the potential costs to achieve your plan when picking the venue. You may decide that another venue is just as good and doesn't have the additional costs or time implications.

Size and type of trucks expected

If you want to know what size vehicle you need when planning your event, look at Table 10-2 below. It can be daunting when you're asked for details of the sizes of trucks when you're trying to obtain quotes and you have no idea how much space your kit will take up.

Through some simple maths and some discussions with all of your suppliers, you can establish your basic requirements. Table 10-2 shows you some basic truck capacities.

Table 10-2	Typical truck sizes		
Type of Truck	**Approximate Dimension of Load (Metres)**	**Load Capacity (Kilograms)**	**Number of UK Pallets**
Luton van (long wheel base)	3.9 × 2 × 2.15	1,600–1,800	4 pallets
7.5-tonne truck	8.23 × 2.44 × 3.28	3,000–3,500	10 pallets
18-tonne box truck (HGV)	7.3 × 2.5 × 2.5	9,000	14 pallets
Semi-trailer truck	13.6 × 2.45 × 2.7	48,000	26 pallets

Number of deliveries expected

The larger the event, the more deliveries you're likely to have. The number of trucks arriving, the times at which they'll arrive and how long they'll take to unload are all elements that you need to establish before you arrive on site.

Include this information in your production schedule. You or your production manager needs to consider in what order you want items to arrive. For example, you need the lighting kit delivered before the table decorations. Consider order of importance but also the size of the items: Organise for larger items to arrive first if they won't get in the way during the rest of the build.

Check any restrictions on delivery times; to avoid disturbing local residents, some venues may not let you bring vehicles onto the site after 10 p.m.

If suppliers are sending deliveries by courier or similar, make sure that the items are carefully labelled. It's worth advising the supplier to include your name plus the name of your venue contact too, in case the courier can't track you down, and, most importantly, your mobile number.

Don't forget to consider the de-rig schedule of pick-ups at the same time; the time window for trucks arriving on the de-rig is likely to be much shorter, because everyone wants to get out of the event and back home quickly.

Parking

Having simple and clear parking arrangements is one of those things that you're unlikely to receive compliments for, but you'll definitely be the first to know if you haven't thought through the arrangements properly.

Consider the location of the venue and what you think your audience's main methods of transport will be. If your venue is in a city centre, are your guests more likely to use public transport or will they drive? If your event is in a remote location, people are likely to drive or need coaches arranged.

If you think that parking is required, try to estimate how many people will drive. Is the venue able to accommodate the likely number of vehicles? If not, can other local options be used? Can you do a deal with the local car park for a fixed-rate cost for your attendees?

If you want to restrict the use of the parking facilities to certain people, it may be best to provide pre-paid permits or identity passes. If you take this route, consider how to distribute these permits: Can you send them out with the invitation or ticket?

✔ Try to encourage car sharing; maybe offer a reward for those who do.

✔ Offer free transfers from local transport hubs.

For truck and service vehicle parking you need a different approach. Secure parking is required, often for very large trucks, which affects which car parks you can use.

Speak to staff at your venue about any loading bays that have a secure parking space within. If nothing is available at the venue, don't be afraid to ask local businesses whether you can use their facilities during your event rather than taking your trucks miles off site.

Check height restrictions and security provisions on car parks for service vehicles and trucks.

Key site facilities (infrastructure)

The main difference between permanent and temporary sites is the availability of site infrastructure. In a hotel, you can assume that facilities such as toilets, lighting and a first aid box will be available (although don't take anything for granted in events; always double-check). On a greenfield or temporary structure site, you need to bring everything in.

Regardless of the type of venue, add to your status list the following, even if just to check that you know where they are in the existing venue and that they are adequate.

Toilets

We all take toilets for granted at home and in the office. You do, however, need to spend some time thinking about toilets for your event.

In a permanent venue, you can be confident that the number of toilets and other facilities reflect the capacity of the venue. For temporary venues, you need to work out how many toilets to provide. Refer to a useful document known as the 'purple guide'. The official name is *The Event Safety Guide* by the Health and Safety Executive (HMSO).

Take the following into account:

- ✔ How many people are attending the event?
- ✔ What sort of food and alcohol is being served?
- ✔ For how long do you expect people to be at the event?
- ✔ Are many children attending?

There is a basic formula to establish how many toilets you should have on site, but also ask the opinion of the supplier, whose job it is. Table 10-3 below gives you a guide to the number of toilets to provide.

Table 10-3	Toilet requirements									
	Hours duration									
Number of people	1	2	3	4	5	6	7	8	9	10
1–50	1	1	1	1	2	2	2	2	2	2
51–100	2	2	2	2	2	3	3	3	3	3
101–250	3	3	3	3	4	4	4	6	6	6
251–500	4	4	4	4	6	6	8	8	8	8
501–1000	4	5	6	7	7	8	8	8	9	9
1001–3000	6	10	12	13	14	14	14	15	15	15
3001–4000	9	14	17	19	20	21	21	21	21	22
4001–5000	12	19	23	25	28	28	30	30	30	30
5001+	15	23	32	32	34	35	36	36	36	36

You may save money by having fewer toilets, but what impact will this have on your audience's experience? Also remember to provide facilities for disabled guests.

Also think about attention to detail. What do the inside of the toilets look like? Is it worth printing some branding to put in them? Do you need to bring in some flowers, new hand-wash, and so on, to make them more pleasant?

Good toilet facilities make a big difference to how your guests perceive your event.

Waste management

Events create a lot of waste – however sustainable you plan your event to be – not just from the people who attend your event, but from suppliers too.

In a contained venue, such as a hotel that hosts a conference, you are unlikely to need to dispose of a huge amount of waste. The venue provides sufficient bins and disposes of waste in a standard process. Only really in external venues does waste management become more your responsibility.

Decide whether to provide recycling options. If so, to what extent? Just paper, or glass, plastic, tins and so on? You can then decide how many bins you need to provide on site. To recycle costs more than standard waste management.

By providing appropriate bins, you help to minimise the quantity of waste on the ground, but some people will continue to drop their waste on the floor. The volume of litter increases if your event has a large amount of sampling or leafleting. Consider having litter pickers on the site during and after the event to help clear the site.

Consider contacting local volunteer groups to see whether they can assist.

If working with a local council, you may be able to negotiate for bins and litter pickers as part of the fee. However, ask before the event if there is a fee so you don't get a surprise cost at the end.

If your event is outdoors and you are bringing in portable toilets, you need to consider how to dispose of the human waste. Most companies that provide portable toilets take the waste away as part of the fee. If your event is only for one day, the toilets are unlikely to need to be emptied during the event. If the event is longer than one day, ask your toilet provider how often it will empty the toilets, and how it will do this.

You must leave the site in the state in which you received it; that includes removing rubbish bags.

Storage

People often underestimate the need for storage at an event. If you are producing an event at which there are giveaways, printed leaflets or samples, carefully work out what storage you require.

If your event is the only one happening at a venue, you can use your production office for some of the storage.

If you have a stand at an exhibition, many other exhibitors will also need space. Book the space you require far in advance, to ensure it's as close to your stand as possible. Think about how often you may need to re-stock your stand throughout the day, how much you can physically keep on your stand, and the location of the paid-for storage units.

Ask the supplier of your giveaways, leaflets and such like how many boxes it expects to fill and how it will pack the boxes. Your supplier or printer may be able to predict the number of boxes and pallets. A pallet is a portable platform, made of wood or plastic. Pallets can be moved and stacked (depending on what is on the pallet), most often by forklift trucks. If pallets are being delivered to your event, make sure you have a forklift truck on site to move them off the truck and to where your storage is situated.

A standard pallet size is $120 \times 100 \times 220$ centimetres. If the goods exceed these dimensions, typically by overhanging the pallet, the pallet is considered an oversized pallet and there may be knock-on implications for transportation and storage, due to the irregular size.

Pallet sizes differ in different markets. Check with your supplier to find out where the pallets are coming from.

Selecting and Contracting the Venue

Based on your original criteria and the evaluation of all your site visit data, you are hopefully in a position to select a venue. Make this decision in consultation with other people in your team, because it may have an impact far beyond just the production of the event. For example, whilst one venue may be perfect based on your criteria, your sales team may now need to change the opening hours, and therefore you need to select a different venue.

Next make sure that a contract is in place that details all of the plans, expectations and costs involved. Spend some time questioning the venue manager and reading the contract carefully. If you're not thorough, hidden extras such as corkage charges or management fees may slip by without you noticing – until you get the final bill, that is.

I recommend getting a second opinion on a contract; this is always a wise move. If you can ask someone with a legal background, all the better but any other person can help. Others may interpret clauses differently to you, and you then have the opportunity to go back to the venue to clarify the meaning.

Always establish clear cancellation costs with the venue and communicate these with your client.

An area that often trips people up is the cancellation clause charges. Whilst you may have every intention that your event will take place no matter what, you do need to be able to assess the financial implication if you did need to cancel the event or move it to another venue. Your client needs to know the cost up front rather than when trying to change venues late in the planning process.

Agreements with venues are another element of events that should be in writing. If the venue manager has promised you something, make sure it's in the contract; if the venue manager is hesitant about putting it in the contract, ask why.

Chapter 11

Who Does What: Front and Back of House

In This Chapter

▶ What is the difference between front and back of house?

▶ Hosts with the most at your event

▶ Briefing your team at the start of the show

▶ Clear communication on site

*A*s you manage more and more events, you're likely to start to get to know the variety of suppliers and freelancers who are specialists in specific roles. A good team makes the difference between a stressful and a successful event. There's no easy way to source freelancers, but they have a habit of finding you; it won't be long before you have so many offers that you won't know what to do with them.

If you're able to have a producer and/or production manager as part of your team (see Chapter 4), they will manage teams of lighting designers, sound operators, carpenters and security staff. These all report into the production manager, and the rest report to the producer or you.

In this chapter, I talk you through each of the different roles that you may need on show day and how to facilitate good team management on site. Chapter 4 gives you more information on the team you will need to help you with the planning, but it's always useful if you can involve any of the people mentioned in this chapter in the planning too.

Back of House

I can't say enough times how important your team is when you're planning an event and, especially, on the actual show day. *Back of house* refers to all those team members who your guests never know are there if everything goes smoothly. They're the ones who help you make everything happen, from the lights shining on the right part of the stage to the security staff being told when to let the crowds into the event site.

The size and type of event you're organising dictates the scale of the back-of-house team you require. You may meet some of them on the first day of your build, and some may be long-term partners on site, but remember how important team morale is. There's more on this in Chapter 4.

Lighting and sound designers

Most events that you plan have some basic element of lighting design and sound effects. The designers and operators may be part of the in-house team at the venue or you may need to bring them in. Before your event, bring a lighting and sound designer to the venue to see what you intend to do and to create a lighting and sound plan. Once you have a lighting plan, for example, someone who is an operator rather than a designer can then run the lighting during your show.

If you are able to hire a producer (see Chapter 4), your producer helps to direct the designers on site.

Graphics operators

A graphics operator helps design and create content for your event. More traditionally required in corporate events, graphics operators aren't likely to appear on your supplier list on a brand experience roadshow at a shopping centre. You probably need at least a couple of days pre-event for a graphics operator to help pull together presentation slides for your speakers. You also need to make sure your graphics operator is on site during your event; not only are there likely to be last-minute changes by your speaker that alter the order of the slides, but also they will help change any content on screens as required during the actual session.

 If you have basic presentation-software skills, you can complete the pre-event part of this role. (You may still want to consider hiring a graphics operator if you have a large number of slides to format and pull together for a big conference.)

During your event, your graphics operator works with your producer to ensure that every time your speaker needs a certain slide on display, it is on screen.

Set carpenters and riggers

The carpenters and riggers help put your set and stage together. If you have a stage, these guys help build it on site. Riggers and local crew are important: There are always more things that need positioning and moving from one place to another than you expect. Often a carpenter can recommend some riggers and local crew who they are happy working with. If not, loads of national companies exist.

Carpenters are often referred to as *chippies*.

Event control

Particularly on larger outdoor events where there are many radio communication channels, somebody needs to listen to all of them and make sure the messages are reaching the right people; that person is the event controller. For smaller events, you generally don't need an event controller.

Typically, the event controller sits in a portacabin or tent (marked clearly as Event Control) with all the communications channels open and a laptop. The event controller's job is to record all activity throughout the day, whether there are any security incidents, details of the weather, the number of visitors currently on site – basically anything of interest that you would like to know about after the event. One of the event controller's main responsibilities is to liaise with security staff and ensure that all relevant information is communicated.

Imagine you're running a family festival and a small child goes missing. The child is found, so all is well. If, however, the parent complains after the event about how the incident was handled, it's important to have a record of the exact time the child was declared missing, the actions taken and the time at which the child was found. As with everything in events, a paper trail always helps.

Show caller

A show caller may be used at events with speakers or some sort of audio-visual aspect – mainly conferences and awards ceremonies, but also stage shows at outdoor events. A running order has been written, everyone is in place, but who's going to make sure that everyone keeps to time? You're likely to be with your client or boss, talking through what's happening.

Someone else needs to be there with a clipboard and microphone, telling your crew how long until they need to have your star guest on stage.

For stage shows, a show caller cues up the walk-in music, speakers, videos, lighting designs and effects and so on. This person gives a countdown to the sound desk to ensure that as the lights change and someone walks to the lectern, the appropriate music is playing.

An experienced show caller doesn't have to be hugely involved in the planning process; provide a version of the production schedule and running order before the day starts, and an experienced show caller is good to go.

If someone in house is fulfilling the role of show caller, involve them in the planning process so they know the schedule and running order inside out.

Runner

Depending on the size of the event, make sure at least one person is a *runner*, someone whose responsibility it is to do all the little jobs that crop up during the event. It will depend not only on the size but how many elements there are to your event. If you have a conference in one room for 100 people, you are likely to only need one runner. If your event incorporates a conference, exhibition and gala dinner, even if all only for 100 people, it is likely you may need 2 or 3 to cover each element of the event. However well planned the event is, there is always something that needs to be bought or moved from one end of the venue to the other.

This broad remit needs to be someone's primary role. It's a great role for a volunteer.

Venue staff

Unless you're hosting your event at your own office or building, it's likely that the venue has some of its own staff present. If it's a dry-hire venue (where you hire the venue and none of the kit or furniture), this may just be an event co-ordinator for the venue, whose job is to ensure you stick to your contract and maintain all the health and safety rules that you've agreed to.

The venue staff need to report in to you, but they also occasionally act as a client if they want you to do something. As long as you adhere to your contract, you're not obliged to follow every order or request from venue staff. Remember, however, that venue staff can also make your life a lot more difficult than needs be if you don't have a good relationship with them.

If you're using some of the venue's internal technical team, it's important to be clear about who's in charge, because they may think that, on their turf, they know best. Now it's extremely likely that they *do* know best, because they know their kit and their venue, but it's important for your production manager (see Chapter 4) on site to ensure that they complete tasks in the way and the order planned.

A technical meeting before being on site and then on the show day is a good way of eliminating any potential problems with venue staff.

Front of House

Part of your team will interact with your guests, delegates or audience. This may be someone who takes down registration details or a person who serves at a bar. Depending on the venue, some of these people will be from the venue and some will need to be hired directly.

Brand ambassadors/hosts

Brand ambassadors, or hosts as they are often called in more corporate environments, are potentially the most under-rated part of your team. The brand ambassadors are the first people who your delegates and guests meet; they are the face of your event and/or brand. Anyone who represents your company or event on show day needs to be a good ambassador. This team needs to be hired in from a staffing agency.

If your event is one at which very little technical information is being discussed, consider recruiting hosts who are students studying a relevant field at a local university. Being a host offers students good experience and potentially a chance to network for their future too.

When selecting the team, consider what the brand would look like if it were a person. You need to create an army of people to bring your client's brand to life – their look, their personality, the language they use, the clothes they wear, all affect the impression that they make on the guests.

Whether it is a smartly dressed registration host at a conference or gala dinner, or a young, trendy looking guy on a skateboard, you need to select these people carefully to ensure the image of the brand and/or event is upheld.

Depending on the type of event, your hosts have different roles. They will welcome guests into an environment, whether that's taking a name of an invited guest at a registration desk or encouraging a young family to take part in a brand experience on a stand in a shopping centre. Hosts may be used as human signage (see Chapter 7) around an event, provide expert advice on products, or roam with microphones for question and answer sessions.

Your client may request that hosts are people from their organisation. The client's team may know the company, brand and/or event inside out and may be great at organising meetings internally, but they're not trained to speak to guests or members of the public. Sometimes it's best to leave the host role to the professionals!

You need to organise a briefing event for the brand ambassadors and hosts prior to the event to talk them through their roles but also to give them basic information about the brand or client messaging, so they can reflect the event in the right way when talking to guests.

'Voice of God'

'Voice of God' is a funny name; it refers to the person making announcements over a sound system to get the attention of your guests, but is not the pre-senter or host on a stage. There's no focal point for the guests or audience to look at, but they receive clear, directional information. A voice of God is mainly used in corporate events when trying to gather an audience in a room or welcome the host on stage.

The voice of God is a small role and can be done by you or any of your team members if they're happy to. No prior training is required: The person simply reads from a pre-prepared script into a microphone, although a clear voice obviously helps.

Timing plans often list these announcements as VOGs.

If you've ever seen the *National Lottery* on TV, Alan Dedicoat is referred to as the 'Voice of the Balls'. The voice of God is a similar concept. People don't know what this person looks like and they're unlikely to know his or her name, but they know they should trust this voice.

Waiters

Providing food for your guests is important at most events. You're likely to use the venue catering team, or you may consider bringing in an external caterer, depending on your requirements. Catering options are discussed more in Chapter 7.

Remember to request waiters from your supplier to serve the food at your event.

It's best, when possible, to source waiters and waitresses from your actual caterer rather than independently, because the waiting staff will be used to working with the caterer, and will understand the processes and standards required.

It's not necessary to meet the waiting staff before the event; however, if you want to reassure yourself about their standard of service, ask to visit another event that your caterers are supplying to see them in action.

Security staff

Not all events require a security team, but if you decide that you need them at your event, remember that they are an important part of your front and back of house team. Chapter 12 gives further information on security requirements and options. Security staff need to interact with your guests and audiences at points, and must be briefed about how you want them to behave on site.

Working with Your Team On Site

As human beings, we are programmed to need interaction with others, and thrive when in a group. This is what should happen on show day: You will hopefully thrive under pressure and with seeing the team of people around you all doing their jobs. One of the most common reasons for people wanting to work in events is because they feel that all the hard work is worth it when the event happens and they can see it all come together.

Whether your team is you plus one or you plus 100, teamwork gets you through the day. We spend so much time planning events for the visitor or guest but often forget to think about the team who will make it happen. The experience that your team has during the day is just as important. All it takes is for one grumpy graphics operator to not put the slides on at the correct point in the conference, and big problems start to happen – just because you've not kept your crew happy.

Ensuring clear team communication on the day

When planning a successful event, you spend a lot of time communicating with various people. This doesn't stop during the live event: Communicate with your client, your team and your audience when required.

Brief the team

Clearly defined roles and responsibilities help the smooth running of the show day. Whenever possible, get all the team to meet before the day itself, so everyone knows everyone else and understands the different types of role that a successful event requires; it's important that the team members empathise with each other.

Briefing the team is vitally important; plan into your production schedule 10–30 minutes at the beginning of the event for briefing everyone together. (See Chapter 9 for more about scheduling.) You may run through the schedule that everyone's already received, but this may also be a good opportunity to update the team on any developments in the last few hours. At this point, ask the key team members to stand up and introduce themselves; these simple things at the start of the day really do help make the team feel more joined up.

You also need to organise a health and safety briefing. The type of event dictates who gives the briefing. If you're doing a large public event, you may have a health and safety officer on site who can give the briefing, or your production manager may be able to do this at more technology-focused events. In some cases, you may need to give the briefing yourself. The main points to cover are:

- ✔ Emergency exits in the venue
- ✔ The procedure to follow in an emergency, dictated by the venue or your health and safety officer
- ✔ Who the trained first aider is and how to contact them
- ✔ Any specific risks at the event or venue

Lines of communication

A basic organisation chart on a wall in the production office can help with the smooth running of the day. If people know who does what, they're likely to talk to the person who can answer their question quickly and most effectively.

In Figure 11-1 I detail some of the roles and responsibilities that you need to have under control on show day.

If you have a small team, some people can take on more than one role.

Radio communication

For a large event spread across multiple rooms, or in a large outdoor space, you may struggle to locate some of your team. Particularly in conferences when silence is required in a room during a presentation, it's not really appropriate for the production manager to ask the producer to ask the lighting technician loudly whether he or she would like a cup of coffee!

SAFETY MANAGEMENT STRUCTURE

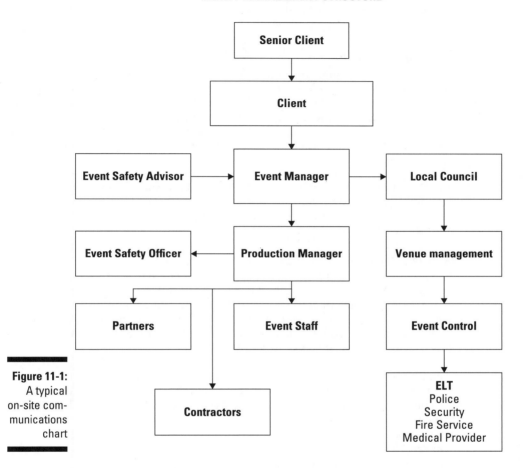

Figure 11-1:
A typical
on-site com-
munications
chart

More important requirements include queuing up content, presenters and/or bands, establishing crew members' locations on site and also assisting in any security or first aid issues. Walkie-talkies help enormously. A show caller can handle these roles when your budget allows for it.

For large events, you can set up multiple channels on radios for the different teams and workstreams, such as production, client, technical, security, and so on. By having these individual channels, you limit the number of requests and conversations over the radios to just those that each team needs to hear. On most radios it's possible to speak to all people on whichever channel when necessary; this feature is mainly used when there's a security alert.

All elements of an event have a cost associated, but radio communication is a small cost in the grand scheme of things and hugely helps with the smooth running of the event. You also protect your voice from a day of shouting – and let's be honest, everyone feels more important when they are wearing a radio mic and holding a clipboard!

Identifying your team

Being able to remember the names of all of your team on site is a great skill and makes the crew and any volunteer helpers feel truly part of the team. If you're working on a small event and you know your team well, you'll have no problem recognising them on site. However, during larger events, people may work for you on the show day who you've never met before; the likelihood of you remembering their names is pretty slim with everything else you have to think about.

But it's not only you who needs to recognise the team working at the event; any members of security on site need to be able to quickly find specific people, or a supplier may need to find someone to discuss moving a vehicle from the loading bay.

Basic identification

A relatively cheap and easy way of identifying people is with a name badge or *lanyard*. A lanyard is a length of cord or ribbon that you wear around your neck holding a piece of card or plastic containing information about your access requirements and your identification. The cards can either be professionally printed or you can make them yourself. Most large stationers sell lanyards and plastic sleeves for name badges.

Consider what you intend to do for your guests at the same time and take the same approach for cost savings. For example, if you're doing lanyards for your staff and guests, it will be cheaper to organise and order them at the same time.

Branded identification

If you have a little more budget to spend, you can consider having matching branded T-shirts printed. There are many companies available that you can find from looking on the Internet, or start with a print shop local to you. Printed T-shirts can cost anything from £4–10, depending on their quality.

If you're ever in Nandos check out their staff members' T-shirts which have phrases such as 'Spicy Bird'! on them. Image is important and sets the tone of the event, so what your crew looks like makes an impact.

If you are organising branded T-shirts for the team working on the event, make sure you buy each member more than one each. If you're working five days straight on site, no one will have a chance to do any laundry.

Looking after your team

The importance of a happy team cannot be overestimated. One easy way to keep the team happy is to provide plenty of food. (See Chapter 7 where I look at catering options.) As Napoleon Bonaparte famously said, 'An army marches on its stomach.' Working long hours, particularly when doing manual labour and running around, as people do in event management, is tiring work and makes for a hungry team.

Always include in the production schedule the times and location of crew catering; the last thing you want is 25 people coming up to you individually and asking the same question.

It may be beneficial for you to pre-empt the inevitable a little further and provide meal tokens to each crew member. This way you can manage who's entitled to what and give your caterer a little bit of an easier job by not having to try to remember who has already been fed. Simple raffle tickets would suffice or mock up a small bit of text that you can print out multiple times and cut up for distribution.

Snacks, tea and coffee and a dry and warm room are basic requirements, but it's amazing how many people forget the team that are putting on the event as they focus on the guests. The event can't happen without either group, so the crew deserve the same attention as the guests.

Part IV
Considering Potential Problems

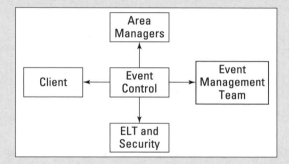

In this part . . .

✔ Understand your responsibilities on health and safety, and learn about your duty of care towards your guests.

✔ Gain a working knowledge of health and safety legislation.

✔ Get to grips with potential hazards, and the intricacies of risk assessment and risk management.

✔ Make proper provision for the weather and other possible events beyond your control.

✔ Develop a plan to make sure everything and everyone turns up on time – no matter what.

Chapter 12

Keeping Healthy, Safe and Secure

. . . .

In This Chapter

▶ Understanding what you're responsible for

▶ Creating an event safety plan

▶ What should be in a risk assessment?

▶ Remembering fire safety

▶ Protecting children and the public from harm

▶ Assessing your security requirements

. . . .

Keeping everyone at your event, including your team, healthy, safe and secure on site is your main responsibility, regardless of your objectives for putting on the event. This area can take a while to get your head around, because there are so many elements to consider, but if you don't follow the basic steps, you risk an accident to a member of your team, a member of the general public, people in your business (including your employer), your client or even yourself.

You have a duty of care when planning your event, and you need to take responsibility if any incidents or accidents occur. You may decide to hire an event health and safety officer, who can advise you specifically. In this chapter, I guide you through the various regulations you need to be aware of, and outline practical steps to ensure you create a safe environment around your event.

Your Health and Safety Responsibilities

A wise person once said, 'Safety doesn't happen by accident.' You need to be aware of a significant amount of health and safety legislation. I provide an overview below. If your budget extends to a production manager and/or an event safety officer, this person can advise and support you to put processes into place to adhere to the legal requirements. Health and safety may sound dull, but stick with me; your event will benefit and your audience will be full of happy and healthy individuals.

If you are likely to organise large public events, spend some time familiarising yourself with *The Event Safety Guide* by the Health and Safety Executive, known in the industry as the 'purple guide'.

Complying with the Health and Safety at Work Act (1974)

When organising an event, you have a duty of care to your event team to remove or minimise any risks that you can identify. You're responsible for the team working at the event as well as any guests or delegates who attend your event.

The Health and Safety at Work Act (1974) contains many sections, but you need to bear two in particular in mind.

- ✔ **Section 2:** This covers the health and safety of employees, stating that 'It shall be the duty of every employer to ensure, so far as is reasonably practicable, the health, safety and welfare at work of all his employees.' Check out the full details at www.legislation.gov.uk/ukpga/1974/37/section/2

- ✔ **Section 3:** The main thrust of this section is the responsibility the event organiser has to guests and other non-staff members. As it says: 'It shall be the duty of every employer . . . to ensure . . . that persons not in his employment . . . are not thereby exposed to risks to their health and safety.' Take a look at www.legislation.gov.uk/ukpga/1974/37/section/3 for the inside track.

Responsible drinking into the night

It's your responsibility to speak to the local authorities before your event. Agree on how you can implement measures during the event to ensure that any guests under the influence of alcohol don't interrupt the peace in a public place. Below are some suggestions that help satisfy the local authorities that you're putting useful processes in place:

- ✔ Serve all drinks in plastic bottles or receptacles

- ✔ Take measures to prevent open bottles or other drinks containers being carried beyond the licensed premises

- ✔ Place restrictions on bringing glass bottles and alcohol into the licensed premises, where appropriate

- ✔ Restrict drinks promotions

- ✔ Use an appropriate number of stewards or other security staff at access and exit points and in other appropriate locations

✔ Conduct search procedures if deemed necessary upon consultation with the police

✔ Light the event arena during hours of darkness

While working with local authorities, you're likely to have to provide information for and attend a Safety Advisory Group (SAG) meeting. The local authority and emergency services generally hold SAGs monthly to discuss upcoming events and any concerns they have over public safety.

Protecting children from harm

You may work in events for years and never manage an event where children attend, but the first event you do teaches you a lot! Children add a whole other dimension to event management, and child safety is one major part of that. As the event manager, putting steps into place to protect children from harm is essential, even if parents are also attending the event.

Any paid team members who will interact with children need to be checked by the Criminal Records Bureau (CRB) to see whether they have any convictions, cautions, reprimands and warnings on the Police National Computer.

Put a detailed emergency communication plan in place. This example is from a family festival:

Brief all the team at the start of the day on the procedure.

✔ If a lost child is discovered, that child will remain in the location in which he or she become separated from the adult, to try and expedite reuniting them. The member of event staff who discovered the lost child will remain with the child, along with one other member of staff who will have been summoned by radio. No member of staff will be left alone with a child.

The area manager will inform Event Control of the lost child, using an agreed code word such as 'Petra'.

  • Petra Major means parents have lost a child.

  • Petra Minor means the child has approached staff because he or she has lost its parents.

✔ If there is a lost child, Event Control will radio all staff and inform them to close all exits. Exits will remain closed until the situation is resolved. Adults can exit as long as they are not accompanied by children.

✔ All radio-holding staff to wear earpieces so no radio communication can be heard by the public. In the event of a lost child – and with parental consent – a description of the child will be given to all radio-holding staff so they can help find the child.

✔ Public address announcements about lost children will be general in nature and not give any specific information about particular children. 'Any parents and guardians who have become/may find themselves separated from young children in their care should contact one of the event representatives in a blue or green hi-vis jacket.'

✔ Only in exceptional circumstances should it be necessary to make a public address announcement to contact a lost child. 'If (name) is in the event arena will they please identify themselves to a member of the venue security for assistance.'

✔ The event team – with the parent – will make a decision on when to notify the police. A decision to notify the police will follow the communication to stewards and a thorough search of the site, and if a child has not been found within a two-hour window following notification, if not sooner.

✔ If there is on-site police presence, the event manager and event control will liaise initially with site police.

Some steps that you can take to help minimise potential issues include:

✔ Upon entry to the site, offer parents sticky labels on which to write a mobile telephone number, so they can be contacted if separated from their child.

✔ Create a 'lost children' area manned by trained and police-checked staff. Limit access to the area and ensure that it is well hidden from passers-by. Before parents can claim their lost child, a form should be filled out and signed to ensure that the child is being reunited with his or her parents or carers.

✔ If an event is unsuitable for children of a particular age, state this in all publicity and promotion. Fully brief all stewards and security staff at access points about any age restriction policies.

✔ If the event is purely child focused, do not give access to adults who are not accompanied by a child.

✔ Ensure robust proof-of-age provisions, including signage at all venues within licensed premise, where alcohol or age-restricted activities are taking place.

Fire safety

Fire safety is important at any event. Consider the following:

✔ Ensure sufficient fire-fighting equipment is in place.

✔ Check fire detection and alarm systems.

✔ Identify sources of fire ignition.

✔ Provide sufficient fire exits.

✔ Put in place procedures for waste disposal.

Fire exits and emergency vehicle routes must never be blocked or obstructed.

If you plan to use fireworks or pyrotechnics (indoor fireworks), you must have a risk assessment in place; this provides information on storing the fireworks and on separation distances when setting them up.

Ensure that all stewards know where fire safety equipment is and how to use it.

Assessing your security requirements

In 2001, the Private Security Industry Act was passed, which details the legal responsibilities for those connected with the events industry. If you use a reputable security firm, you don't need to worry too much about the details of the Act.

Consider three options when planning your security provision: Security guards, stewards and volunteers. You can use all three roles at one event, in different levels.

The level of security that you need is affected by the:

✔ Number of guests

✔ Number of entry points

✔ Age and demographic of your guests

✔ Amount of alcohol available

✔ Number of VIPs attending

Burning down the house: A cautionary tale

For a gala dinner in a large marquee, an event organiser sourced designer candelabras to be positioned on each of the 30 tables. The candelabras were not fire-retardant; two hours into the event, the candles had burnt down considerably and set fire in turn to each and every candelabra. The event had to be stopped and the marquee evacuated.

Security guards

Ensure that any security guards on site have the appropriate Security Industry Authority (SIA) licence. There are various levels of licences depending on the role that the individual needs to take. For example door supervisors, close protection, security guards. A local security firm can recommend what levels of licence you need for your event.

The industry standard is one member of security staff to 100 people for an indoor event, and one member of security staff to 250 people at an outdoor event.

Stewards

Stewards can perform many tasks at your event that they do not require a licence for, and as such are slightly cheaper than security staff. Stewards can undertake the following tasks, plus many more:

- ✔ Directing guests around a site to areas such as toilets, first aid points and refreshment stands
- ✔ Assisting in crowd management and people flow around *pinch points* (narrow or easily obstructed areas)
- ✔ Directing guests to seating areas by checking tickets
- ✔ Keeping crowds clear of emergency exits
- ✔ Providing assistance if an evacuation procedure is put in place

Security firms can normally also provide stewards as well as security staff. Just speak to your security supplier for advice.

Provide all stewards with coloured safety bibs, for example in orange or yellow, to make them easily identifiable on site.

Volunteers

If you want to keep costs down, consider volunteers; they are a great opportunity to ensure good people management on site and enable people in the local area to get involved.

Pick your volunteers carefully, though; make sure you or someone in your team meets each volunteer before he or she goes on site. You may not be paying them, but your volunteers still represent you and your client at the event.

If volunteers on site are doing similar activities to a steward, they don't require an SIA licence but can't receive any reward, benefit or payment in kind. Payment of out-of-pocket expenses (such as for travelling to and from the event) is not considered payment in kind so is allowed.

Complying with the Equality Act 2010

The Equality Act 2010 gives people with special needs equal rights to attend, participate in and enjoy all events. As the event organiser, it's your responsibility to ensure you comply with the Act and guide your client through the options and processes.

A disabled person is defined as someone who has a physical or mental impairment which has an effect on his or her ability to carry out normal day-day-day activities. This includes people who:

- ✔ Are blind or visually impaired.
- ✔ Are deaf or hard of hearing.
- ✔ Have heart conditions.
- ✔ Have learning disabilities.
- ✔ Have mobility and manual dexterity problems.
- ✔ Have experienced mental health problems.
- ✔ Have dyslexia.
- ✔ Have epilepsy.
- ✔ Have incontinence.

The code explains the duties that service providers such as you have to:

- ✔ Not treat disabled people less favourably than non-disabled people.
- ✔ Make reasonable adjustments to your services so that disabled people can access them.

Not only is it illegal not to comply, but it would be costly in terms of the bad PR that it may generate. The impact of not complying with the Equality Act, and the legal implications, mean that the requirements of the Act can be a daunting area to tackle for the first time.

You can follow some basic steps, and don't forget that your team is likely to include someone who's more experienced than you, whether a production manager, the venue manager or even a caterer.

If you hire a venue, the venue manager is responsible for ensuring that the venue meets the required standards. You do, however, have a duty to make sure that you believe that the venue is taking every possible step to ensure that the physical features of the venue have been made as accessible as possible.

Around 10 million disabled people live in the UK. Disabled people are likely to make up a large proportion of your target market.

Ensuring accessibility

'Access' to an event doesn't refer to just physical access, but also the information that's provided.

In terms of physical access, you need to provide:

- Ramps for wheelchair users
- Wheelchair-accessible toilets
- Raised viewing platforms to allow those using wheelchairs to raise them above standing height

Providing information

Consider providing your information in alternative formats such as braille or audio. Even just providing information in a larger font size (such as 14-point size and above) helps those with visual impairments to access your information. Not only disabled visitors benefit; all your guests do.

The Royal National Institute for the Blind (RNIB) can advise on who to contact to arrange transcriptions if required.

Lighting effects

On television and in the cinema, you may have heard warnings about flash photography or strobe lighting. If your event is going to have anything similar, consider how you inform people with conditions such as epilepsy or tinnitus.

A simple sign on entry and a short announcement before the lighting effects start is sufficient.

Briefing staff

It's not enough to just make sure that all the physical elements are in place; you need to brief your team to be aware of the implications. Even if your team only consists of one other person, make sure that person is aware if you are expecting any disabled guests, and knows how to accommodate the person in your event.

Catering safely for your team and guests

When booking caterers for your event, ensure that they are currently achieving the standards required by the Food Safety (General Food Hygiene) Regulations 1995. To adhere to these standards, the caterers will have to ensure that their equipment meets the following basic requirements. The facilities should:

✔ Be clean and maintained properly, so that everything works.

✔ Be designed and constructed to enable them to be kept clean and hygienic.

✔ Have an adequate supply of drinking water.

✔ Have suitable controls against pests, particularly scavengers like rats.

✔ Have adequate lighting, whether natural or electric.

✔ Be properly ventilated, whether by natural or mechanical means.

✔ Have clean toilets that do not lead directly into food rooms.

✔ Have adequate handwashing facilities.

✔ Be provided with sufficient drainage.

You need to provide clean water for the caterers, not just for handwashing but for boiling water for food preparation, and so on.

The Working At Height regulations (2005)

These regulations do not ban ladders, but say you can use ladders only when you have ruled out all other safer alternatives for work at height. A risk assessment must show that the task is low risk and of short duration, or that features of the site make other equipment inappropriate. If so, you can use ladders.

Personal Protective Equipment (PPE)

PPE is all equipment that is intended to be worn or held by a person at work, and that protects them from one or more risks to their health and safety. Such equipment may include warm- and wet-weather clothing, as well as more common items such as hard hats, protective footwear, gloves, climbing harnesses and ear defenders.

Provide PPE 'only as a last resort' when a risk assessment deems the use of such equipment necessary.

At a conference in Indonesia for a leading bank, the British event management company arrived to find the local crew wearing flip-flops whilst on site – not safe and definitely didn't adhere to their agreed risk assessment!

Making Sure All the Paperwork is in Place

To be a good event manager, you have got to learn to love paperwork. It's not an appealing thought, I appreciate, but you will thank me in the end.

The process of thinking through what's required in the paperwork and the process of writing it hugely helps with the health and safety aspects of your event.

Certain types of document are applicable more to certain types of events. For example, an event safety plan is for large events mainly in a public place; you're unlikely to have to compile one for a conference or press launch inside an existing venue.

You need to complete all paperwork before your event and, more often than not, you aren't given permission to do the event unless the venue and local authority have seen and approved the paperwork.

When you go on site for the build of your event, make sure you have an event manager pack. This contains:

- Production schedule
- Risk assessment and method statement
- Any permits required for music usage
- Temporary event licence
- Copies of all contracts and agreement letters with suppliers and the venue

This pack is a record of all of the necessary documents to put the event on, in case anybody needs to refer to, for example, the health and safety procedures. In a rather large folder, which will take the best part of an hour to print and compile, you're likely to have hundreds of pieces of paper. It is, however, good practice to create this record.

In an ideal situation, you don't need to open the folder during the whole event. You can guarantee, though, that if you don't have your event manager pack, you will be asked to show something. Even though you may have your laptop with you, on which you've stored all these documents, I still suggest printing one copy of everything and storing the folder in a secure place. If a fire officer comes to check your evacuation plans, you can quickly show a print version without having to start up your laptop.

Creating an Event Safety Plan

Create an event safety plan well in advance of any large or public-facing events. Depending on how much time you have been given from your client for the whole planning process, ideally create this plan a few months in advance, then circulate it to the following groups:

- Client
- Venue

- Police
- Fire and rescue service
- Ambulance service
- Local enforcement authority

It's not unusual for several drafts of the event safety plan to be produced to take account of all the safety elements of the event and the associated procedures. Don't worry if you're on version 6 by the time it's approved!

The event safety plan contains information under the following headings:

- **Event overview:** This is to help put into context what the event is for and for whom. Referring back to your original brief will help you write this section. See Chapter 1 for more information on this.

- **Venue overview:** This should cover information such as the contact/directional details, a floor plan and any specific access information. (See Chapter 10 for information on questions you should ask whilst on a site visit and therefore the information you should then provide to suppliers.)

- **Risk assessment:** This shows all readers that you have considered all the potential risks, but more importantly how you are minimising or removing those risks. See later in this chapter for more information on how to write a risk assessment.

- **Event health, safety and welfare:** As covered throughout this chapter, there are various methods that can be used to ensure your team's and guest's welfare at your event. The reader of this document will not need to know every individual plan, but more an overview that you are aware of what is required and any specific details that may be pertinent to the local authorities.

- **Stage, temporary structures and infrastructure:** Provide an overview of any major structure, of their manufacturer and any health and safety notes such as wind speed ratings. See Chapter 10 for more information about site infrastructure.

- **Electrical systems:** Information on the level of power that is required and how this is being provided and maintained on site.

- **Food, refreshments and traders:** You are likely to provide food for your guests but also for your crew. Give information in the event safety plan about the food – not whether it will be lamb or chicken, but how many caterers you will have on site and the types of food-preparation techniques they will be using. See Chapter 7 for more information on catering.

- **Waste disposal:** Detail your plan for this – whether you will be having recycling bins, how often these will be emptied and whether you are employing litter pickers, for example.

✔ **Security/stewarding:** Include information on how many staff will be on site and any particular processes they will need to follow. There is information earlier in this chapter on different security options.

✔ **Crowd/traffic management:** This will be of particular interest to the local authorities who will want to ensure that you have taken adequate precautions to manage large movements of people. See later in this chapter for methods of crowd management at events.

✔ **Organisation and contractors:** Chapters 4 and 11 cover the team members that you will have on-site and you should include a little information on these in your event safety plan. An organisation chart (see Chapter 4) will help show outside readers how your on-site team will be structured and who will be responsible for what.

✔ **Communications:** In Chapter 11 you will find information about on-site communication with your team and guests. A basic overview of this should be provided in your event safety plan.

✔ **Medical/first aid provision:** Detail who on site will be available to provide first aid attention and how they can be contacted. Later in this chapter I give you some options about who you should consider having on site.

✔ **Fire precautions and equipment:** Your health and safety advisor and production manager will be able to help you fill in this section of the event safety plan. Readers will want to know what your exit routes are, how many extinguishers you have, where they are and who will use them in case of an emergency.

✔ **Sanitary accommodation:** Include information on how many toilets are provided and how often they will be serviced during your event.

✔ **Emergency procedures:** This is an area where the local authorities will want to see lots of detail and feel confident that you are responsible enough to deal with emergencies on site. This chapter provides insight into the procedures that need to be considered and documented.

✔ **Event inspection:** Cover when and whom will inspect your site and sign off the site in terms of structures and health and safety. See Chapter 9 for more information on the order of this process on site.

✔ **Accident reporting and investigation:** At the end of this chapter you will find some information on how to deal with accidents and what needs to be done on site. An overview of your process needs to be included.

✔ **Provisions for people with special needs:** Adhering to the Equality Act is important. See earlier in this chapter for some basic pointers. Provide information in your event safety plan as to what visitors with various special needs will need to do.

▸ **Contingency plans:** Show the local authorities that you have considered all the main potential issues by putting contingency plan examples in your event safety plan. Chapter 13 provides more information on what these should cover.

Undertaking risk assessments

A risk assessment focuses your thinking around health and safety on your site. It can be defined as the identification, evaluation, and calculation of the levels of risks involved in a situation, how this compares to acceptable benchmarks, and what remedial action for reducing the risk need to be taken.

Many standard templates are available, such as the one in Figure 12-1. You can expect a risk assessment to look a lot more uniform than a contingency plan, for example, although both documents cover much the same areas.

A suitable and sufficient risk assessment is a legal requirement under the Health and Safety at Work Act. Your risk assessment should focus your health and safety management of your event site.

If your budget allows, employ a specialist company to write this document for you.

RISK ASSESSMENT FORM

Date Assessed:	Assessor's Name & Title:	Location/Event:	Stand Number:
Contact Telephone Number:	Mobile Number:	Email Address:	

Hazard Identified:	Person(s) at Risk:	Low, Medium or High	Control Measures In Place Or Required:	Residual Risk Level
Slips, trips & falls	Contractors	Low	All cables etc. will besecured away behind stock walling so as not to present a trip hazard. Cables to plinth to be taped to floor or rubber ramp used.	Low
Heavy lifting	Contractors	Medium	All contractors to adhere to safety guidelines when lifting heavy goods	
Materials used, fire hazard	Staff Visitors Contactors	Low	All materials used are in line with guidelines and meet fire ratings	Low
Structural	Staff Visitors Contactors	Low	Stock walling to be braced and weighted at back to prevent toppling over	Low
Tools – Injury	Contractors	Medium	Health and Safety Regulations to be adhered to by all contractors with First Aid kit on site. No Tools are to be left unattended and all tools will be cordless.	Medium

Figure 12-1:
A risk assessment template

To accurately assess risk:

1. **Identify the hazards.**

   Consider and make a list of risks such as:

- Slips, trips and fall hazards
- Vehicle movement on-site
- Fire hazards and risks
- Manual labour
- Working-at-height risks
- Sound levels
- Crowd management
- Event-specific risks such as handling dangerous animals or quad biking

2. **Decide who might be harmed and how.**

   Consider groups such as:

   - Audience
   - Members of the public not attending the event
   - Contractors
   - Exhibitors/performers/presenters, and so on
   - Stewards/volunteers
   - Employees
   - Special-care groups such as children, the elderly or disabled people

3. **Evaluate the risks and decide on precautions.**

   The risks need to be classified into high, medium and low. If the risk can't be removed entirely, you need to consider how to bring the risk down to an acceptable level. You may have the following risks:

   - High-risk: Back injuries during manual handling.
   - Medium-risk: Cutting hands during litter collection
   - Low-risk: Bins being too full during the event. (A low-risk item isn't included in the risk assessment; it's just assessed during the planning stage.)

   The simplest style of risk assessment is simply broken down into high, medium and low risk by using your judgement. Another approach to calculating this is to use the formula: Risk rating = severity × likelihood of the incident happening. See Table 12-1 for how to calculate risk in this way.

4. **Record your findings and implement them.**

5. **Review your assessment and update it if necessary.**

Table 12-1	Calculating a risk rating		
Severity	**Severity Likelihood**		
Low = 1	1	2	3
Medium = 2	2	4	6
High = 3	3	6	9

The risk ratings you can see in Table 12-1 are categorised as follows:

- 6–9 = High risk – action required to reduce risk

- 3–5 = Medium risk – seek to reduce risk further

- 1–2 = Low risk – no action, but continue to monitor

The severity of a risk is defined as follows:

- High = Fatality or major injury causing long-term disability

- Medium = Injury or illness causing short-term disability

- Low = Other injury or illness

Likelihood of risk falls into three categories:

- High = Certain or near certain

- Medium = Reasonably likely

- Low = Seldom or never

Figure 12-2 shows part of a completed risk assessment.

RISK ASSESSMENT–Event Specific Risks										
Hazard	Ref:	To whom:	Uncontrolled Risk *Severity x Likelihood = Risk rating*			Minimise risk by:	Residual risk: *Severity x Likelihood = Risk rating*			Further action needed:
			S	L	R		S	L	R	
Competence: All Event Management staff should be competent to carry out the tasks they are asked to perform. If not, they may be exposing themselves to hazards they are unaware of, and therefore may injure themselves needlessly.	G-1	Staff, freelancers, contractors and the general public.	3	3	H	All Sledge staff's competence for tasks is carried out as part of the Company's training process. All training records are regularly reviewed by Line Managers.	2	1	L	
Schedule Management: There is a risk that if any party starts to fall outside the schedule, the impact on other workers may increase the risk of an accident.	G-2	Staff, freelancers, contractors and the general public.	2	3	H	The Production Manager will ensure that the schedule is adhered to as closely as possible. In the event that the schedule becomes impractical, a revised schedule must be discussed in consultation with all parties. The Production Manager will issue the Call Sheet prior to the event.	1	1	L	All Sub -Contractors should ensure that the Production Manager has a single point of contact within each department. In the event of a Sub -Contractor being no longer able to work within the schedule, they must inform the Production Manager as soon as possible. All Sub contractors should ensure that copies of the Call Sheet are passed to all their staff before starting work on Site.

Figure 12-2: Part of a completed risk assessment

Having emergency procedures in place

A variety of incidents may occur at your event that require you or your team to invoke an emergency procedure. In the event of a major incident, it may be necessary to evacuate the entire event site or individual areas of the event site. An emergency evacuation carries its own risks and should only be undertaken when absolutely necessary.

It's impossible to predict every situation that may necessitate the evacuation of the event site, and it's not possible to have prescriptive procedures for every eventuality or details of how an evacuation would take place. These example emergency procedures therefore set out the framework for action, taking into consideration the configuration of the site and the event infrastructure.

Whilst you may be the responsible person, you don't manage everything on your own.

Before arriving on site, think through what the communication process should be if an incident occurs. In an emergency situation, it's useful to have one point of contact. For example, see Figure 12-3.

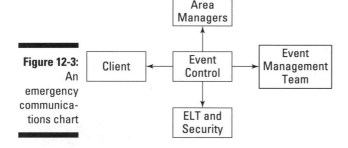

Figure 12-3: An emergency communications chart

Manage your wider team's health and safety too

As the event organiser, you're responsible for the actions of your contractors. It's therefore important that you obtain the following documents from your contractors and keep them on file in case any incidents occur and they need to be investigated:

- Health and safety policy
- Risk assessments
- Method statements

✔ Certification for materials used, for example, fire rating certificates for fabric chairs

✔ Structural engineers' certificates

✔ Public liability insurance policy

Negotiating the First Aid Minefield

To identify what level of first aid cover you require, it's always prudent to consider the following:

✔ Whether the event is indoor or outdoor as weather can have a big impact on ground conditions

✔ Time of year

✔ Duration of event

✔ Audience profile

✔ Proximity of the nearest accident and emergency department

✔ Availability of alcohol

In general, the more people, the more alcohol is available, the greater the extremity of weather possible and the further away the local Accident and Emergency hospital department, the more first aid presence you will need on site.

Whilst it's good practice for you to be first-aid trained, have someone else who is responsible for first aid on show day. You will have many things to consider, and many fully trained organisations can help.

At an internal venue, such as a conference centre or hotel, a trained first aider is likely to be on site – check this before the event. If a trained first aider is available, you don't need to arrange for additional support. If you have a production manager on site, you may find that this person is first-aid trained, but check this.

If you're hosting an event in a public or outdoor space, the Red Cross and St John's Ambulance both offer event services for a small fee. They are experts in their field and are reassuring names for your audience to see. It's possible to book first-aiders, ambulances and even cycle-response teams to attend your event. Other groups also offer a first-aid service, of course; speak to the local authority where the event will take place and ask who it uses for local public events.

Where there are no significant risks, at small events provide two first aiders per 1,000 people.

Managing Crowds

Good crowd management can completely change the experience that someone has at an event. Can you think of any events at which you were herded or trodden on in the queue? Scrums are most common when you're queuing for music festivals or while people are waiting to see a celebrity. How much more enjoyable would your experience have been without a stiletto in your toe?

In essence, crowd management is as it sounds: Managing the flow of large groups of people around a site, safely and securely.

As detailed by the Health and Safety Executive on their website (www.hse.gov.uk), the hazards that large numbers of people can pose are:

- Crushing between people
- Crushing against fixed structures, such as barriers
- Trampling underfoot
- Surging, swaying or rushing
- Aggressive behaviour
- Dangerous behaviour, such as climbing on equipment or throwing objects

Occupancy capacities

Ensure that your venue is large enough to accommodate your guests. When deciding the capacity with the venue, take into account the following:

- Layout of the venue/space
- Viewing areas
- Seating arrangements
- Site/venue infrastructure
- Fire exits/routes
- Circulation areas and customer flow

The 2010 Love Parade disaster

The 2010 Love Parade, an electronic dance music festival in Germany, is a prime example of the disastrous consequences of bad crowd management.

To manage the crowds and direct people to the one ramped access point into the event, 3,200 police were on hand. The capacity of the venue was 250,000 but over 1.3 million people tried to attend the event. Police told visitors to turn around because of the overcrowding, but people ignored the instructions and continued to access the event.

Twenty-one people died on the 24 July from suffocation, with over 500 people being injured.

This incident could have been avoided. It was concluded that not one single mistake caused the disaster but a mixture of many factors:

- The site was too small for the event

- The site opened late, and so people were already queuing up

- The access route was unsuitable for the expected number of attendees, due to a major pinch point on the ramp

- Large numbers of queuing people had limited access to refreshments and toilet facilities

- No entertainment was present outside the main site, thus there was little to distract the attendees

- There was no PA system across the access points

- When the police stopped people entering, their physical position also restricted people exiting the site

- The start of the evacuation procedure was delayed because of a limited number of communication channels

Some nationally recognised occupancy capacities, as advised by the Health and Safety Executive, are:

- Standing audience: One person per 0.5 square metres

- Seated audience: One person per 1 square metre

- Gala dinner: One person per 1.5 square metres

- Queuing lanes: One person per 0.65 square metres

Assessing the situation

Crowd management can be daunting, but as with many things in events, it's all about putting yourself in your audience's shoes. If you can begin to understand what's going through your guests' heads, you can get a good idea of what may work and what won't.

A crowded house: Getting capacity wrong

A company organising a fashion show for London Fashion Week booked an old warehouse in Covent Garden for its show. The company didn't calculate the maximum audience capacity. Two hours before the show, the local fire safety officer visited. Based on the number of guests expected, the officer worked out the maximum audience capacity; the company received an enforcement notice and had to cancel the event, because there was insufficient space in the venue to accommodate all of the guests.

For award ceremonies and festivals, for example, the push of the crowd towards the stage when the gates open may be the issue – not the queuing system while everyone is waiting.

At events for which large numbers of children (or drunk people!) queue, individuals may keep making trips to the toilet and then push back into the queue, often upsetting the people around them.

The HSE also recognises the following hazards presented by venues, so think about your plans and which hazards may affect your event:

- Slipping or tripping due to inadequately lit areas or poorly maintained floors and the build-up of rubbish
- Moving vehicles sharing the same route as pedestrians
- Collapse of a structure such as a fence or barrier, which falls onto the crowd
- People being pushed against objects such as unguarded hot cooking equipment on a food stall
- Objects, such as stalls, that obstruct movement and cause congestion during busy periods
- Crowd movements obstructed by people queuing at bars and such like
- Cross-flows as people cut through the crowd to get to other areas, such as toilets
- Failure of equipment, such as turnstiles
- Sources of fire, such as cooking equipment

Simple methods of crowd management

The main challenge for crowd management tends to be when queues form – at entry, at a bar, for toilets, and so on. The techniques to use to manage crowds in each of these areas are largely the same.

Human power

Having volunteers, stewards and security staff, if correctly briefed and identified, help with crowd management. The level of risk that your audience poses in terms of crowd management helps dictate the type of personnel to involve in the process.

Having people telling visitors where to go and when to stop can create a more immediate impact than any amount of signage or barriers.

Queuing systems

A good queuing system is one of the first things that your guests see, and their experience of this can impact how they remember and feel about the whole event – first impressions count, as we know.

The number of people expected and the entry points to your event dictate the type of queuing system to use. If you have one long access road, you're likely to employ a single queue system because there isn't space for a zig-zag pattern. If you have a wider space, a zig-zag approach is easier and gives a more efficient use of space.

Don't forget to allow space in your queuing system for your audience to exit your event if needed through the same point.

Unless you're likely to put on many similar events, it's worth hiring the ropes and posts. This equipment can take up a lot of space and is also likely to incur storage costs, so it's often more cost-effective to hire it in.

Crowd/pedestrian barriers

Crowd barriers are low barriers that create a physical and psychological barrier. People could easily jump over the barriers, but they act as a deterrent and encourage crowds to follow a certain path. Barriers are often hooked together to create a zig-zag path to maximise the queuing space. If you've ever been to Disneyland, it's the kind of queuing system they have there.

Rope and post

Posts linked by ropes are an excellent option for more formal-looking queuing systems. You often see rope barriers at museums, art galleries and VIP entrances to clubs and exhibitions. Options include a traditional twisted rope with metal posts, or there are now also retractable nylon or plastic versions too.

Stage barriers

If your event includes a production on stage that's likely to generate a lot of interest from your audience, erect a crowd barrier to prevent members of the public accessing the stage. Mojo barriers are a type of barrier that have a base that points towards the audience; as people in the crowd move forward, they stand on the base, so the barrier can't be pushed forward.

Accidents Do Happen

Accidents happen. We know this, but many can be prevented. (I cover examples of how to prevent them earlier in this chapter.) Understanding that accidents can and do happen at events can help with the shock when one does happen. Although an accident at your event is never a nice experience, don't blame yourself and instead focus on fixing the situation.

What to do in the event of an accident?

If you're the responsible person, you need to follow several steps if an accident or incident occurs during your event:

- ✔ Make the scene safe by removing any immediate dangers such as fallen debris and clearing people from the area. You will need to decide whether the injured person should be moved or not based on the severity of their injuries, but the area should be cleared of other people just in case.

- ✔ Contact the appropriate emergency services, either by phone or, if they are on site, through the venue management if appropriate (follow your emergency procedure).

- ✔ Adopt a treatment-before-facts approach; that is, make sure the emergency services obtain access to the accident scene, and so on.

- ✔ Start a written log; any notepaper suffices. Keep it with you at all times so you can note down any observations you have, such as the progress of the injured person and any treatment you have provided

✔ Preserve the scene and any equipment or tools involved, where possible.

✔ Inform the company's managing director, health and safety manager, insurer and client.

✔ Keep everyone who was involved in the accident or incident on site.

How serious is the accident?

Understanding the different levels of incident that can happen enables you to take the appropriate action and document it correctly. Here are some standard definitions that event personnel understand:

✔ **Minor injuries:** Require on-site treatment, but no need for a visit to an Accident and Emergency department.

✔ **Significant injuries:** Treatment required; it's recommended that the casualty is taken to the Accident and Emergency department.

✔ **Major injuries:** An injury that requires admission to hospital for more than a few hours, for example a broken bone or burn.

✔ **Fatality:** A fatality that happens on your site or within a few days of activity at your event.

✔ **Property damage:** Damage to third party property during the event build, show or de-rig.

Documenting any accidents

If an accident happens at your event, document the details. Paper trails are important, especially if you are sued and a claim is made that you did not protect your guests from potential risks. Report anything more serious than a minor injury to your insurance company for its records, even if the person involved doesn't threaten to sue at the time.

When treatment is in progress and the site is secure again, it's your responsibility to investigate the accident or incident. The six questions you need to ask are:

✔ What happened?

✔ Why did it happen?

✔ When did it happen?

✔ How did it happen?

✔ Where did it happen?

✔ Who was involved?

It's important to establish and record only facts, not hearsay. Then pass on this information to your directors, client, insurance company, and so on.

Figure 12-4 shows an example of an accident reporting form; it has basic sections for you to fill in. You may not know all the answers initially, but aim to complete the documentation as soon as possible after the incident.

Accident Report: Client and Job

Reference Number:	Name	Type of Accident	Action	Investigated

Figure 12-4:
Example accident reporting form

Not just broken bones

It's not just the thought of someone being injured that you should consider. You should make health and safety a priority for three main reasons, shown in Table 12-2. It can often feel like a tick-box exercise and sometimes the health and safety industry get a bad reputation for trying to stop 'fun', but very good reasons exist for their restrictions.

Table 12-2	Reasons why good health and safety are priorities	
Personal: The impact on the individual	*Economic: The financial impact on the business and/or event*	*Legal: The impact of a civil and or criminal prosecution*
Pain and suffering	**Insured:**	Court Costs
Mental strain	Medical compensation	Prosecution fines
Loss of earnings	Employer liability	Civil actions
Extra expenditure	Public liability	Compensation
Continued disability	**Uninsured:**	Bad publicity
Incapacity to work	Lost time	Criminal records
Loss or shortening of life	Investigation time	Notices
Effect on dependants	Cost of labour replacement	HSE attention
Effect on outside activities	Retraining	
	Repair	
	Loss of client confidence	

Chapter 13

Fail to Prepare, Prepare to Fail! Contingency Planning

*T*he nature of live events means that anything can happen. Event managers don't have the power to see into the future; however, you can make some good predictions and ensure that you have a plan if any of those come about.

Risks exist when you put on an event, because you can't control everything around you and every one of your guests and suppliers. Putting in place plans to control these risks is what is called contingency planning, and it's a valuable process.

Beyond risk management, which I cover in detail in Chapter 12, there's also the process of saying 'What if . . . ?' for many other potential situations. These are the slightly bigger, more content-based what-ifs, rather than health and safety focused ones – such as items not being delivered on time or traffic delaying the arrival of your star guest, or weather causing havoc. Putting in place solutions to these what-ifs is what we call contingency planning.

Four Steps to Being in Control

When organising an event, the fun bit is thinking through all the nice bits that make it come to life for your guests. The last thing you want to be thinking about is all the problems that might happen, but actually this is a really important step in putting on an event. Below, I describe the fundamental stages in contingency planning. I deal with how to write a risk assessment in more detail in Chapter 12. The documentation for each activity is likely to take a different format.

Four stages to risk management exist: Identify, assess, plan and review.

Identifying the risk

Risks can be internal – from within the project, such as a lack of ticket sales – or external, for example a fire at the venue for the event. External risks are more difficult to identify, because there are so many potential ones. You can't identify them all, but it may be worth grouping them by the impact they may have; for example, you can group fire at the venue with flooding of the venue and double-booking of the venue, because in all cases the venue is unusable.

Document each of the risks that could happen and draw up a scale of how likely each is.

Assessing the impact that these risks may have on your event

This step involves identifying the consequences for your event if the risk becomes reality. For example, if you didn't sell enough tickets to your event, the impacts may be a really empty-looking room and negative press, not being able to cover the cost of the event, or even having vast amounts of food and drink left over.

Making a plan

Identify the most likely scenarios and develop a plan to reduce the impact they would have. The ideal scenario is that, by the end of your event, you've not actioned any of these plans. It may feel like it was a waste of time creating these plans, but you can guarantee that if you didn't spend the time doing them, one of those scenarios would happen! It's a bit like insurance: You need it, but you hope you don't need to use it.

Communicate your contingency plans to the team.

Ensure that all your contingency plan documentation is distributed and discussed at the start of the planning process. All your hard work preparing for these scenarios is wasted if no one knows what to do in each situation.

Testing the plan (if you can)

This is a sneaky fifth step; it's one to consider, but not one that's often completed. More often than not, it's not physically possible to test the plan if the situation hasn't occurred.

Maybe one of your concerns is that a projector doesn't work in a complex, wide-screen video projection and you want to test your back-up projector. Find a space you can run the entire video show and actively try losing power on one or two of your projectors to see how quickly your back-up projectors kick in.

Other situations such as crowd management issues or acts of God are difficult to replicate to practise your plan of action. In these cases, you need to work the plan through theoretically and hope the situation never arises!

Identifying a member of the team to take responsibility if any of these situations occurs is also important. The person is likely to be a different one for each risk, and you're likely to be the person who retains ultimate control.

Keep reading to find out about some of the potential risks you should plan for.

Reviewing the risks

This is a continual process and needs reviewing over the course of your preparations. As you get closer to your event day, you may now be able to discount certain risks that you identified and which have now passed. However, a new weather forecast or a virus going around that threatens to make your crew ill may present new risks. As time passes, the risks change.

You need to communicate to the team any changes that you make to your plans. Don't be tempted to just send an updated document by email, because the chances are the recipients won't read it. Try to book a face-to-face meeting with your team to run through the details.

Contingency Planning

This is 'What if . . . ?' scenario planning, and it's an opportunity to make use of any pessimistic team members you have. Put them all in a room and ask them to come up with as many what-ifs as they can.

Planning for potential risks early in the process gives you time for good communication with your team, but also adds potential costs into your budget.

One of the main solutions to most problems is having a little extra time. Even if you're not quite sure which alternative approach to select, allow yourself plenty of time in your planning to give you the opportunity to think.

Contingency planning gets easier with time. Experience is invaluable in event planning, and over time you're likely to learn from so many mistakes and problems that you start to know which solutions suit your events better. A production manager, if you're able to have one helping with your event, can also advise on contingency planning.

The potential risks to consider when writing your contingency plan can be grouped as follows:

- ✔ **Physical:** Any accident, fire, flood or other natural disaster that would have an impact on your equipment, buildings or stock.

- ✔ **Team:** Your team is only human, so illness, grievances or industrial action may affect them.

- ✔ **Legal:** What might someone sue you for is the easiest question here. Or are you confident that the competition you plan to run is legal? It's best to not leave matters such as this down to chance.

- ✔ **Technical:** Everyone relies so heavily on technology now that they often assume it will always work. Think about how you'd run a barcode registration process without a computer or barcode reader that works.

- ✔ **Political:** Riots, protests, campaigning and changes in corporate policy can all affect the success of your event. If, on the day of your event promoting the launch of a new car, you read a new press release stating that the tax of that type of vehicle will increase by 25 per cent, what do you do?

Unlike risk assessments, where there's a common approach to the layout of the form, contingency plans are less uniform. Due to the slightly more detailed nature of the potential scenarios, a contingency plan is more likely to be a discursive document rather than a table. As with all communication in events, though, it's best to talk through the scenarios and not rely on your team reading a document.

Contingency plan scenarios tend to be less immediate or accident focused (like risk assessments) and more gradual, allowing slightly more time to plan the solution.

Potential Problems

The following sections cover some of the risks to consider. This is by no means an exhaustive list, and the risks may not be relevant to your event, but hopefully this section gives you a headstart when thinking about your contingency planning.

I don't care what the weatherman says . . .

The weather can be one of the biggest areas for concern for your client and therefore for you. Preparation really does help, and most situations can be managed quickly and easily. Not just 'bad' weather can cause you problems; any extreme weather can have an impact on your event.

The weather in another country can also have an impact. Major storms across the other side of the world may delay the arrival of your guests, hosts or even some of your kit. You can't prevent a natural disaster, but you can still ensure that people have a good experience. If some of your audience can't attend, consider live-streaming your event so they can still see what's going on. Publicise your Twitter feed so that those unable to attend can still interact and ask questions. If you have the budget and are feeling really generous, you can even see whether a local café or venue can provide beverages or gifts, to give a little unexpected special service to those who wanted to attend your event.

Contingency site planning

When planning an outdoor event, it's potentially worth considering finding two venues, so that you have a contingency site. If you encounter major problems in the run-up to the event, in theory you have a plan B.

Arranging such a site is easier said than done though, because your planning for the event is specific to the venue. If you could move to a different site, don't consider that this would be an easy option. Every single element of your planning would need to be revisited; most importantly, think through the impact this would have on your guests and budget. Also, having a back-up site is often an expensive approach, because you need to pay venue fees for two sites. A back-up is also rarely required if you put into place solid contingency plans for the site that you've secured.

Indoor sites in extreme weather

Not only outdoor events are affected by the weather. If you expect a really hot day and are using an indoor venue, check that its air conditioning works. A room full of hot people is not likely to be a room full of engaged people: Everyone will be too busy trying to cool themselves down. Provide extra water, ideally iced water, throughout the day if you struggle to reduce the temperature in the venue.

Attention to detail wins here. If it's raining on the day of the event, make sure you provide plenty of places for people to store their umbrellas and wet coats, rather than encouraging people to put them on the backs of their chairs.

Blue Peter's Big Olympic Tour

To celebrate the Olympic torch relay, Blue Peter and BBC Learning followed the relay and took a mini festival to sites around the country each Saturday during the period.

June 2012 will be remembered as one of the wettest summers on record. The week that the tour was due to go to the Isle of Wight, awful weather was reported to be spreading south. The event was due to be built on the Wednesday, Thursday and Friday; the event day was the Saturday, with a live TV broadcast happening at 9:30 a.m. On the Tuesday, it was decided that the Isle of Wight site was too wet and waterlogged to host an event for 5,000–9,000 people.

A new site had to be found, not only so the event could happen, but also so that the live TV show could be broadcast. A team was dispatched to the south coast to find an alternative. No other options were available on the Isle of Wight, because the whole island had suffered unprecedented rain. The event needed to take place in a nearby region to capitalise on the Olympic torch passing by. A site was identified in Bournemouth, and on the Wednesday

morning all suppliers were re-routed to the new event site. There were no plans, and some new suppliers needed to be sourced. An urgent marketing plan was put into place to inform all ticket holders and potential visitors that the site had changed.

The change of plan did, of course, cost extra money – for accommodation costs that couldn't be recouped, additional transport costs from suppliers, and additional time on the Tuesday and Wednesday for the team to visit the new site to see whether it was viable.

Whilst the event was organised in less than 24 hours, it was still successful, and is a great example of how, where there is a will, there is a way to make something happen.

The site in Bournemouth is unlikely ever to have been selected as a contingency site before the event, because no one would have predicted that the whole Isle of Wight would be unusable.

If you are faced with a similar situation, you just need to consider how far your visitors would be willing to travel.

Dealing with no-shows

If one of your key speakers or celebrities fails to turn up, all may not be lost. The time of the no-show is the critical part here: If you find out more than 24 hours before your event is due to start, you may be able to find an alternative. The stand-in is unlikely to be the same calibre as the original, but may reduce their rate if not already scheduled to work that evening.

If your no-show is literally a no-notice no-show, then you need to think on your feet. What else is happening in your event? Can you rearrange some of the running order to give yourself time to find a stand-in, or can you extend someone else's element to fill the time slot? If a band doesn't turn up, can you just get the DJ to play for longer? If your surprise guest doesn't turn up to present an award, well, he or she was a surprise anyway, so no one will notice if your client presents that award too. If your keynote speaker doesn't turn up, can you promote the next speaker to the top spot?

You can also consider identifying a member of your team or the client team who is confident enough to stand on stage and present, to swoop in and save the day if absolutely necessary.

If you do have a no-show and you think that the audience will notice, communicate at the start of the event that this person sends apologies but can no longer attend. The audience will then be a little more sympathetic if the delivery isn't quite as expected.

To prevent no-shows, ensure you have watertight contracts in place with your performers that make it is so costly for them not to turn up that they don't even consider it.

Running out of food

Imagine that your marketing for an event is so successful that more people turn up than you expected. Sounds great in theory, and your client will no doubt be very happy, but you may regret your caution when you said 'Let's not over-cater.' I believe that most situations can be saved if you provide audiences with drinks and/or food. If these aren't available, you may have a problem.

You are likely to discover pretty quickly if there are more people arriving than expected by the flow of people through registration. If you think this is a potential scenario, make sure you either stand close to or are in close contact with your registration desk. Discuss these options with your caterer as soon as you've noticed a higher level of registrations than expected to maximise the time available to fix the situation. Consider the following solutions:

- ✔ Splitting portions
- ✔ Producing more food
- ✔ Sending someone out to a supermarket, ASAP

In this kind of situation, it's often sensible to take money out of the equation, and sort it out with your client later. The price is often a small one to avoid having hundreds of unhappy guests. If you use our guide in Chapter 7 on how much food to allow per person, this action should only ever be required if more people arrive than expected.

CASE STUDY

Ottawa Bluesfest 2011: Face to face with Mother Nature

The Bluesfest in Ottawa, Canada, was among a number of events in the summer of 2011 at which the stage collapsed. No one was severely injured, thanks to most of the rigging landing on a truck nearby.

How could the organisers have avoided the incident? Well, the reports pointed mainly towards a severe storm that hit the event site and was not expected by event organisers. No other part of the event site sustained damaged, showing that the affected area was isolated and therefore the incident was difficult to predict.

What led to the collapse of the stage may never be known. The lessons you can take from this are to take Mother Nature seriously, but to also consider all the possible implications of an outdoor event.

The team minimised the impact of this incident by following a strict emergency exit plan to remove all the crew and audience from the site, so that no further damage or injuries happened with freak gusts of wind. Communication in this situation was vital.

Coping with structural collapses

Perfect planning – attention to weight loading and wind speeds – can almost entirely eliminate the risk of something happening to your structure. But, of course, anything can happen in events. All it takes is for one piece of kit to be faulty or for one person not to do his or her job properly, and you can find yourself in a dangerous situation.

Ensuring that a structural engineer signs off your structures helps minimise the risk of them collapsing. You will be able to source an engineer through the venue, the council or through your Production Manager. But if your structure actually collapses, what do you do? Well it all depends whether anyone was in or on your structure when it collapsed.

- ✔ If no one is involved in the incident, ensure that the area is made safe and the supplier of the structure is contacted. The supplier should send a crew immediately to remove the structure and, if possible, bring an alternative option. If the collapse happens during show day, the supplier may not be able to remove the structure easily, but it should be covered and taped off so that no one can access it.

- ✔ If someone is on or in your structure when it collapses, follow your agreed event safety plan, using the emergency communication chart that you agreed with your venue. (See Chapter 12 for more on this.)

Managing delayed deliveries

Imagine the scene: Your event goes exactly to plan and everyone has a great day. Is this a good scene? This is still possible, even if some of your kit doesn't arrive on time. It of course depends on how critical that piece of kit is in your plans; assuming the item is not the most important thing, but is still pretty important, solutions can be found. Mobile phones and the power of the Internet have revolutionised the events industry, particularly when it comes to finding solutions fast.

If your supplier doesn't deliver a projector for your event, phone other local suppliers, phone the local school even – who else may have a projector that you can borrow? If no one has a projector, why not use a TV screen (depending on the size of your audience)? Most screens can now be hooked up to a smartphone or tablet device to play content. It may be a lot quicker to download the presentation from an email to play on a screen than to change the whole format of your event.

If the sound system doesn't work because part of the kit is missing, why not go acoustic and claim that was always the plan? You can have subtitles running along the screen if the presenter can't shout loudly enough. Again, audience size has an impact on which ideas are feasible, but if it's appropriate, give it a go.

Now, if part of your set is missing, try to find someone with a creative brain nearby. Then consider how you can use any props, theming or branding to make best use of what you do have. It's amazing how good you can make something look; considering that your audience probably don't know what your set was supposed to look like, how can they know it's different?

Handling show day over-runs

You may have the perfectly timed running order, but sometimes presenters talk for too long. You can do only so much in this type of situation; short of walking on stage and dragging the person off, if he or she ignores your prompts, you're stuck.

If you can see a presenter over-running, and you've tried everything you can think of to remove the person from the stage, quickly turn your thoughts to the impact on the rest of the day:

✔ **Other speakers, entertainers and so on are likely to over-run too.**
Check whether they can wait until their new start time. They may have other places to go to.

> ✔ **Speak to your catering team.** Does the over-run mean that dinner is going to be later? If so, can the caterers slow down the process, or do you risk having sub-standard catering?
>
> ✔ **Consider how everyone will get home.** Have you booked transport that you need to change? Does this now mean that everyone is going to hit the rush hour?

The only ways to minimise the likelihood of an over-run are to give a thorough briefing about timings and to allow some contingency time in your running order. As you know, it's a live event – anything can happen! Maybe ask the client to go onto the stage and thank the presenter to encourage him or her to leave.

When darkness falls: Power supply failure

A power failure in an existing venue isn't often a huge cause for concern, but it should be considered, particularly when outside or when a vast amount of technology in a room is using a large amount of power. Some ways exist to reduce the risk.

A piece of kit called an *uninterruptible power supply* (UPS) provides power when the main source fails. Think of it as a big battery that replaces the main power in emergency situations.

Standby generators are often used when in outside venues, and allow for near-instantaneous transfer to the new power source. Generators often run on diesel and make a noise.

As in any emergency situation, communication is important. If your venue is suddenly plunged into darkness, ensure you speak to your audience. This may have to be through shouting if all power and therefore microphones have been cut off. Ensure that members of your audience don't panic, and explain what steps are being followed.

Hurry along now: Getting timings wrong

The Brit Awards made the headlines in 2012 when ITV cut off Adele's acceptance speech because the show was running late. Adele responded by making an obscene gesture, forcing ITV to apologise for the incident. As an event organiser, you can appreciate that asking James Corden, the presenter, to go on stage and hurry her along was not intended to create such a reaction.

Insuring Success: Getting the Right Cover

You probably have insurance for your house and your car in your personal life, so you're protected against the unexpected and costly situations that can arise. You need to take the same precautions in your working life, too. Your client will require you to, and the venue you are hosting your event in will insist that you have adequate insurance to provide cover in the event of an accident. If you don't have such insurance, you often are unable to actually plan and manage an event.

Depending on the scale of company you work in, insurance should be something that it already has. If you have one, speak to your finance director about the provisions your company has in place. Various types of insurance are available, with public liability being the one you're most likely be asked about.

- **Employers' liability insurance.** If you employ staff, you must take out employers' liability insurance by law. This cover is designed to protect the interests of employees, in terms of illness or accident at work.

- **Professional indemnity insurance.** If you hire a professional, for example an accountant or project manager, to work on your event, you may want to check that he or she holds adequate professional indemnity insurance. Professional indemnity insurance is particularly important when you are considering health and safety advisors, for example. This type of insurance enables a company to meet the cost of claims against it for any of the following:

  - Any negligent act, error or omission

  - Unintentional libel, slander or defamation

  - Implied statutory terms (such as in relation to the Sale of Goods Act 1979)

  - Unintentional breach of confidence, confidential duty or misuse of information

  - Loss of documents or data entrusted to the insured

  - Unintentional infringement of intellectual property rights

Public liability

For events, you need public liability insurance. This type of insurance covers you if a customer or member of the public suffers a loss or injury as a result of your event. A venue or your client may advise you that you need £2 million, £5 million or £10 million cover. The amount of cover is dictated by the size of your event and the number of people attending. You can extend your insurance policy, which is useful, for example, if you know you'll do one large event a year but normally only arrange small meetings. Speak to your insurance company to see what it can offer you.

Specialist insurance

You may have all the above types of insurance and be adequately covered in most situations. For certain events, however, you may be dealing with specialist and valuable kit; for example, a limited-edition-specification projector or a historical piece of content that your client entrusts to your care. You can add on cover to your insurance policy. It may cost that bit extra, but you can charge this on to your client. It's always better to be prepared than to cut corners and regret it afterwards. There is no set amount or way to calculate this cost accurately so ensure you speak to insurers for accurate quotes.

Keeping Your Sanity in Check

The main thing to remember is to breathe – so simple, but so important! I hear of people who've been working at an event and have barely been to the toilet, because they're just too busy. You're *not* too busy to go to the toilet! You're not that indispensable! Remember that you're a lot more effective on site if you're functioning like you would on any other day; a bit of adrenalin is always a good thing, but keeping your sanity should be your personal goal for the day.

Top tips for surviving the day:

- **Have a stash of sweets and energy drinks.** Whilst having crew catering is important, you still can't beat eating and drinking unhealthy, sugary foods to give you the energy to keep going! After eating a Mars bar, anything seems possible!

- **Keep essential documents to hand.** Write your production schedule and contact lists (see Chapter 9 for more information on these) on one of those big sticky sheets and stick it to the wall for you and all your team to see.

  Also have another sheet that you can add to throughout the day if you notice any small things that need sorting – we call this *snagging*.

- **Expect the unexpected.** You've spent months planning a solution to every potential issue, so you can near-on guarantee that something happens that you never imagined. It's inevitable, so don't worry about it. When it happens, switch into problem-solving mode and work out your plan. Don't worry about feeling guilty or pointing fingers until after the event; just fix it.

Part V
On the Day and Beyond

*1. Please select the day, time, and subject of the specific session you are evaluating

Day: `Please select ⇕`

TIme: `Please select ⇕`

Session: `Please select ⇕`

*2. Please rate the following aspects of the session content

	Excellent	Good	Fair	Poor	Terrible	n/a
Did this session meet your expectations	●	●	●	●	●	●
Was the level of instruction appropriate	●	●	●	●	●	●
Was the length of time appropriate	●	●	●	●	●	●
Did the class begin on time	●	●	●	●	●	●
Was all of the equipment working properly	●	●	●	●	●	●
How would you rate the handouts	●	●	●	●	●	●

*3. Please rate the following aspects of the Presenter

	Excellent	Good	Fair	Poor	Terrible	n/a
Presenter's knowledge of the subject	●	●	●	●	●	●
Presenter's actively invited questions	●	●	●	●	●	●
Presenter answered the question posed	●	●	●	●	●	●
Presenter's preparedness for the seesion	●	●	●	●	●	●
Presenter's professional speaking skills	●	●	●	●	●	●
How would you rate the overall skills of the Presenter	●	●	●	●	●	●

4. Any other suggestions or comments to help us improve future sessions?

For Dummies can help you get started with a huge range of subjects. Visit
www.dummies.com to learn more and do more with *For Dummies*.

In this part . . .

- ✔ Measure the success of your event accurately and honestly, and use it to calculate return on investment.

- ✔ Acquire customer feedback across a range of formats and using different methods.

- ✔ Understand the importance of face-to-face feedback.

- ✔ Reflect on how the event went, and consider what you could do better next time.

- ✔ Make the most of post-event follow-up and opportunities for marketing and community development.

Chapter 14

Measuring the Success of Your Event

*M*arketing disciplines such as TV and digital marketing have very clear and widely accepted forms of measurement; the events industry doesn't. The lack of accepted forms of measurement can work to your advantage, though: You can use a more tailored measurement process and provide information in the most appropriate and useful way for you and your client.

This chapter talks you through what is meant by measurement, what you can measure and the methods you can use to do it. Whilst it is an area that you're likely to focus on more after your event than during the rush of planning the event production, having a clearly identified plan up front means you don't miss any opportunities to gather information.

The Importance of Meeting Objectives

In Chapter 1 I talked about how important it is to have a clear set of objectives before you start planning your event. These clear objectives make it easier to see whether you've achieved your objectives after the event.

You and your client are likely to have agreed objectives in your scope of works (see Chapter 4) that not only cover the impact of your event on the target market but also your ability as an event manager.

Go back through the original objectives one by one and tick off each objective, or provide feedback on it, if appropriate, making sure you note down any other factors that should be recorded.

It goes without saying how important it is for your reputation as an event manager that you do everything in your power to achieve your objectives and give your client confidence to trust you with future events.

Reviewing the brief and budget

Your objectives should cover all elements of the brief, and therefore the budget. If, however, your objectives focus on change of behaviour for employees or consumers and not on the actual event delivery, don't forget to review any change in behaviour that you have influenced too.

If you've kept your client updated on budget changes regularly through the planning process, reviewing the budget is relatively easy and involves a summary of all previous communications.

Going back to the original brief is useful, because often in event planning the client changes the brief over time as he or she sees further opportunities or has internal or external pressures to change the scope slightly. I find that looking back at the original brief with the client in conjunction with what was delivered helps your client to see how you've coped with a changing brief – and, ideally, with no complaints!

Accounting for external influences

If a situation arises for which you have a contingency plan (see Chapter 13), many of your objectives may have become obsolete. Most clients understand this and allow you to re-analyse the success of the event using slightly more relaxed criteria, probably focusing on how you dealt with the situation.

It's useful for you to note down any changes to the plan due to external influences, so that if you need to compare this event against future events, you are comparing like with like.

When thinking about the evaluation, it's useful to be aware of any other activity your client is running at the time, for example TV or press campaigns, and whether any competitors are doing anything similar. Other campaigns can have an impact on how your event performs against its objectives. For example, if the brand is running a TV campaign alongside event activity, positive perceptions and awareness of the brand may be enhanced not solely because of the event.

Making a Measurement Plan

Measurement of the impact of an event is much more common in consumer-facing events than in the world of internal employee-focused events. This, however, doesn't mean that you shouldn't try to measure the success of an internal conference, because it helps justify to your client that the budget was well spent, and for your client to justify this internally to his or her finance director.

The four main benefits of measuring the success of your event are:

✔ Justifying the event budget.

✔ Justifying or extending the budget for the next event.

✔ Identifying areas for improvement in the next event.

✔ Providing your client with insight about its brand or company.

Methodology options

With so many methods of evaluation available, working out what's best for you can take some time. Two main types of research are used, with numerous methods – some methods crossing both areas of research. They are *quantitative* and *qualitative* research.

✔ **Quantitative research** focuses on numbers or quantities, and results are based on numerical analysis and statistics. Often, these studies have many participants – over a thousand people in a quantitative research study is not unusual. A large number of participants is ideal, because this gives the analysis more statistical power.

The larger the sample size, the better, because the result is more likely to be accurate. Try not to go below a sample size of 100 when conducting quantitative research.

Which of the four main quantitative methodologies you choose to use generally depends on the nature and size of your campaign, often in addition to the budget available.

✔ **Qualitative research** studies focus on differences in quality rather than differences in quantity. The results collected are word based. Qualitative studies are likely to have fewer participants than quantitative studies, due to the depth of data collected and the time needed to analyse it.

Qualitative research adds an additional layer of understanding to the quantitative research. For example, you can ask what respondents found good or bad about the event, and why they would or would not recommend it to a friend, and so on.

Face-to-face research

Face-to-face research can be conducted at the event site. It's a useful method for obtaining immediate feedback, and is generally used to gauge people's perception of the event rather than to measure metrics such as brand awareness and brand perception, because on-site branding may skew this.

Telephone research

In order to conduct telephone research, you first collect consumers' names and telephone numbers at the event. You or a member of your team then contact the respondents a couple of weeks later.

Not every consumer who provides contact details is happy to take part in the follow-up interview, therefore it's important to collect enough contact details for the overall number of completed interviews required.

Telephone research is more often used to obtain qualitative feedback. Further information is provided later in this chapter in a section called 'Follow-up phone-call interview'.

As a general rule, one in every five consumers will participate in the follow-up call.

Online research

For this type of research, consumers' names and email addresses are collected at the event and a survey is sent to respondents by email following the event. An email survey has the advantage that you can include images of the activity or brand logos.

Generally, 1 in 50 of the people sent a survey by email participate. Therefore, this approach is only appropriate for events on a large scale or that take place over a long period.

Mobile and smartphone surveys

You can collect mobile numbers at the event. This approach has the advantage that you can contact people on the go, and respondents can complete the digital survey at a time that suits them. The survey needs to be short. Mobile phone surveys are less relevant if you want to interview older respondents, for example those aged over 65 who use mobile phones less than younger people do.

Control samples

When conducting quantitative research, often you use a control group of respondents in order to understand whether the event has achieved its objectives. (For example, if the event was designed to raise awareness of a brand, then post-event brand awareness should be higher among attendees than among the control group.)

The control group should be matched as closely to possible to those who attend your event. For example, if your event targets female middle managers at accounting firms, between the ages of 30 and 45, your control group should be made up of the same type of person with the only difference being that they don't attend the event. It can also be important to match attendees and the controls in terms of behaviour. For example, if the event is a sporting event, then it's important to ensure that members of the control group are interested in sport.

If you're only interested in understanding perception of the event itself, you only need to interview attendees of the event – no control group is required.

The control sample size should be large enough to give robust results, and no fewer than about 100 respondents.

Observation

A great method of evaluation to use when you have a limited budget is to watch and listen to your audience at your event. You're likely to be very busy during the event, so use a team of volunteers to help you out. To not affect the behaviour of your audience, the observers need to fit into the audience. Brief your observers carefully so that they all look for the same things and know how to record their observations accurately.

Focus groups

A focus group is a small-group gathering conducted specifically to collect information from the group members. During a focus group discussion, between 6 and 12 people who are similar in one or more ways are guided through a facilitated discussion on a clearly defined topic. Focus groups are not often used to assess the impact of an event but more often used in the planning process of the event to identify possible themes.

Follow-up phone-call interview

If your questions and key performance indicators relate to post-event opinions and actions, it may be useful to ask recipients their opinions 2–3 weeks after the event, so they are not swayed by the event being so at the front of their minds. Phone interviews are more personal, so you need to overcome some potential hurdles:

- People don't always like telephone solicitation, and may hang up on you.
- People may not want to give out their phone numbers.
- The process takes a considerable amount of time and resources.

The following is an example phone script that you can adapt to use for your follow-up interviews: Insert questions/items specific to your event.

Hi, my name is _____ and I am calling from the event planning committee from the Make it in Great Britain event at the Science Museum in London. I was just wondering whether you have a few minutes to talk to me about the event you attended on July 30th.

First, I'd like to thank you for taking the time to speak to me. Is there anything that stands out in your mind, good or bad, about the Make it in Great Britain exhibition?

Do you have any comments or suggestions about the:

> • Size of the exhibition?

> • Level of detail?

> • Web app?

> • Volunteers?

Do you now feel better informed about British manufacturing?

Thank you again for taking the time to speak to me, and if anything else comes to mind that you think may help us to improve this event, please feel free to contact me at _____.

This doesn't have to be just over the phone; if you have the resources, you can arrange to visit people and hold in-depth interviews.

Questionnaires

Questionnaires are simple and effective tools for collecting information from a large number of people. People understand and are comfortable with the questionnaire format. The process of collecting information is low cost in that it can be done by volunteers or through online surveys. The more expensive part is the collation of the information.

You can use two types of question to generate different types of information (quantitative and qualitative). You can construct *open* or *closed* questions.

Closed questions have a limited number of responses from which a respondent may choose. One advantage of closed questions is that they're typically easier to analyse than open-ended questions.

An example of a closed question is: 'How did you travel to the event today?' The answers may be: Car, train, taxi, on foot, a mixture, or other.

An open question doesn't require a respondent to choose from a set of possible responses, and respondents are encouraged to answer in as much depth as they like. Open questions provide more information, but they're more difficult to analyse.

An example of an open question is: 'What was your favourite moment of the event?'

Where possible, try to use a mixture of forced-choice and open-ended questions.

When analysing forced-choice questions, it's common to calculate the percentage of respondents who selected a particular response. With open-ended questions, you need to look for themes or common answers.

Loads of free online tools are available which allow you to set up free surveys and provide basic reporting on figures, such as SurveyMonkey (`www.survey monkey.co.uk`).

Figure 14-1 shows an example of a basic questionnaire that you can use for evaluating the success of a conference. The questions need to be focused very much around your objectives and any aspects about which you had concerns when planning, so that you can clarify what was successful.

*1. Please select the day, time, and subject of the specific session you are evaluating

Day: Please select
TIme:
Session:

*2. Please rate the following aspects of the session content

	Excellent	Good	Fair	Poor	Terrible	n/a
Did this session meet your expectations	●	●	●	●	●	●
Was the level of instruction appropriate	●	●	●	●	●	●
Was the length of time appropriate	●	●	●	●	●	●
Did the class begin on time	●	●	●	●	●	●
Was all of the equipment working properly	●	●	●	●	●	●
How would you rate the handouts	●	●	●	●	●	●

*3. Please rate the following aspects of the Presenter

	Excellent	Good	Fair	Poor	Terrible	n/a
Presenter's knowledge of the subject	●	●	●	●	●	●
Presenter's actively invited questions	●	●	●	●	●	●
Presenter answered the question posed	●	●	●	●	●	●
Presenter's preparedness for the seesion	●	●	●	●	●	●
Presenter's professional speaking skills	●	●	●	●	●	●
How would you rate the overall skills of the Presenter	●	●	●	●	●	●

4. Any other suggestions or comments to help us improve future sessions?

Figure 14-1:
Event evaluation questionnaire.

Standard metrics for measuring brand experience events

Using metrics to measure consumer-facing events is more common and easier to do than measuring the impact of internal employee-focused events. Every event and marketing campaign is different, but here is a list of some of the standard metrics against which events are measured:

- **Brand awareness:** Thinking about manufacturer X, which brands can you think of? Which of the following brands are you aware of?

- **Word of mouth:** Which of the following have you done in the past few weeks? Have you told someone else about the activity X or recommended brand X? How many people have you recommended it to?

- **Consideration:** How likely are you to consider purchasing brand X or product X in the future: Very likely, quite likely, not very likely, not at all likely? Alternatively, a more direct question is: Have you purchased brand X in the past few weeks?

- **Brand perception:** How do you rate brand X on a scale of 1–10, with 1 being the least positive score and 10 being the most positive?

- **Brand equity:** X is a brand I love. X is a brand for people like me.

- **Perception of the event:** Overall, what was your opinion of event X: Excellent, very good, good, poor or very poor? Why do you say that? What do you think was the key message of the event?

Standard metrics for measuring employee-focused events

The purpose of events focused on people inside the client's organisation tends to be to communicate information to employees or to motivate employees. Employees are a captive audience, and you should be able to conduct research before and after the event so that you can see the direct impact of any change.

- **Employee satisfaction:** Are you happy in your role? Are you happy working with your team?

- **Information cascade:** Do you understand the reason for the event? What were your key take-outs? What would you have liked to have seen or to have been done differently?

Putting your results into context

When you've found out the answers to some of your key questions, it's difficult to know whether the outcome is good or bad unless you have something to compare it against. Through extensive research across many experiential campaigns, industry experts BDRC Continental have found some key metrics against which you can measure the success of your event to see how well it compares with the average:

- ✔ Spontaneous brand awareness shows an uplift of 90 per cent.
- ✔ Spontaneous advertising awareness shows an uplift of 300 per cent.
- ✔ Of those who attended, 51 per cent go on to recommend the brand to an average of four people.
- ✔ The likelihood of purchasing the brand increases by 90 per cent.

As you complete more and more events for your clients, you can build up your own metrics for each client and see how you are improving the impact of events over time.

Measurement beyond attendees

Remember that your event may have a greater reach than just those in attendance, not only through any pre-event marketing that you've done, but also by the actual visitors to your event becoming 'brand ambassadors' for your client's brand. Brand ambassadors in this sense are not quite the same as those that you may hire for your event; in essence, they support the brand and tell other people about it without being paid, so are in fact the more valuable brand ambassadors.

Word of mouth is the primary factor behind 20 to 50 per cent of all purchasing decisions, so satisfaction from all of your guests is important.

By asking the right questions, with regards to recommendation, you can quantify the additional reach of the activity (the *amplification figure*) through word of mouth. You can see an example of this in Figure 14-2.

Who can evaluate?

There is an art to evaluating data. If your budget can stretch to it, I recommend briefing a measurement company to run this part of the event for you. Explaining to your client the level of information that it will receive on its target market may help in this process.

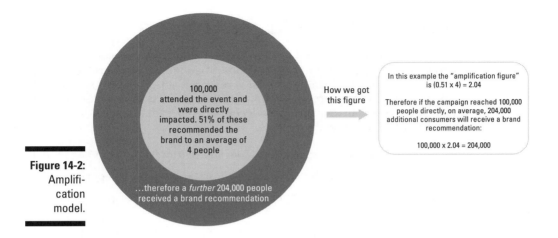

In this example the "amplification figure" is (0.51 x 4) = 2.04

Therefore if the campaign reached 100,000 people directly, on average, 204,000 additional consumers will receive a brand recommendation:

100,000 x 2.04 = 204,000

100,000 attended the event and were directly impacted. 51% of these recommended the brand to an average of 4 people

How we got this figure

...therefore a *further* 204,000 people received a brand recommendation

Figure 14-2: Amplification model.

However, if your budget can't stretch to paying a measurement company, you can follow some basic steps yourself to obtain a basic understanding of the success of the event.

Measuring online social success

If you run an online marketing campaign as part of your event, remember to measure its success and learn from this area of your event management too.

You can use various tools to measure online success, depending on what methods you used in the first place:

- ✔ **Event website:** Google Analytics is a great tool for assessing the traffic on your event website, if you have one.

- ✔ **Twitter:** Programmes such as HootSuite easily compile information about key statistics of growth and interactivity of followers (check out www.hootsuite.com). Basic things such as the number of Twitter mentions can show how much people are interacting with your brand, and what they say is useful to know too.

- ✔ **Facebook:** If you use Facebook in your marketing campaign, you can use various tools to monitor and measure the success of your activity after the event. Facebook Insights is a good option for this.

The impact of a successful online marketing campaign is also known as *social buzz*.

CASE STUDY

NIVEA Visage brand awareness roadshow

An event manager was briefed to help raise the awareness of the NIVEA range through live events and justify the expenditure post-event. The event manager decided to brief an agency to help with the research, but had to be very clear about the objectives of the campaign and what information the client was trying to understand.

- ✔ **Campaign objectives:** To raise awareness of the NIVEA Visage range to increase the perception of the brand as having 'face-care expertise' and to encourage people to purchase.

- ✔ **Concept:** NIVEA undertook a brand experience roadshow which visited 11 shopping centres across the UK. Individual skincare consultations were given to determine which products within the NIVEA Visage range were most suitable for each customer. All consumers who visited the stand received a complimentary gift bag containing samples of NIVEA Visage products.

- ✔ **Research:** A sample of people who attended the NIVEA Visage activity and a demographically matched sample of people who did not were interviewed. The matched groups

ensured that any differences in results could be attributed to the activity itself.

The results were:

- ✔ Consumers who attended the activity were more likely to be aware of all products within the NIVEA Visage range. Significant shifts in awareness were seen for five of the eight products.

- ✔ The campaign successfully encouraged people's perception of NIVEA Visage as an expert in facial skincare.

- ✔ The number of people considering a future purchase of NIVEA Visage significantly increased as a result of the activity: The number of consumers considering a purchase nearly doubled. Those who did not attend the activity were more likely to consider competitor brands Olay and Simple.

- ✔ Of the exposed sample, 35 per cent claimed to have already purchased Nivea products as a result of attending the Nivea Visage activity.

Had this research not been done, the extent of the impact of the event would not have been known.

Measuring PR reach

With PR being a great tool, you may have included it in your event plan. If so, you need to measure the success of PR too. You normally measure PR success by how many pieces of coverage you've secured (that is, how many times the event was mentioned in print or online). A value is then sometimes put on this coverage by calculating what it would have cost to buy the same amount of advertising space. This is called the *advertising value equivalent*. You calculate it like this:

Advertising value equivalent = Cost of placing similar advertisement/Cost of PR campaign

If one of your objectives is around a cause or need in the market place, journalists may focus on the need rather than on your key message – your event strapline – so identify how many journalists included all the key messages.

If you tried to find advocates or champions to support your event, you can place a value on them. For example, if high-profile champions attended a press launch, you can calculate not only the press coverage but also the money you saved by not paying for their attendance. The same goes for anyone who gives free radio interviews for your press plan.

What Your Analysis Should Look Like

How you present your findings is down to you and your client. I'm a fan of charts and graphs to show the impact or change in people's behaviour visually, but some people prefer the numbers in tabular fashion on a page or even just an executive summary of what the findings mean. Your client may need to circulate the information internally, so discuss whether he or she has a preferred method for that.

Another method that I find easy to use and easy to understand for your client is to use the format of your status report (see Chapter 4). Your status report should have covered all areas of your event, including the management and budget. Rather than the columns of 'Action' and 'By whom/when?', change to 'What worked well' and 'Areas for development'.

De-brief meeting

Your client's focus is likely to shift after the event as he or she catches up on all the other work. It can therefore be difficult for you to secure some of your client's time to evaluate the event. It's worth your client dedicating the time to evaluating the event, because you may have collated some interesting information – your client may benefit from hearing your analysis.

Try whenever possible to insist on a face-to-face meeting to de-brief the event, rather than just sending your findings by email. Planning the event was likely to have been a team effort, so make it a team effort to evaluate it.

Always try to start the meeting by focusing on how much you enjoyed the event, despite its challenges, and how you achieved a good result. Mention that, as with anything, areas for improvement exist for next time. This sets the tone for the meeting as a positive, supportive conversation.

Send the de-brief template to your client to fill in before the event, and take your completed copy to the meeting so that opinions from both sides are presented in the same format.

Calculating your return on investment

Return on investment (ROI) is a form of measurement in a totally financial sense. Depending on your event objectives, ROI may or may not become part of your post-event measurement. I talk more about ROI in Chapter 5. If you think you should cover ROI in your measurement and evaluation assessment for your client, don't be afraid to ask how your client wants it presented.

If one of the objectives for the event was to capture details of potential customers, the very number of people's details captured and the number of conversions to sales in the coming months provide a really good measure of success and ROI.

Considering industry awards

Although you can use strong ROIs to reassure your client that the event reached its objectives, as an event manager you also want to know that your event is one of the best examples of a success story. This not only helps to secure new clients but also to give you the confidence that you're doing a good job.

The industry offers many awards for events. The application process tends to occur around May to July; the awards ceremonies are then normally in September and October. Sign up to the industry websites and they then send emails to let you know when the application process is due to start. Check out eventia.org.uk, eventawards.com and marketingweekawards. co.uk. Most awards schemes charge you to enter and to attend the ceremony (they are a profitable area of event management themselves!), so consider carefully whether you have a good chance of winning.

Chapter 15

Building on the Event

In This Chapter

▶ How it's okay to make mistakes – just make sure you learn from them

▶ Making use of leftover stationery after your event

▶ Continuing the conversation with your guests when they leave the event

▶ Making use of photos and videos that your guests create

*A*n event manager's job can sometimes seems like it's never ending: Not only do you need to think about organising the event and making sure it all runs as intended on the day, but you also need a plan for after the event. Being prepared for the time after the event is, however, the step that can take you from being a good event manager to a great event manager. Clients like to know that you've thought of everything, and even if they don't have any budget for post-event plans or follow up activations, or any need for it, the fact that you've posed certain questions reflects well on you.

Learning from Your Mistakes

No event is perfect, but that isn't a bad thing: There's always room for improvement. No doubt, during the planning process you thought, 'I wish I'd done that differently' or 'If only I could have met that person two weeks ago.'

When writing your de-brief notes for your client, also write a set of notes that are for your eyes only. Ask yourself what went wrong on your side that your client wasn't aware of. For example, did you incur rush charges because you forgot to send the approved content to the printers early enough?

Event managers are often compared to swans; the scurrying of feet below the water is what you should focus on when improving your methods for your next event.

Ask your suppliers and other team members, volunteers, and others for feedback on your processes and approach, and see whether they can identify any areas for you to focus on more next time.

Mistakes help us develop, so always make sure you learn from them and use this knowledge in your next event.

I once was doing a pre-event mail-out to potential attendees. All the artwork was approved, I sent it to print and then 5 days later I got a call from the Post Office, who refused to deliver my 500 packs. I'd included an RSVP postcard but used the wrong franking mark and the post office had done a spot check and had discovered it just in time. The printers had to re-print them all, and the delivery was delayed by another 4 days. The cost to my event budget was hundreds of pounds in profit, because I couldn't pass the cost on to the client. I've never made such a mistake since, and always make a point of checking artwork carefully. The Post Office don't mind if you ask it to approve your franking marks.

Making Good Use of Your Supplies

However carefully you plan your event, there are always things left over, whether that's pens, bottles of water or lanyards. If you get a chance before the event – but if not, definitely soon after – ask your client what he or she wants to do with leftover supplies. Often your client doesn't have time to decide and looks to you to make some suggestions.

Dealing with leftovers

How you handle leftovers all comes down to what they comprise:

- **Stationery:** Put back into your PA (Project assistant/administrator) case and keep with you for the next event. This case should be like your practical DIY event survival kit. See Chapter 18 for advice on what else to include in your PA case/event kit.

- **Water bottles:** If they are branded, suggest that your client uses them at the next event or in the reception for other members of staff. If non-branded, see whether your client is happy to donate them to a local charity event.

- **Food:** If perishable, check whether your caterer provides food to local homeless charities. If non-perishable, such as sweets, then consider the next possible event at which they could be used.

- **Child props or toys:** If your event is child focused and you have an element such as a ball pit or dressing-up box as part of your experiential stand, see whether your client will give any appropriate parts to a local school or children's charity.

Remind your client that unless a decision is made quickly, you may have to charge storage costs, depending on the quantity of supplies.

Making things to last

One of the questions to ask your client during the briefing process is what to do with everything such as the set, branding, furniture, and so on after the event. The answer to this simple question can have a huge impact on how you brief your suppliers and how you manage the event.

The answer is often dictated by how much your client knows about its future event plans. If it knows that it is doing another similar event in two weeks' time, it's probably worth keeping everything. Naturally, roadshows that use a vehicle or similar to house the event experience need to be built to last.

Think about how many people you expect to go through your experience. Speak to your supplier about which materials will stand up to the footfall. Your footfall may be so high that maintaining or replacing certain elements on a regular basis is easier than building everything to last the entire duration.

Generally, it always costs more to make a set or stage to last more than one show, and often it's not worth it due to the increased labour costs to break it down carefully and then the storage costs.

Post-event Marketing

Speaking to your guests or audience after your event is often left out of the planning process. As an event manager, it isn't your main role to focus on this post-event activity, but I recommend at least starting a conversation with your client about options for after the event. The numerous benefits include:

- ✔ Widening the reach of your event by getting people talking, particularly on social networks about your event.
- ✔ Building a brand for your event and spreading the word – especially important if the event will be a regular one that you want to grow year on year.
- ✔ Providing a good opportunity to offer special deals or discounts to people who attended the event, to encourage post-event purchases.
- ✔ Making the impact of the event more long term; for example, after an internal event for your employees, you want to remind them a few times of the purpose of that event to ensure a long-term behaviour change.

> ✔ Helping you to differentiate yourself from competing events and giving you a competitive advantage if you exploit all post-event marketing opportunities.

If your client has employed a PR and/or digital agency, make sure you have a meeting with it as soon as you can, to discuss the future options.

Encourage the conversation to continue online by offering the space and directions for people on how to do that. Promote the event's official social sites to try to encourage people to say what they want to say officially.

Don't let the story stop at home-time!

I was always taught to be thankful for what I received, and have always been an avid thank-you letter writer. Write not only to your suppliers and partners during the event-planning process, but also thank your guests or audience too.

Send an email or a letter or even post a simple message of thanks on your guests' social network sites to show gratitude for their support.

Contact everyone and thank them, but also let them know further information, ask them for feedback, inform them of future events that they may be interested in, offer them a voucher, and so on.

For some public events, contacting everyone is not possible if you haven't collected contact details, but why would you put on an event and not collect these details? Try to always extend the conversation beyond just that one event moment.

A basic CRM process

Your client may have a customer relationship management system, which monitors their relationship with existing and potential customers. The process of marketing to this database of customers is often called Customer Relationship Marketing (CRM). It can take many forms, and the complexity is dictated by the budget available and the involvement that the customer has in the purchase process. For example, if you are promoting a car, the customer's involvement in the purchase process will be much greater than buying toilet roll, owing to the high purchase price and the fact that their decision will have a long-term impact. Therefore there is likely to be a far more complex and developed CRM system for an automotive client than for a fast moving consumer goods (FMCG) brand.

If your event is customer focused rather than for employees, ask your client if all the customers who attended your event are included in a CRM system, which is in essence a big database or excel spreadsheet of all your customers with details on their interactions with the client's company and any offers or recommendations that have been made to them. If so, you can use this system to send thank-you emails and also to share other information.

Feedback on feedback

You may have gathered all the feedback you need from your guests to do a full evaluation of the event, but how will they know that you've listened to their feedback? Feed back on their feedback: If your guests are really passionate about a certain topic, show that you listened to them and took action. For example, if guests comment there wasn't enough time for networking, ensure that if you run the event again you tell them that more time is available for networking. They will appreciate this.

Using photos and video content

Nowadays, a huge amount of content is created at events without you even trying. Many people have smartphones with photo and video capabilities, and the number of people who upload information to the Internet during and after their visit still amazes me. Whether it's content that you organised or content from other people, it's valuable for future activity.

Can you edit all the content together to create a day-at-a-glance type video (2–3 minutes that capture all the main parts of the day), or maybe upload small snippets to your website for people who missed a particular session and want to hear a specific seminar or band?

Encourage people to share their content and to share links to yours; it's a very cheap form of post-event promotion, and a photo or video always shows more than a few lines of text.

For the most part, videos and photos that are on the Internet are in the public arena and can be used, but you need to check copyright restrictions before using someone else's content.

Planning follow-up events

Hopefully your client is so happy with the event that you worked on together that he or she wants to plan another one. This is great news and obviously means that you've done a good job and that your client has bought into the power of face-to-face communication.

Make sure that you receive a good brief to show whether it's the next stage of the first event or delivering an entirely separate message. For example, if you organised a conference for 100 senior leaders of an organisation and your client then asks you to organise events for the 300 middle managers, is it to cascade the original senior leader messages or for a new purpose? Being really clear up front helps you decide whether you can re-use content and graphics, so helps you write a clearer first version of the budget.

If your client doesn't suggest a follow-up event, there's no reason why you can't! Why not suggest that you follow up your exhibition with smaller exhibits that tour to a regional audience so that more people can interact with them?

Part VI
The Part of Tens

In this part . . .

✔ Discover the people you can't do without with our handy list of essential suppliers.

✔ Get a handle on a range of online resources that can make your life easier.

✔ Develop your event day survival kit with our list of ten essential items to have with you when the event kicks off.

✔ Find out how to get a toehold in the industry with our list of tips on career development.

Chapter 16

Ten Types of Suppliers You Need in Your Address Book

*I*n the run-up to an event and during the show day, you rely on lots of people. Having a good set of suppliers who are happy to help you and not charge you the earth for it is invaluable. Start building up your supplier list so that you've dealt with each of the following types of supplier, and have at least one supplier in each area who you trust.

Amazing with AV

Audio-visual elements once used to be a luxury at events, when just a whiteboard and some posters would do. Now, audio-visual equipment is essential at every event and can easily be something that makes or breaks the experience. Many venues have in-house teams and kit that you need to use, but another supplier who can bring in additional equipment to give your event that wow factor is always worth having.

Start by having a chat with the in-house team about who they worked with previously. A recommendation is always the best place to start.

Make sure that the team you meet are happy to help and that their kit is relatively new and that they have plenty of it.

Catering with Class

People remember really good food at an event, but not as much as they remember really bad food.

For many events you don't have a huge choice of caterers – the caterer will be the in-house supplier. However, you can work with the caterer, do tastings and request alterations if the food doesn't match your high standards.

Remember to ask the caterers what dietary requirements they can cater for. For example, if many of the events that you host are for young children or at the other extreme, CEOs, make sure the caterer has an appropriate range to cater for your audience; young children aren't often fans of risotto or steak. The same goes for cultural and religious requirements. Always consider your audience.

Sourcing Stunning Props

Where can you find a life-like telephone box, a giant fake camel or a table-sized reel of cotton? Well that's exactly the kind of request that you can fulfil when you have a good prop company in your phone book.

Give a brief to a prop company and it can come up with a whole list of suggestions for you and help with inspiration. A prop company can even recommend what worked before, and it can make you a prop if the perfect prop doesn't exist yet.

If you have a last-minute requirement, speak to local amateur theatre groups or the local theatre to see what they have in their store rooms.

A few well-placed props can make a huge difference to an event. With a decent prop company, it just takes a couple of phone calls.

Providing Print

More and more events are reducing the amount of printed material required by moving the entire event collateral across to devices such as tablets. This reduces the number of packs you need, but there will be for many years yet a requirement for print in events: lanyards, branded uniforms, directional signage around the venue, and branding for the set and staging.

A good printer who is not only cheap but is flexible is a great asset. Your printer should be local to your office, a local one to your venue is also worth finding to deal with any last-minute requests.

Then you need to find someone to bring it all to you quickly . . .

Getting it There: Couriers to Trust

It's amazing how many things you end up couriering in events; in an age of technology, a lot of last-minute deliveries still need to be made. A reliable courier who goes that extra mile can get you out of many tight spots. When you've left the outfit that your star host is due to wear in the office, a good courier can jump on a bike, meet one of your colleagues at the office and bring you the outfit quicker than you can say 'Where's the closest Marks and Spencer?'

Blooming Great: Finding a Florist

Floristry is an art; it's tempting to forget this fact when trying to save money during event planning. Floral design is a lot more complex than putting a bunch of flowers in a vase. To create memorable centrepieces and stage set displays takes a skilled florist with a good brief.

If you brief the florist early enough, you can often have displays in the exact colours of your client's brand.

Entertain Me: Sourcing Talent

When you've agreed with your client to have a speaker or entertainment for your audience, you can then have a difficult job of trying to work out who's appropriate, who's available and who you can afford within your budget.

A good speaker or entertainment company can take your brief and write a list of potential options that are within your budget. The company is likely to give you a mini biography with a photo, which you can drop straight into a presentation for your client.

It's often worth asking for a few examples of people outside your budget; your client may find additional budget for entertainment if he or she (or your client's boss) is a big fan of the more expensive option.

A good relationship with this type of company helps you get out of difficult situations, such as when a speaker drops out at the last minute; such a company is in the best position to come up with a contingency plan.

Manning All Posts: Working with a Staffing Agency

Not all events need hosts, but if all the volunteers your client promised don't turn up on the day, you need a back-up plan. Your client will normally agree to the cost if there is no other option than hiring staff. If you have a relationship with this company and use it regularly, the further it will go beyond the call of duty to find you a team at short notice.

Such companies are much better partners when you don't work with them at the last minute though. Having a partner who can provide you with the perfect face to your client's event goes a long way. A registration host is the first person that many of your audience interact with, so this person's professionalism and appearance go a long way to cementing a positive experience in your guest's memory.

Addressing the Chair (and Table)

Conferences require a lot of furniture, and not all venues have the chairs you want at your disposal. A good furniture supplier opens your eyes to more unique and memorable furniture that you can use at your event.

It isn't just chairs for a conference, though: Your furniture supplier can also supply cloakroom rails, trestle tables for registration and even bean bags.

Whilst a supplier is unlikely to help get you out of a tight spot if you suddenly realise that you need 200 chairs, a good relationship may reduce late-night pick-up costs or help you afford the designer-look furniture that your client wants but can't afford to buy.

Seeking Fulfilment

Although you won't need them for every event, a *fulfilment house* can help you put together goody bags or information packs. Stuffing five different items into a tote bag doesn't take that long, but when you have 4,999 more to do, it's a very good job to hand over to a fulfilment house. A fulfilment house does exactly that, the time-consuming simple jobs that you haven't got time for. That can be anything from stuffing goody bags to making up hundreds of pieces of flat-pack furniture.

Such companies are used to last-minute requests and often have good relationships with printers and suppliers of merchandise through the constant back and forth of deliveries.

premier may change your mind. Or take Lance Armstrong, for example, with Nike withdrawing its sponsorship of him when he was stripped of his titles.

Key news sites include the BBC (www.bbc.co.uk) and Sky News (news.sky.com).

Always Take the Weather with You

Knowing what the weather will be like in the run-up to and during your event is important, even if it will be indoors. For example, we've all experienced trying to get around in the snow, and know how many times we've given up trying to get out of the house.

If you are aware of the weather forecast, you may be able to make some last-minute tweaks to your schedule. For example, in hot weather you might offer ice-lollies and ice-cold elderflower cordial to guests when they arrive, rather than tea and coffee, which may be unappealing.

If you have any guests or deliveries coming from overseas, also keep an eye on the weather in other countries. During the ash cloud situation in 2010, when ash from the Icelandic volcano Eyjafjallajökull closed down British airspace, I experienced a delay of over two weeks in getting some gold dog leashes. These were vital for a brand experience event for a dog-food manufacturer, so I had to postpone the start date to wait for the deliveries. Through regularly checking the weather sites, however, we were able to update the client on potential options.

Check out the Meteorological Office website at www.metoffice.gov.uk for the most up-to-date weather info..

Google.co.uk

Organising an event before the invention of search engines was a tough job. Now, to find a supplier that can deliver 2,000 branded gold and pink sun hats with hanging purple corks, you just use a search engine and make some phone calls. Search engines are a great tool when you are looking for obscure things or to help you build up your knowledge when you enter the industry.

Planning Your Route

I constantly check train times on www.nationalrail.co.uk, whether it's for meetings or to work out how easy it is for my guests to travel from where

Chapter 17

Ten Online Resources For Event Planners

In This Chapter

▶ Keeping in the loop on changes to health and safety policy

▶ Receiving up-to-date news and weather information

▶ Avoiding logistical nightmares

▶ Getting to know your industry

*T*he Internet has made event planning much easier – there are so many online resources that you can now use to gather information quickly. Set the websites in the list below as bookmarks on your computer. Try to get into the habit of checking some of these websites every morning when you arrive at work.

Keeping Safe with the HSE Purple Guide

This is an important website (and guide) to be aware of when you are planning an event. This document is published by the Health and Safety Executive (HSE) and provides recommended guidelines to follow. The information on which to base your health and safety decisions is very clear. The guide is especially useful when you're hosting outdoor public events. Find it at www.hse.gov.uk/pubns/priced/hsg195.pdf.

Staying In Touch with the News

Being aware of any situations that may affect your event is important.

For example, if you are thinking of using a celebrity to present an award or perform at your event, knowing that he or she created havoc at a movie they live to potential event sites. Having a good idea about which connections around the country are easy and which are difficult saves you a lot of time in the long run.

For example, Stoke-on-Trent may sound like a good mid-point when hosting an event for your northern and southern call centre teams. When you look at the train connections, however, you may see that both teams have a very long journey, and actually Manchester may be more appropriate; even though it is further north the train speeds from London are faster.

Checking public transport sites just before your event is also a good idea, to find out whether there are any holdups such as signalling failures, broken-down trains or other incidents. You should also check for roadworks, or other delays that could affect driving, on sites such as the AA (www.theaa.com/route-planner/index.jsp) or the RAC (www.rac.co.uk/route-planner). If you know of delays, you can phone your speaker, for example, and find out whether he or she is affected. By checking, you have slightly more time to work out a contingency plan than if you found out 20 minutes before the speaker was due to go on stage. If a large proportion of your guests are likely to be late, it may be worth delaying the start time so people don't miss any information.

Checking Out The Competition

Keep an eye open for other events that may compete with yours. Depending on the type of event, listings sites like www.timeout.com can be a great source of information. Competing events aren't only those that are similar to yours – they include anything that your audience may be interested in at the same time as your event. So whilst the Queen's Diamond Jubilee may not sound like it competes with your exhibition about healthcare, if it's on at the same time, a lot of your audience may give priority to experiencing the Jubilee because it's a once-in-a-lifetime opportunity.

Finding the Perfect Venue

Sometimes all you need is a bit of inspiration when trying to find the perfect venue for your event. Venue-sourcing sites, such as www.funkyvenues.co.uk, are a great tool to find venues you hadn't even thought about. Why limit yourself to a hotel when you can use a castle or a boat or a sports ground? Use a search engine to try to find a couple of sites that have a variety of options for you to look through. (Think of the sites as a venue version of Pinterest.)

Staying Up to Date with the Trade

Keeping up to date with other events happening in your industry gives you an important and insightful focus. Clients trust you more if you can refer to what their competitors are doing without having to say you'll get back to them. Knowing what other events are being put on also gives you inspiration when planning your own events.

There are many marketing industry websites. And don't forget to look at your competitors' own company websites. One of the key ones you should check out is www.eventmagazine.co.uk.

Minding Your Business

Check out www.gov.uk/browse/business. If you are a self-employed event manager, this site gives you a vast amount of advice about how to set up and run your business. The website also includes useful information about event licensing (see Chapter 12 for more information on the licences you will need when putting on events with live entertainment or alcohol) and around importing and exporting. It's a one-stop shop to find the guidelines that all local councils use.

Sustaining an Interest in Event Sustainability

This website (www.iso20121.org) is one to look at when you want to improve your event management business rather than directly improve your event delivery. ISO 20121 is an international standard that specifies the requirements for an event sustainability management system to improve the sustainability of events. The aim is for the event to have a minimal impact on the environment around them, whether that be the physical environment, the people or the local economy.

The website provides basic information on how to ensure that you are acting sustainably through being financially successful, socially responsible and reducing your environmental footprint.

Chapter 18

Ten Things to Have in Your Event Kit during the Build and Show Day

In This Chapter

▶ Branding your events through cable ties

▶ Combatting the effects of sleep deprivation

▶ Making sure your team don't get sunburnt

▶ Solving the lead singer's wardrobe malfunction

*B*eing a good event planner is all about being prepared. You can't always predict every scenario but you can be as prepared as you possibly can; think of it like being a good Girl Guide or Scout. Pack a rucksack or a small suitcase of things that you may need. Below is a list of items to keep in your pack all the time. Depending on the event, you may want to tweak this list slightly. Regardless of this list, always make sure you have your phone and laptop (plus charger!) with you.

USB Sticks

During corporate events, you are likely to need to transfer documents from machine to machine or print them: For example logos, intro films or production schedules. Having a couple of USB sticks to hand makes this process a lot easier, and the copy gives you a back-up in case a file is corrupted.

Try to obtain branded USB sticks, so that if a stick is lost, someone who finds it knows where to send it.

A Printer and Paper

You may think that printers are bulky, but some compact printers are great to take around from event to event. For any type of event, you still need paper, even in this technology-driven world. With a printer and paper, you can re-print your updated running orders and scripts multiple times.

A printer with a built-in scanner is even more useful.

General Stationery

Pens and paper clips, rulers, calculators and so on are always useful to have to hand. Your production office, where you hide during your event, should be similar to your normal office. Bring all the things you normally have, to reduce the stress significantly.

Envelopes are also really handy to easily file petty cash and receipts and for any confidential documentation that you need to give individuals.

Scissors are useful throughout your event. A sharp pair of scissors can be used like a scalpel or to cut fabric. Make sure you store them safely.

Cable Ties

A cable tie is a long piece of plastic with a hole at one end; by feeding the plastic tape through the hole at the end, you can hold various things together. Cable ties are great for putting up securing cables (as the name suggests!) or branding. All the branding around a festival site fence is normally secured with cable ties. You can buy various lengths and colours of cable tie from any hardware store.

Lotions for the Great Outdoors

Everyone is taught at school that protection from the sun is important; however, few people follow what they're taught into adulthood. If you're hosting an outdoor event and you have a team of people working with you, make sure that everyone is adequately protected. Have suntan lotion of the highest possible SPF rating. If your team get sunburnt, they set a bad example to the audience but also risk being ill.

Consider insect repellent along the same lines; you are of little use if you spend the entire time itching. At a recent event in Scotland, near the coast, at sunset, the team were putting the final touches to the site for the next day's festival. A swarm of mosquitoes came across the water and started attacking the team, who hadn't put insect repellent on. Everyone made sure they were protected the following evening on the de-rig!

Snacks

Food and drinks are always a welcome addition to any event kit. You and your team need energy throughout the build, show day and de-rig of your events. Have a small box of snacks to keep everyone's morale up during the long hours.

A Basic First Aid Kit

During many events, you have a health and safety officer on site; at other times you may just need to fix a small injury, such as a paper cut from all that re-printing you're doing. A first aid kit may even just be needed to provide painkillers to soothe the headache caused by too many coffees and too little sleep for you or your team.

Bin Bags

However green an event you intend to run, you always create rubbish and there never seems to be a bin when you need it. Rather than carrying bins from event to event for your back-of-house areas, just take some bin bags and put them either over the backs of chairs or on handles to keep your areas tidy.

Safety Pins

Safety pins are useful if you have any costumes or fabric props that may need last-minute adjustments. All it takes is for a seam or zip to break to cause panic. If you have a handy box of safety pins, panic can be avoided.

Staple Gun and Staples

Staple guns are really easy to use and can fix a variety of materials together. Whilst you may have a team of people helping you, sometimes you just need to get stuck in yourself and help staple branding to walls.

Chapter 19

About Ten Tips for Building a Career in Event Management

*E*vent management is one of the few industries that doesn't require formal training, but is also one of the most competitive industries to join. It's a tough industry, and you need to be fully committed to your career, otherwise the idea of all the long days and long nights that lie ahead is not appealing.

Show Initiative at Getting Relevant Experience

Employers look for skills rather than just qualifications, but they also want to see passion and commitment. Try planning a small event with your friends. Maybe try organising a fundraising comedy or auction event for a local charity. Not only do you find out whether event management is a job you can do, you can also do some networking and research to get yourself started, and meet influential people – and you raise money for charity.

Try to contact an event manager and offer to help in your spare time. Whilst you may not get a job at the company, you at least gain some valuable experience that you can talk about in an interview.

Volunteer Your Way into Events

Huge numbers of events happen every year. Why not volunteer to help at some of them? Summer events such as festivals often look for people to help with basic roles on site. Not only do you get some experience and insight into how an event is planned, but you're likely to end up with free tickets to that event, so when you're not working you can have a wander around. These roles are extremely popular, so make sure you get in early, sometimes a year in advance.

Speak to a venue to find out what events are coming up and contact the management company to see if you can help with work on site.

Whilst paid placements and internships are the ideal, with so much competition the investment of a couple of weeks of your time is worth it for some first-hand experience, even if it doesn't help pay the bills yet.

Do You Qualify for a Career in Event Management?

Although a qualification is not essential for a career in event management, a course is a good method to help you decide whether you're interested in event management.

Hundreds of courses are available, from short evening courses up to degrees. Contact your local council and do some research online to identify the most convenient place in which to learn. Many local councils run and subsidise basic courses in event management.

Through your studies you may meet like-minded people who may be good contacts in the future.

It's All About Who You Know

It's true in events that it's not what you know but who you know. Many experienced event managers are looking for the right job and not focusing on building up their network of contacts.

Do some research to find out where networking sessions run in your area. It doesn't need to be an event management networking session; you may be surprised how many people know someone in events. You just need to meet and speak to enough of these potential contacts.

Remember to approach these networking sessions in a professional manner, a bit like going for an interview. Anyone you meet is only going to put effort into helping you if you seem worth the effort and doing so isn't going to be of detriment to them.

Use networking tools such as LinkedIn to connect to people and to stay in contact. Once you've met somebody who you think may help you meet the right people, remember not to let your enthusiasm get ahead of you. Other people have their own jobs to do, and are hopefully doing you a favour.

Targeted Marketing

Look through industry press, such as *Marketing, Campaign, Event Magazine* and *Conference & Incentive Travel*, and try to focus on those companies that are doing well and which you are interested in working for.

Find contact details online through networking tools and through phoning up the company switchboard, and make contact, referencing the article you have read and why you are interested in the company.

Timely and relevant contact will seem a lot more genuine than a copied and pasted email from someone who is contacting all potential employers.

Remember to change the name of the agency in your covering email. It sounds simple, but I've seen a vast number of incorrectly addressed emails; if you send one, you won't even be invited for an interview.

Be Open to Other Entry Points

You may have a clear idea of what type of event management company you want to work for. Your ideal role may be in a big event agency, it may be an in-house role at a venue, it may be what we call in agencies 'client side' (in other words, in the company who the event is for – the brand), or it may be that you want to set up in business on your own.

If your approaches are getting nowhere, widen your search. Look at getting an office manager role in an events company or a sales role at a venue. By working in the environment but not necessarily in the right role, you have your foot in the door when a job comes up. You have a much better chance of getting the role you want if you already work within the business. Working in an events company also gives you the opportunity to help plan the events, even if this isn't your main role.

You Don't Need to Always Go It Alone

Many businesses looking to recruit event managers use a recruitment company to help with the process of marketing the role, sifting through potential applicants and sometimes even doing the first stage of the interview.

Sign up to some agencies and see what roles they have; they may not have something suitable straight away, but if you have a good relationship with the agency, it will remember you when a suitable role comes up. Take the time to see what client base it has, though; make sure it's the type of company you want to work for.

For junior roles in the industry, many companies prefer to employ someone directly, due to the commission they have to pay the recruiter. So it's always worth going direct too.

Don't Give Up!

It's a tough industry with a huge amount of competition, so you may find it difficult to get into a suitable company immediately when you decide this is the career for you. However, it's a large industry with many types of events and roles within those events, so if you know what you're aiming for, persistence pays.

• D •

About the Author

Laura Capell is Managing Director of Sledge Ltd, one of the most successful events companies in London. She was voted one of the top 35 under 35 in the industry by *Conference and Incentive Travel* magazine.

Author's Acknowledgments

The two women that had the confidence in me at the start of this writing process were Raichelle Weller and Claire Ruston. Thank you both for having the faith in me to achieve what felt like at the time, an impossible task. To Simon Bell, and the rest of the team at Wiley, thanks for having the patience to work with someone who had vowed after university to never write anything longer than 10,000 words again and who is used to writing everything in bullet points rather than full sentences.

I am especially grateful to Nic Cooper and the rest of the Sledge team for providing me with countless anecdotes and advice to help make this book as useful as possible. The team make going to work every day feel like a pleasure not a job. To my sister Rachel who I work with and who has read and reviewed every chapter of this book, thank you for putting up with having your sister as your boss.

My thanks go to my secret weapons – my team of partners who are specialists in all the things I am not, I thank Alan Law from AFL Associates and Becki Reynard from BDRC Continental who have been invaluable in ensuring that the finer details are correct and who have helped create and evaluate some fantastic, award-winning events over the years.

Thank you to my friends and family who have never complained about the unsociable hours that the events industry has forced me to do and who have always been on hand to support and listen to my late night stories over a glass of wine. Your constant encouragement has helped me to enjoy and relish the ridiculousness of the industry. Thank you to my clients and all the partners that I have worked with over the years. The team really is important in events and those people that I have stood with in a muddy field in the rain or running round with at a conference centre in the middle of the night, I thank you, I hope I have re-counted your learnings accurately and that this book does justice to the hard work that we all do to make each event come to life. I hope I continue to learn every day.

Last of all, thank you James who has motivated me through this writing process, cooked me countless dinners whilst I'm trying to come up with the right words and who has given me the confidence that I know what I'm talking about. I couldn't and wouldn't have done it without you.

I hope that I have made you all proud.

Publisher's Acknowledgments

We're proud of this book; please send us your comments at `http://dummies.custhelp.com`. For other comments, please contact our Customer Care Department within the U.S. at 877-762-2974, outside the U.S. at (001) 317-572-3993, or fax 317-572-4002.

Some of the people who helped bring this book to market include the following:

Project and Development Editor: Simon Bell

Commissioning Editor: Claire Ruston

Assistant Editor: Ben Kemble

Copy Editor: Mary White

Technical Editor: Helen Wood

Production Manager: Daniel Mersey

Publisher: Miles Kendall

Cover Photos: © Nicolas Hansen / iStock Images

Project Coordinator: Kristie Rees

Index